Law, Legal Culture and Society

This volume addresses the pluralistic identity of the legal order. It argues that the mutual reflexivity of the different ways society perceives law and law perceives society eclipses the unique formal identity of written law. It advances a distinctive approach to the plural ways in which legal cultures work in a modern society, through the metaphor of the mirror. As a mirror of society, it distinguishes between the structure and function of legal culture within the legal system, and the external representation of law in society. This duality is further problematized in relation to the increasing transnationalisation of law.

Based on a multi-level interpretation of the concept of legal culture, the work is divided into three parts: the first addresses the mutual reflections of social and legal norms that support a pluralist representation of internal legal cultures, the second concentrates on the external legal cultures that constantly enable pragmatic adjustments of the legal order to its social environment, and the third concludes the book with a theoretical discussion of the issues presented.

Alberto Febbrajo is Senior Professor of Sociology of Law at the Department of Law, University of Macerata, Italy.

Studies in the Sociology of Law

The objectives of Studies in the Sociology of Law are threefold. First, the series aims to deepen the analysis of the socio-legal problems related to the enlarged European Union and the different paths of its constitutional process and policy. Second, it examines the many facets of legal cultures within and outside the European context in a comparative perspective and in an open debate with extra European scholarship. Third, it reconsiders the historical legacy of socio-legal thought while dealing with the broader dynamic and the new challenges of contemporary societies.

Titles in the series:

Law and Intersystemic Communication
Understanding 'Structural Coupling'
Edited by Alberto Febbrajo and Gorm Harste

Sociology of Constitutions
A Paradoxical Perspective
Edited by Alberto Febbrajo and Giancarlo Corsi

Law, Legal Culture and Society
Mirrored Identities of the Legal Order
Edited by Alberto Febbrajo

For more information about this series, please visit: www.routledge.com/Studies-in-the-Sociology-of-Law/book-series/ASHSER1365

Law, Legal Culture and Society

Mirrored Identities of the Legal Order

Edited by Alberto Febbrajo

Routledge
Taylor & Francis Group
LONDON AND NEW YORK

First published 2019 by Routledge

2 Park Square, Milton Park, Abingdon, Oxfordshire OX14 4RN
52 Vanderbilt Avenue, New York, NY 10017

Routledge is an imprint of the Taylor & Francis Group, an informa business

First issued in paperback 2020

British Library Cataloguing-in-Publication Data
A catalogue record for this book is available from the British Library

Library of Congress Cataloging-in-Publication Data
Names: Febbrajo, Alberto, editor.
Title: Law, legal culture and society: mirrored identities of the legal order / edited by Alberto Febbrajo.
Description: New York, NY: Routledge, 2018. |
Series: Studies in the sociology of law |
Includes bibliographical references and index.
Identifiers: LCCN 2018004293 |
ISBN 978-1-138-48836-6 (hardback)
Subjects: LCSH: Sociological jurisprudence. | Legal polycentricity.
Classification: LCC K370 .L3884 2018 | DDC 340/.115—dc23
LC record available at https://lccn.loc.gov/2018004293

ISBN: 978-1-138-48836-6 (hbk)
ISBN: 978-0-367-58887-8 (pbk)

Typeset in Galliard
by codeMantra

Contents

Contents

Figures and tables

Figures

Tables

Contributors

André-Jean Arnaud (1936–2015) Emeritus Director of Research at the CNRS (Centre National de la Recherche Scientifique), Director of RED&S (Réseau Européen Droit et Société), Paris, France

Lasha Bregvadze LLM (EALT), MA (IISL), PhD in Law, Professor in Sociology of Law, Ilia State University and Director, Tsereteli Institute of State and Law, Tbilisi, Georgia

Karl Dahlstrand Ph.D. in Sociology of Law, Lund University, Sweden

Alberto Febbrajo Senior Professor of Sociology of Law, University of Macerata, Italy

Tércio Sampaio Ferraz Jr. Senior Professor of Philosophy of Law in the Faculdade de Direito da Universidade de São Paulo and in the Pontifícia Universidade Católica de São Paulo, Brazil

Pedro Rubim Borges Fortes Professor of Law, Getúlio Vargas Foundation, Law School, Rio de Janeiro, Brazil, and Research Associate, Centre for Socio-Legal Studies, University of Oxford, UK.

Håkan Hydén Senior Professor of Sociology of Law, Lund University, Fellow of the Royal Academy of Arts and Sciences, Sweden

Karl-Heinz Ladeur Senior Professor of Public Law, University of Bremen, Germany

Niklas Luhmann (1927–1998), Emeritus Professor of Sociology, University of Bielefeld, Germany

Jack Meakin postdoctoral Fellow at the University of Glasgow, UK

Anton Schütz Senior Lecturer in Law, Birkbeck, University of London, UK

Introduction

Alberto Febbrajo

This volume is about legal culture: about how society perceives law and how law perceives society. Legal culture constitutes an important key for understanding, on the one hand, if and how legal norms are able to influence social norms and, on the other, if and how social norms are able to influence legal norms.

Legal culture is functionally equivalent to a virtual bridge that makes it possible to analyse the fundamental subject matter of sociology of law: the reciprocal connections between law and society.

This ubiquity of the concept raises a preliminary question: can a way be found to introduce some distinctions that would allow us to engage with this pervasive field of research?

According to a very general definition, the concept of legal culture constitutes a point of reference for a number of different but *convergent* elements. It basically "refers to ideas, values, expectations and attitudes *towards* law and legal institutions".[1] Each of these elements can be placed at various levels of abstraction, ranging from the more abstract *ideas* and *values* to the bilateral *expectations* and the concrete individual *attitudes*. The same author specifies that this cluster of different orientations towards law is what "some public or some part of the public holds", thus recognising the possibility of a *plurality* of legal cultures connected to the legal order.

Legal culture is also defined in a complementary fashion as the description of "relatively stable patterns of legally-oriented social behaviours".[2] This definition suggests that, in addition to written legal norms and unstable normative orientations of single actors, every society has an intermediate level of generalised cultural patterns, called legal cultures, to be monitored by empirical tools for the purpose of explaining law in action.

A further distinction between *internal* legal cultures, typically embodied by professional legal actors, and *external* legal cultures, mainly represented by popular perceptions of law, accounts for an important dichotomy in the manifold meanings of legal cultures. As a matter of fact, the complex machine of a legal order requires legal cultures that, something like the god Janus, are oriented to elements located both inside and outside the legal perspective. Following this distinction legal orders appear to be supported by a *formal legality* based on a 'normation of normation'. This allows to combine substantial renewal with procedural continuity. On the other hand the issue of *social legitimation* is of at least equal

1 L.M. Friedman, 'Is There a Modern Legal Culture?' in *Ratio Juris*, vol. 7, 1994, pp. 117–31 [my italics].

2 Cf D. Nelken, 'Using the Concept of Legal Culture' in *Australian Journal of Legal Philosophy*, vol. 29, 2004, 1 ff. In this context, Nelken observes that "legal culture finds its place at the empirical level of the way law is conceived and lived rather than at the universal level of the natural law; legal culture maps the existence of different concepts of law rather than establish a general concept of law".

importance because it is only if legal norms are generally perceived as acceptable that they can successfully maintain social order.

The mutual connection between formal legality and social legitimation ensures the re-entry of external cultural elements into the legal system. Legal culture reflects not only the one-dimensional self-portraits of official law, but also the mutual interactions of internal and external representations of law. This means that the various different elements of a definition of legal culture are not definitely in or outside the legal order, but are reciprocally oriented in a reflexive way.

Starting from these premises, which allow for mutual overlaps and intersections between internal and external perspectives, this volume does not approach legal cultures through sharp distinctions between what is inside and what is outside legal orders. The rigid image of a 'border' that draws clear-cut differentiations between what is lawful and what is not, is replaced here by the image of a 'mirror', which introduces the idea of a circular relation.[3] Legal culture appears to be produced by a set of different mirrors through which not only an official or a popular image of law is perceived, but also a plurality of images of law and of cultural patterns that emerge in different concrete situations. The legal cultures diffused in a particular society are the main reasons why legal norms acquire different contents, or at least different colours, in order to be better adapted through official or unofficial interpretations to the social contexts in which they operate.

It is important here to underline that every element of a dynamic, flexible and pluralistic concept of legal culture reflects not only normative but also cognitive orientations. In the circular connection of legal norms with society and of society with legal norms, the social image of law and the content of legal norms learn from each other.[4]

Socio-legal scholars are aware that, without the mediation of legal cultures capable of reflecting social norms, legal norms cannot both produce *and* control a coherent social order.[5] They must proclaim neither the superiority of law nor the superiority of society. The definitive architect of social order is thus neither law nor society, but a legal culture flexible enough to register the effects of legal norms and to elaborate socially acceptable adjustments. The premise of a legal order that is completely neutral since it is oriented exclusively to official legal norms, or completely partisan since it is oriented exclusively to a superior presupposed natural law, appears to the general public, as well as to legal professionals, at odds with the everyday life of law. This explains why, in the real functioning of modern legal orders, legal cultures are – paradoxically enough – both, *explanans* and *explanandum*, the source and the solution of basic socio-legal problems, such as those of the social origin

3 Cf, the use of the word 'mirror' in R. Cotterrell, *Law, Culture and Society. Legal Ideas in the Mirror of Social Theory*, Routledge, 2006. The circulation of news among people who in turn, with a sort of mirror effect, inform other people is a simple example of reflexivity; in this context a more complex example of reflexivity is represented by the attempt to distinguish between two kinds of news (official news reflected by professionals and fake news disseminated without any kind of control).

4 N. Luhmann, *Theory of Society*, vol. II, Stanford University Press, 2013, 318. From a communicative perspective Luhmann observes, that public opinion "acts as a mirror that is backed by another mirror. The information provider sees himself and other transmitters in the medium of current information. The recipient of information sees himself and other recipients, and gradually learns what he has to take highly selective note of if he is to participate in the given social context,". These two mirrors of the "information provider" and of the "recipient of the information" could represent the internal and external points of view.

5 This was the principal argument of a legal realism open to the observation of different cultural variables and not concentrated on legally relevant behaviours. Cf. Krzysztof Motyka, 'Law and Sociology: The Petrażyckian Perspective'. In Michael Freeman (ed.) *Law and Sociology. Current Legal Issues 2005*. Oxford: Oxford University Press, 2006, pp. 119–140.

of law, of the effectiveness of legal norms on society or of the development of legal institution in their social environment.

The pluralistic combinations of social and legal elements reflected by legal culture are decisive for defining the real 'impact'[6] of law on society and vice versa. Legal norms must select, stabilise and change their contents in order to adapt them to widely accepted lifestyles through the relevant but not completely controllable support of mass media and new technologies. This leads the legal order to a complex identity produced by the interplay of different legal cultures which are mutually reflected in different social sectors.

Adding further complexity to contemporary legal orders, increasing transnational trends seem nowadays to call for a more embedded legal culture than in the past in the cognitive search for possible normative convergences, not only within but also among states. Sociology of law has thus to observe the different ways in which legal cultures can absorb the *dis*order inevitably produced by the plurality of social and legal norms that coexist in a transnational perspective.

On the basis of this interpretation of the concept of legal culture, the present volume is articulated into three parts. The first part addresses the structural reflection of both internal and external perspectives and is intended to outline a pluralist self-representation of the legal order. The second part addresses the functional connections that require a constant pragmatic adjustment of the legal order to its social environment. Finally, an Appendix proposes two important contributions of Niklas Luhmann, which offer an analysis of the previously discussed issues from the perspective of a general systems theory.

Each author focuses on a specific semantic key in order to contribute to defining the plurality of the cultural mirrors through which the relations between law and society take shape.

Opening the first part, the chapter by Håkan Hydén expands the concept of *anatomy* generally used as an umbrella term for scientific approaches to the structure of living organisms, and tries to establish the foundation of a normative theory of society on this basis. Referring critically to Durkheim's theory of social facts, Hydén underlines that norms and legal cultures are highly differentiated (public norms, private regulations, norms connected to institutions of different kinds). Understanding society's normative anatomy calls for us to notice that norms follow habits, customs, attitudes, beliefs and models of behaviour in specific situations. We thus have to explore the normative set-up for different organisms of society. In particular, the author suggests a matrix that illustrates the relations between different types of norms and institutions and claims that there are pathologic tendencies in society related to what Jürgen Habermas has addressed as a relation between a lifeworld and a system that colonises and distorts it.

In the second chapter, Alberto Febbrajo develops a *typology* of models of legal culture, focusing attention on four aspects of the life of legal orders. He distinguishes a traditional legal culture that contributes to the stabilisation of the legal order on the basis of customs culturally embedded in a certain community (legal culture of memory), a reactive legal culture that contributes to the selection of possible interventions of judges and/or of public opinion against deviant behaviours (legal culture of defence), an innovative legal culture that contributes to the inter-systemic compatibility of new legislations (legal culture of variation) and a global legal culture that contributes to the transnational dialogue concerning universal values (legal culture of communication). All these models of legal

6 On this complex concept that calls for an interdisciplinary approach, cf. recently L.M. Friedman, *Impact. How Law Affects Behaviour*, Harvard University Press, Cambridge, 2016.

culture have different temporal orientations: to the past in the case of traditions, to the present in the case of sanctions, to the future in the case of innovative legislations and to a sort of hyper-present in the case of a transnational law supported neither by deeply rooted memories nor by clearly defined projects. Each of these concepts of legal culture is represented through ideal typical combinations of social and legal norms that include specific lines of research.

In the third chapter, Pedro Fortes proposes innovative conceptual tools for contemporary systems theory. He concentrates on the image of a *kaleidoscope* in order to illustrate the multiple combinations of mirrors in a legal system. Making several references to the work of Niklas Luhmann, Fortes suggests that the concepts of autopoiesis, structural coupling and self-referential coding could be revised according to the empirical observation of law and legal cultures in contemporary society. In this context, the chapter invites a reappraisal of the legal system as a pluripoietic organisation and the constitutional state is presented as a case of structural grouping between law, politics, economics and religion. This means that the legal system's internal operations collect a variety of reflexive legal cultures so that legal claims may receive different normative answers. On this basis, the chapter sets out to identify how different mirrors could construct a multidimensional concept of law, accentuating the distance from the positivist approach to legal phenomena and embracing influences from hermeneutics and other interdisciplinary studies.

Lasha Bregvadze focuses on the history of the notion of legal culture, going back much farther than generally supposed, namely, to Johann Caspar Bluntschli, an 18th-century international lawyer. He developed the concept from the fundamental distinction between nature, seen as an external force, and culture, seen as a societal power. Starting from this point of reference, the author outlines a concept of *transnational legal culture* that combines the nature/culture dichotomy, as formulated by Bluntschli, with autopoietic systems theory. The idea of a homogenous global legal culture is thus criticised, and the notion of transnational legal culture is formulated on the basis of different types of social systems (interactions, organisations, societal subsystems). These are presented as the 'locations' where transnational legal cultures emerge, encompassing and influencing social structures. In this context, global legal culture (generally reconstructed from a Western perspective) seems to be no more than a fiction used as a political and ideological instrument. The multiplicity of transnational legal cultures emerges and shapes functional domains of law beyond the state. If there can be law without the state, there is no law without legal cultures. A global living law is thus mediated and maintained by the living legal culture of transnational sectors.

In the fifth contribution, Anton Schütz, turning the page on the theme of right and its long hegemony over legal theory, claims that law as we know it relies upon rights' Hohfeldian mirror image, i.e. upon duty and *officium*. Legal modernity is irredeemably indebted in these concepts when it reconsiders the ambiguous distinction between official and unofficial law, legal and social norms and legal positivism and sociology. The European legal tradition at large can thus be characterized as a series of footnotes to the concept of *officium*. Anton Schütz selects two different perspectives for developing a detailed inquiry of this issue. The first is represented by philosopher Giorgio Agamben, who, in his recently completed work *Homo Sacer*, applies Foucaultian archaeo- and genealogical methods and sees in the double decision of Western culture to entrust ethics on duty, and duty on law, the most worrying of its steps; the second is represented by the sociologist and private lawyer Gunther Teubner, who specifically referring to the work of Luhmann tries to demonstrate that if the rule and the rationality of law are the end, duty needs to be endorsed as a means and a condition. The sophisticated mirrors used by both authors contradict each other underlining the presence of several blind spots in the current representation of the role of legal culture.

In the opening chapter of the second part, André-Jean Arnaud underlines the strategic importance of the notion of *normative force* that may enable the traditional approach to studies in law to be overhauled, suggesting a renewed understanding of the role of legal and social norms and, consequently, of legal cultures. Jurists have to admit that different normative forces inside and outside the realm of law are able to determine the impact of legal norms on social reality. As Arnaud says, "it is only by moving away from a positivist epistemological approach" that we can actually consider the concept of 'normative force'. Its underlying epistemological thinking about norms is a veritable paradigm, and socio-legal studies are obliged to have recourse to the theories of complexity because only complex legal thinking can enable one to cope with both the diversity of social norms and the multiplicity of contemporary legal regulations. This opens up a strict connection between the concept of normative force and the concept of political intelligence. Both are capable of improving public policies through a mixed cognitive and normative approach that takes the 'creative forces' and the 'receptive forces' of law into consideration, together with "the practical collisions between legal norms and the ones that emerge in other fields, from ethics to politics via economics".

In the following chapter, Tércio Sampaio Ferraz proposes to reconsider the concept of legal culture, starting from the flexible concept of *topos*. What ensures the maintenance of a legal system is not a rigid and deductive legal culture but a style of thought, according to which problems provide the ground for argumentation, reasoning and decisions in terms of a theory of viewpoints (*loci*, *topoi*). This means that principles, more than norms, offer a wide repertoire (e.g. at constitutional level) that ease the task of the *ars inveniendi* of the legal interpreter. In general, a model of legal culture based not on hierarchical norms but on principles and *topoi* seems to be better able to overcome the difficulties of a jurisdictional exercise that is only apparently neutralised politically by the principle of the division of powers. Arguments could thus be presented as techniques for 'flexibly' ensuring the unity of the system, as instruments of the completeness of the law. Now jurists have to face a scenario where the borders drawn between legal and extra-legal regulations are muddled not only because of the mobility of some actors, but also because economic and political activities are developing a structurally and functionally undifferentiated logic between public and private technocracy. This underlines the importance of the use of *topoi* in today's legal cultures.

Jack Meakin considers that the prevailing understanding of *judicial adjudication* rests on a culturally based belief in the possibility to avoid and control external intrusions. As a matter of fact, theoretical over-reliance on judicial practice is controlled by judicially legalistic filters. The resulting self-imposed neutrality is analysed along with Pierre Bourdieu's understanding of the juridical field's capacity to universalise personal values and perpetuate the myth of neutral judging as an expected social fact. Through an exploration of legal cultures, it becomes clear that professional agents cannot decide in the manner proposed by neutrality. Rather, they come to deliberation engaging their categories of perception, which are profoundly influenced by the legal cultures prevailing in different situations. This enables a specific investigation into the influence of subjectivities on the perception of the right to religious freedom in English and Welsh law. The result of these case studies is the validation of the hypothesis that the conception of adjudicative practice entails the effective role of legal cultures. Personal values affect the judicial framing of disputes even when the law's higher authority is invoked.

Karl Dahlstrand's chapter starts by tackling the crucial question of how damages for violations through crimes are determined by law. Non-pecuniary damages caused by crimes are a dominating type in many countries and are supported by different legal cultures. There are fundamental uncertainties in Sweden's law of torts surrounding in particular the *computation of damages* and what is really meant by 'violation' in a legal sense. 'How to compensate the irreplaceable' is only one way to formulate the problem and underlines a form of incommensurability between the violation and the compensation. The results of this empirical study do not simply highlight a 'gap problem' between law in books and law in action but illustrate that what can be described as leaking law deals with the application of general rules through contextual interpretations. Therefore the question is *how* the law leaks rather than *if* it does. The chapter considers theoretical aspects of the question inspired by analytical jurisprudence. In particular, relating to Wittgenstein's late discussion about the 'rule-following paradox', it underlines that the law shifts from being a matter of representation (what *is* the law) to a matter of expression, language and discourse (law seen in the mode of a perpetual *becoming*).

In the final chapter Karl-Heinz Ladeur develops an approach that attempts to build a cultural bridge between transnational and domestic administrative law using the concept of *global network*. To the extent to which one can talk about an established field of this type of research in Germany, it is possible to observe different approaches in the discussion of the traditional ways in which "matters" undergoing a process of administrative internationalisation are presented. The focus of the corresponding legal cultures thus seems to be fragmented into a plurality of different mutually-reflecting mirrors. After having demonstrated that there is a close link between the evolution of administrative law in postmodernity and the emergence of a global administrative law, the basic institutions of administrative law appear as the product of the autonomous rationality of administration. This sheds new light on the questions of the accountability and the legitimation of transnational networks which, as a sort of 'network of network', play the important role of allowing social knowledge otherwise dispersed to be collected and used in a flexible way that breaks with the traditional hierarchical legal culture, considered inadequate in conditions of globalisation.

The Appendix features two early contributions of Luhmann to the systems theoretical re-description of a pluralistic model of legal culture. In the first of these chapters,[7] Luhmann concentrates on the problematic concept of *sociological observation*. This concept is crucial for defining strategies and limits of a possible reconstruction of legal cultures. In a self-referential system that constitutes the system's unity, legal culture, be it considered as a result of the autopoiesis of a legal system, has to respect the conditions of the system's existence and its ability to communicate with the environment without losing specific identity and functional purposes. The difficulty starts "if what can only be described by means of a distinction cannot distinguish itself against the distinction". This raises a paradox that could affect every kind of legal culture, internal or external, because deciding whether something is legal or illegal "would mean questioning the right (or wrong) of distinguishing between right or wrong". In that case, the autopoietic communication of law in the everyday life of legal systems can not only offer a de-paradoxification of the apparently illogical connection "legal because illegal", but also recognise the important role of different kinds of legal cultures for the evolution of law.

7 First published in *European Yearbook in the Sociology of Law*, Mailand: Giuffrè, 1988, 23–42.

The second contribution of Luhmann[8] focuses on what is probably the most crucial concept for the definition of legal culture: *reflexivity.* Starting from the approach adopted by Spencer Brown, the question raised is "how can the world observe itself?" There seems to be no solution to this problem because of the "undifferentiatedness" of the world, which "does not leave something out". But for society, a possible solution is a 'reflexive' differentiation. This does not mean that parts of the environment could "increasingly and uninhibitedly" flow into the legal system. Luhmann rejects the possibility of a legal culture considered as an external entity that enters into the life of a legal order and argues that, through a parallel circuit of self-application and self-consciousness, law can "solve problems to which it gave rise itself". So it is possible to imagine a level of "regulation of self-regulation", of "reflexivity of reflexivity", according to which legal cultures are represented as the result of the reiteration of different processes of externalisation and internalisation.

This volume appears mostly oriented, in a pluralistic framework, to the general systems theory as it was developed by Niklas Luhmann. I must underline that a tribute to Luhmann, who passed away 20 years ago, seems to be an obvious duty for socio-legal scholars today. For older scholars who had the opportunity to meet Luhmann and loved his continuous autopoietical flow of original contributions about a vast number of topics, his untimely demise came as a shock, as if all of a sudden, an intriguing speaker had to leave the room in the midst of his speech. The only possible reaction was to continue the dialogue with him, remembering what he taught us and, in so doing, allow the younger scholars who could not know him personally to study his many writings with care, i.e. well aware of their complexity.

So, it is no coincidence that the general systems theory and Luhmann's terminology are among the most important elements that – explicitly or implicitly – pervade the chapters of this volume presented by two generations of sociologists.

As everyone knows, a theory that is vital refuses to be reproduced faithfully. Here, the possibility has emerged to reconsider the role of legal culture as an essential part of the legal system. "Reflexive law can only be self-reflexive law", said Luhmann, and in this context, legal culture could be seen as a sort of reflexive system beyond the social and the legal one, capable of providing a useful connection between an internal and an external perspective. At the meta-level of a self-critical legal culture, sociology of law might find a way of gradually shifting from a *logic of differentiation*, centred on single legal systems, to a *logic of connection*, more open to the plural, but, to some extent, compatible, orientations to law of social and legal mirrors, within and outside legal systems, in a scenario, still to be adequately defined.

8 First published in G. Teubner and A. Febbrajo (eds.), *European Yearbook in the Sociology of Law*, Mailand: Giuffré, 1991–92, 389–416.

Part I

Towards a reflexive legal culture

1 The normative anatomy of society[1]

Håkan Hydén

Without going into the causal mechanisms of the construction of society, I will reflect in this chapter on society's construction in normative terms and, thereby, try to lay the foundation for a theory based on the strategy of anatomy applied to society. Anatomy is that part of biology that deals with how organisms are built. All living organisms consist of cells that are structured in different types of tissues, which, in turn, build up the organs. Anatomy studies and systematises the knowledge of these structures. Every society is made up of individuals that are structured in different types of social communities. Sociology of law studies and systematises the knowledge of these structures.[2] It is the role of (social) science to deal with how communities are structured, both in terms of social and of system integration.

1. Society as a living object

Durkheim aimed to establish sociology as a science and keep it separate from psychology. He went so far in his efforts to streamline sociology as a social science that he argued that social facts were independent of the individual. To gain support for sociology as a science, Durkheim drew parallels to the (natural) sciences that understood natural facts as being independent of the individual. Durkheim argued that there are social facts with the same ontological base, i.e. existing in society irrespective of the individual. On the contrary, they are something that individuals are forced to relate to. Social facts influence individuals' behaviour. They can be studied as things and, thus, measured in the same way as natural science objects.

Durkheim claimed that sociology as a whole is based on the objective reality of social facts.[3] To be possible, sociology "must above all have an object all of its own, a reality which is not in the domain of the other sciences", and that object is social facts. Durkheim regarded social facts as lying on a continuum.[4] At one end are structural social phenomena, making up the substratum of collective life, such as demographic factors, infrastructure, the form of dwellings, etc. Then there are what can be called institutionalised norms, which may be more or less formal. Here, Durkheim refers to legal and moral rules, religious dogmas, financial systems, etc., i.e. to established beliefs and practices. Finally, occupying the rest of the continuum, Durkheim counted social facts that are not institutionalised, but have the same ascendancy over the individual, mentioning social currents of different kinds as an example.

1 I would like to thank Mats Benner for encouraging comments on the content of the article and John Woodlock for valuable discussions on different aspects of the article and for being helpful with language check.

2 Cotterrell, R., *Law's community: legal theory in sociological perspective*, Clarendon Press, Oxford, 1995.

3 *Lukes, Steven,* Émile Durkheim: his life and work: a historical and critical study, *Penguin, London, 1972 [1985],* pp. 8–10.

4 Ibid.

In his eagerness to argue for sociology as an independent science with its own field of knowledge, Durkheim closed the door to interaction between the individual and society as a potential explanatory factor for human behaviour.[5] As such, what remained were social facts as the explanatory factor in all its nakedness. Social facts became an object of study in itself. In this way, Durkheim lost the ability to generate theories about what governs human behaviour at the collective level: this was the price he had to pay when he fought to establish sociology as a science.

Durkheim's mistake was that he ignored that the knowledge objectives of social science and natural science are not compatible. They cannot be studied in the same manner and with the same theory and methods. To illustrate this, we can make use of a comparison between an atom and an individual. An atom is the minimum unit of an element that defines its chemical properties. The term 'atom', from the Greek ἄτομος, átomos, meaning 'indivisible', was created because the original atomic theory presupposed the atom as indivisible, even though it has long been known that is not the case. The atom can nevertheless be said to symbolise the knowledge object of natural science. If we look at the social sciences, the individual, from the Latin 'Individuum', which, in turn, means indivisible, is an equivalent representation. If we compare these two entities, the atom and the individual, they exhibit many times totally opposite characteristics. The atom holds the same properties, no matter where it occurs over the globe, while individuals differ, depending on context. Individuals from different countries or different ethnic groups have different cultural backgrounds, so behave differently. The atom can be manipulated, as experiments may be conducted to verify its properties and its relationship to other atoms, etc. In terms of individuals, it is often unethical to do experiments or in any case to manipulate the individual. When we study atoms, there is reason to expect them to behave in the same way, all other things being equal. Individuals, on other hand, are equipped with their own will, which means that there is no guarantee that similar circumstances will produce the same results when comparing how individuals choose to react and behave. Individuals are subject to different motives for acting, and this results in different outcomes. This does not mean that individuals sometimes choose to act in the same way. This is particularly the case when they occur under the same structural conditions, which then give rise to similar behaviour. This may also concern common interests. Another example is group pressure that can exert pressure on individuals to act in the same way.

When combined, these circumstances make it more difficult to accumulate knowledge in social science than in the (natural) sciences. There is even the possibility that, if you think you have established certain scientific evidence concerning how individuals behave in a certain context, then this relationship might have changed before the scientific result has been published. Sometimes social sciences are accused of a kind of built-in bias in the assertion of the research results and are blamed for being the actual cause of what was to be explained.

This results in the social sciences having to cut away as much as possible of the contextual factors, giving a psychological bias, or preferring theories established on a high abstract level, thus detaching themselves from the contextual burden. Here we can refer to Marx's surplus value theory. The same judgement can be based on contemporary social theorists, such as Jürgen Habermas and Niklas Luhmann. These theories may be viewed as examples of the Grand theories. Grand Theory is a term invented by the American sociologist C. Wright Mills,[6] who refers to the form of highly abstract theorising in which the formal

5 Cf. the critique by Abrams, Philip in his book *Historical sociology*, Cornell University Press, Ithaca, NY, 1982, p. 25.

6 Mills, C.W., *The sociological imagination*, Oxford University Press, Oxford, 1959.

organisation and arrangement of concepts takes priority over understanding the social world. In his view, Grand Theory was more or less separated from the concrete concerns of everyday life and its variety in time and space. Concepts in our time, such as soft law, governance and the like, have become empty rhetorical spaces. The same goes for a concept like living law, which becomes an explanation without explanatory value in itself.

The theories become immune to empirical load, while becoming more or less empirically vacuous. They even have problems inspiring empirical studies. This is a dilemma for all social science research: either it becomes contextually bound, not least to a certain country, or it loses basic contact with empirical relationships in that its theory floats more or less freely. In the latter case, (social) science tends to develop its own codes and language in the course of time, which becomes the criterion of belonging to an international research environment. You can sometimes even talk about a certain genre. The disadvantage of this relationship is that the theories may be an end in themselves. Science tends to 'chew around' and twist and turn the same old truths, but in new ways, although without science progressing in the form of increased knowledge about the actual conditions.

The difference between the individual's characteristics and the atom puts social science at a disadvantage in comparison to science, and medicine for that matter, which can afford to be much more international and cumulative. There is therefore little doubt about the kind of science that enjoys the best reputation. Within the social sciences, the scholarship surrounding economics comes closest. Building on the idea that all people are equal and, therefore, will react in the same way, all other things being equal (*homo oeconomicus*),[7] one can accumulate knowledge internationally. By changing the context, one can systematise the knowledge of how humans relate to different economic incentives.[8] This resulting simplification from these cases is that human action is not only determined by economic considerations and that not all human beings value things in the same way. The assumption that self-interest is the motive governing all human behaviour situates the economy as a one-dimensional science. But the generalisation on which economics as a science is based gives it an advantage compared to other social sciences in that it claims to be able to comment on various social relations regardless of national context.

As we have seen, in seeking to establish sociology as a science, Durkheim adopted the position that the study object exists outside individual consciences. Sociology would study the world regardless of how it emerged in the human mind. For Durkheim, there was a reality independent of human consciousness. By adopting this position, Durkheim disregarded the question: 'How do social facts as such affect human actions?' Instead, for Durkheim, social facts were collective representations that could be the basis for sociological explanations that satisfy the social science requirement to consider the motives behind human action. Durkheim saw the role of sociology as a science about institutions, their emergence and functioning, mentioning the state, family, property law, contract, punishment and responsibility and arguing that we are ignorant of their causes, their functions and the laws governing their development. However, this is something that later research has attempted

7 *Homo Oeconomicus* is a term that describes the rational human being assumed by some economists when deriving, explaining and verifying theories and models. *Homo oeconomicus*, or economic man, is the figurative human being characterised by the infinite ability to make rational decisions.

8 Rational choice theory assumes that all people actively try to maximise their advantage in any situation, and therefore, consistently try to minimise their losses. The theory is based on the idea that all humans base their decisions on rational calculations, act with rationality when choosing and aim to increase either pleasure or profit. See Gilboa, Itzhak, *Rational choice*, MIT Press, Cambridge, MA, 2012 [2010].

to remedy, not least through the broader scope of specialisation that has taken place in the social sciences in terms of political science, social work, legal science, criminology, etc.

What still seems to be unanswered, however, are questions about how these institutions, construed as social facts, affect the motives for human behaviour, where motive is taken to mean one of two things: either what the image represents (or something that science produces) or a ground or reason for something in itself. With his social-realistic approach, Durkheim was caught in the first position: motives for action were subordinate to the determination of social facts, as something that is capable of exercising "over the individual an external constraint". However, a crucial question for social science is to understand how social facts affect people's motives to act in certain ways, whether it is under social coercion or related to incentives. With this approach, social facts have the potential to lay the foundation for an understanding of the normative anatomy of society. It is by accessing the motives for human action that we find reason to concern ourselves with society's normative anatomy. On this basis, human action can be seen as related to a certain normativity: with this concept we refer to the conditions (social facts), or the climate through which the motives for human action is shaped. The question we must ask ourselves is what motives make us comply with social facts? What is it that makes people feel obliged or wish to act in certain ways?

2. Norms and motives

One assumption for the study of social normativity is that individuals' actions are guided by different motives: psychology as a behavioural science might produce knowledge about the motives individuals have when they act. Sociology of law, as a social science, studies norms in an attempt to understand human action on a collective level in the light of the general motives that make their presence felt in different situations, the situated context. Durkheim offered this kind of explanation in terms of organic-psychic factors that, in his view, are pre-social features of the individual organism.[9] He also discussed psychological explanation in terms of particular or individual, as opposed to general or social conditions. Finally, and most often, he viewed and situated psychological explanations in terms of individual mental states or dispositions.

On a collective level, the motives for human behaviour are embedded in norms. These, in turn, form systems of norms, which are linked to institutions. Norms are seen as an overarching concept containing different categories. For analytical purposes, there is reason to distinguish between (1) law, linked to the state and having a background in institutions belonging to the political system; (2) ideological rules based on party politics, as in Communist regimes; (3) religious rules emanating from a specific religion; (4) rules, underpinned by private agreements and having a background in civil society or the market; (5) social norms, based on the relations between people and with a background in the interactions and communications that takes place between people; and (6) professional norms, which are used to solve specific tasks, usually within a public authority or a private company, and have a background in knowledge developed by science or practical experience. These different systems of norms interfere with each other in a way that creates a kind of trans-normative reflexivity. Within one and the same formal organisation (jurisdiction), nation state, there might be competing norms on the same level, e.g. different legal systems or different religious rules.

That norms have an essential function for society becomes clear if we consider that social community depends on the existence of norms. The notion of social community is based on collaboration of various kinds: collaboration is synchronised by norms and is vital, both

9 Lukes, *Émile Durkheim*, pp. 17–18.

for the individual and for society. Finding themselves outside social interaction is just as devastating for individuals as if the body were deprived of food and nutrition. There are signals from our senses, signals that the brain recognises as patterns that give meaning to the individual. Brain research has shown that a human brain that does not get new visual stimuli creates hallucinations and unrealistic pictures of reality, leading to mental illness.[10] In a normal state of social community, life goes on by itself, without the individual having to think about it. Finding themselves outside social interaction is just as devastating for individuals as if the body were deprived of food and nutrition.

The brain, which we perceive spontaneously as something that we think with, is also, paradoxically, what allows us not to have to think about what (everything) we do.[11] What we do is imprinted in the brain through every individual's stored experience with varied content. A similar process concerns norms, which enable us to act without having to think about it. Taken to a societal level and on the basis of norms as 'action guidelines', the parallel would be that we do not act as individuals but follow existing norms and the normativity based on them. Such norms guide us, often without us even being aware of them. Norms are embedded in how a company or public authority is organised and are also reflected in what we call tradition, often reflected along the lines of something like: do this! This is what we've always done. This is how I have learned that you should act, and so on. In this context, sociologists use the concept of the internalisation of norms, which partly covers the phenomenon. A lot is taken for granted: how we act, norms and sitting as though it were second nature. We need not think about them consciously. Norms are the carriers from one generation to another of information about how to act in different situations. So, norms can be seen as having the function of reducing complexity.[12] They talk about how we should behave in different situations, without considering more closely why. This applies both in everyday life and in professional life. In the former case, we are talking about social norms and, in the latter, about professional norms.[13] The sociologist Göran Therborn has described the function of norms as a question of reducing uncertainty in social life and, thus, contributing to social order, in the sense of predictability.[14] The same applies to the market and civil society in general.

Perhaps the fundamental part that shapes and forms many multicellular animals and is necessary both for their form and mobility is the skeleton. It is a support structure for the organism. The skeleton can be compared to a society's legal system, i.e. systems of norms that are established to define a society and hold it together. Legal rules are the rules adopted and issued by the political system. In his book *Norm and Action*, Georg Henrik von Wright speaks about legal rules in terms of directives.[15] A legal rule differs from other norms by being adopted and mandated in some authoritative order. This includes a requirement that people are brought together in some kind of community, i.e. that a society exists. Within this, there must be a sovereignty with which the community of 'included' individuals is recognised as authorised to issue common rules to the members of the community. What distinguishes legal rules from other norms of society is not only that they are adopted in some order: common to law is that a breach of a norm leads to a predetermined, specified

10 Sylwan, Peter, *Tillit: en bok om meningen i livet: från den stora smällen till morgondagens middagsmat*, Natur och Kultur, Stockholm, 2005.

11 Ibid.

12 Luhmann, Niklas, *Law as a social system*, Oxford University Press, Oxford, 2004.

13 Berger, Peter L. & Luckmann, Thomas, *The social construction of reality: a treatise in the sociology of knowledge*, *Open Road Integrated Media*, New York, 2011.

14 Therborn, Göran, 'Normens vägar och frågetecken', *Sociologisk forskning* 2: 3–15, 1993.

15 Von Wright, Georg Henrik, *Norm and action, a logical inquiry*, Routledge and Kegan Paul, London, 1963.

and agreed sanction. All norms may result in sanctions for breach. The peculiarity of legal provisions, however, is that the sanction is decided and executed by the body that represents the formation: in our kind of society, that is the sovereign state. Groups of states, such as the EU, can also agree on the introduction of legal rules.

For single-celled animals or for species with few cells, the skeleton plays a minor role. The same applies to communities with few members. In such cases, a formalised legal system becomes more or less unnecessary. Society is defined and kept together in such cases by interactions between individuals included in the community. It is relevant here to refer to the distinction drawn by Ferdinand Tönnies between *Gemeinschaft* and *Gesellschaft*.[16] Tönnies distinguished between two types of social groupings: *Gemeinschaft* – often translated as *community* – refers to groupings based on feelings of togetherness and on mutual bonds, which are felt to be a goal to be achieved, while their members are means towards this goal. On the other hand, *Gesellschaft* – often translated as *society* – refers to groups that are sustained because they are instrumental for their members' individual aims and goals. *Gemeinschaft* may be exemplified historically by a family or a neighbourhood in a pre-modern (rural) society; *Gesellschaft* by a joint-stock company or a state in a modern society, i.e. society at the time when Tönnies lived. A clan might be regarded as something in between depending on context. *Gesellschaft* relationships, he argued, arose in an urban and capitalist setting, characterised by individualism and impersonal monetary connections between people. Social ties were often instrumental and superficial, with self-interest and exploitation increasingly the norm. Examples are corporations, states and voluntary associations.

3. Rules of the game and norms of play

In sociology, norms seem to be limited to two aspects: one involves expectations emanating from individuals, where even if this includes the generalized other, they are still related to some sort of sender/transmitter of expectations. However, expectations do not have to emanate from a specific norm-sender. They can arise from the underlying rationality of systems.[17] In this respect, we can talk about the idea or logic behind the game that provides norms of suitable behaviour, which is something different from the rules of the game.[18] The latter are manifest, stable and upheld by judges, like legal rules, while norms tell us how to act in the most rational way,[19] are of a more general character and are implemented by a coach or a leader who represents competence in relation to the specific system in question.[20] Learning these systemic norms, which can be said to belong to different professions, requires education and on-the-job training. Some of them may be characterised as silent or tacit knowledge, while others are developed within different sciences. Most norms have been articulated within, and have a background in, specific sciences. The creation of a profession has to a large extent been a task for educational institutions, whether these are vocational schools or universities.

16 Tönnies, Ferdinand, *Community and civil society*, edited by Jose Harris, translated by Jose Harris and Margaret Hollis, Cambridge University Press, Cambridge, 2001.

17 Cf Banakar, Reza, Can legal sociology account for the normativity of law?, in Baier, Matthias, ed., *Social and legal norms*. Towards a socio-legal Understanding of Normativity, pp. 15–39, with references to Raz, Joseph, Explaining normativity: reason and the will, in *Engaging reasons: on the theory of value and action*, Oxford University Press, Oxford, 1999, pp. 90–117.

18 Hydén, Håkan, *Arbetslivets reglering* (The Regulation of Working Life), Studentlitteratur, Lund, 1985, pp. 28–32.

19 Norms of the game are like legal rules, while guidance about proper or most rational behaviour takes the form of social, economic or technical norms.

20 Cf Max Weber's concept of rational authority, Weber 1968.

Rationalities are thus bound to systems, and the more unambiguously the system is constructed, the stronger the normativity that follows from analyses of the system's relationship to a given empirical reality. This normativity is even more pronounced in systems that are associated with the laws of nature. Phenomena like gravity, thermodynamics, photosynthesis, etc. give rise to knowledge systems about how nature functions in various areas. By understanding how these phenomena operate, one can also give advice about how to act to attain various ends. We can call these imperatives for norms of play. These norms are equally invisible and unknown before they are articulated through science. These systems thus give rise to a sort of conditional normativity. If you want to accomplish something, you have to pay attention to the laws of nature that give rise to prescriptions about how you should act to attain a given goal or secure a given value. If, for example, you want to build a bridge, in order to be successful in this endeavour, you should pay attention to the insights from natural science about things like load-bearing capacities. These insights give us prescriptions about how the bridge should be built if it is to stand up, etc.

The rules of the game point out the playing field; define what behaviour is accepted in the game, and also what is not; how and when success in the game is met; who the players are; etc. In his book *The Law as a Union of Primary and Secondary Rules*,[21] H.L.A Hart uses the same metaphor for thinking: that of the rules in a sporting competition. Hart discusses the idea of 'rules of recognition'. These rules tell us how to identify a law. According to Hart, validity is not determined by whether a rule is obeyed, its morality, or its efficiency, but by whether it fits the criteria set forth by the rule of recognition.[22] This requires an understanding in a sociological way of which norms in society find their way into the legal system, which norms transform themselves from being social norms to become primary rules via secondary rules, using Hart´s terminology.[23]

Despite different ontological and epistemological belongings, there is a relation between legal rules and the norms of play. Hart discusses the idea of 'rules of recognition', which tell us how to identify a law. In modern systems with multiple sources of law, such as a written constitution, legislative enactments and judicial precedents, rules of recognition can be quite complex and require a hierarchy where some types of rules overrule others.[24] However, by far the most important function of the rules of recognition is that they allow us to determine the validity of a rule. Validity is what allows us to determine which norms should be considered laws and, therefore, which norms should create obligations for citizens with an internal perspective to the law.

This is how Hart deals with the problem that Niklas Luhmann described in terms of the border between what is legal and illegal, i.e. what belongs to and what does not belong to the legal system. Denis Galligan has approached the same problem in his book *Law in Modern Society*, where he formulates the aim of the book in the following way: law is a social formation with its own character and features, while at the same time interacting with and being affected by other social formations.[25]

You cannot, however, play the game through knowledge of the game rules alone. The ability to play follows other norms, norms built on knowledge about the logic or rationale of the best way to play the game. In society, we then move from the political arena to economy and technique. To be a good player, you must learn the skill to play, such as how to do

21 H.L. Hart, *The Law as a Union of Primary and Secondary Rules*,

22 Ibid p. 80

23 cf Galligan 2007

24 Hart, *The law as a union*, p. 76.

25 Galligan, Denis, *Law in modern society*, Oxford University Press, Oxford, 2007.

certain tricks with the ball; you must be able to run fast and be physically strong, etc. when playing football. Different games are based on different skills. If we take the example of football, it is primarily a question of using your legs, not your arms, since using the arms is actually prohibited. Some players develop a certain skill to head the ball into goal. You do not use your head for other purposes: you do not have to be educated intellectually or have other qualifications, like being able to swim, to cook food, etc. Game rules are controlled by referees in relation to the game. In relation to society, meanwhile, the legal machinery plays the same role through the police, prosecutors and judges. In parallel, norms about how to play the game are guided by coaches. In society, these norms are fine-tuned through science and then put into operation in different professions. Rules of the game are manifest, stable and upheld by judges, while norms of play tell us how to act in the most rational way. They are of a more general character and implemented by an authority who represents competence in relation to the specific system in question.[26] The learning of what we call norms of play requires education and training on the job. They belong to different professions.

Law is fundamental to the rules of the game. If anyone in an organisation goes beyond those statutes, such acts are not valid. However, when it comes to norms of the play, operations are conducted best in terms of free behaviour within what the criminal law framework established in the form of prohibitions against theft, fraud, embezzlement and other dishonesty. Likewise, the body can be used for any purpose at any time, within the constraints established by the skeleton. It is the various organs and their abilities that determine the direction and development of the organisation's operations. Society develops guidelines and norms about how best to engage in particular activities, originally developed by man through trial and error, which supplanted the experience of a better or a worse way of doing something. In the end, theories and methods have developed within different scientific disciplines. This is particularly true of activities that have been important for man's material development. The type of normativity we are talking about here manifests itself practically within the framework of professional knowledge systems.

When ideas about different management cultures are articulated in business administration, they spread to the corporate world. As a result, professional norms grow within organisations and fill them with content. This can be seen as an explanation for why organisations establish similar administrative systems, hire the same consultant and build similar systems for command and control.[27] Similar norms are disseminated among organisations when they hire people with a similar education or employ professional experts. Meyer and Rowan described the establishment of norms in terms of rationalised myths: expectations are taken for granted and do not even have to be articulated to serve as norms.[28] Meyer and Rowan argued that rationalised myths are widespread and are considered to be self-evident. They seem to be institutionalised typologies, classifications and interpretations that Berger and Luckmann argued have a rule-like status and form a socially constructed reality. Organisations are developed and designed by individuals acting on behalf of the organisation to follow the social facts that exert a social coercion on their choice of actions.[29]

It is possible to draw up a matrix showing the relations between the different types of norms and institutions. A graph based on what has been said above would look as follows (Figure 1.1):

26 Ibid

27 Jönsson, Lars-Eric, Persson, Anders & Sahlin, Kerstin, Institution, Liber, Malmö, 2011 p. 84.

28 Meyer, John W. & Rowan, Brian, 'Institutionalized organizations: formal structure as myth and ceremony', Organisationer, S. 146–169, 2002.

29 Berger, Peter L. & Luckmann, Thomas, *The social construction of reality (Electronic): a treatise in the sociology of knowledge*, Open Road Integrated Media, New York, 2011.

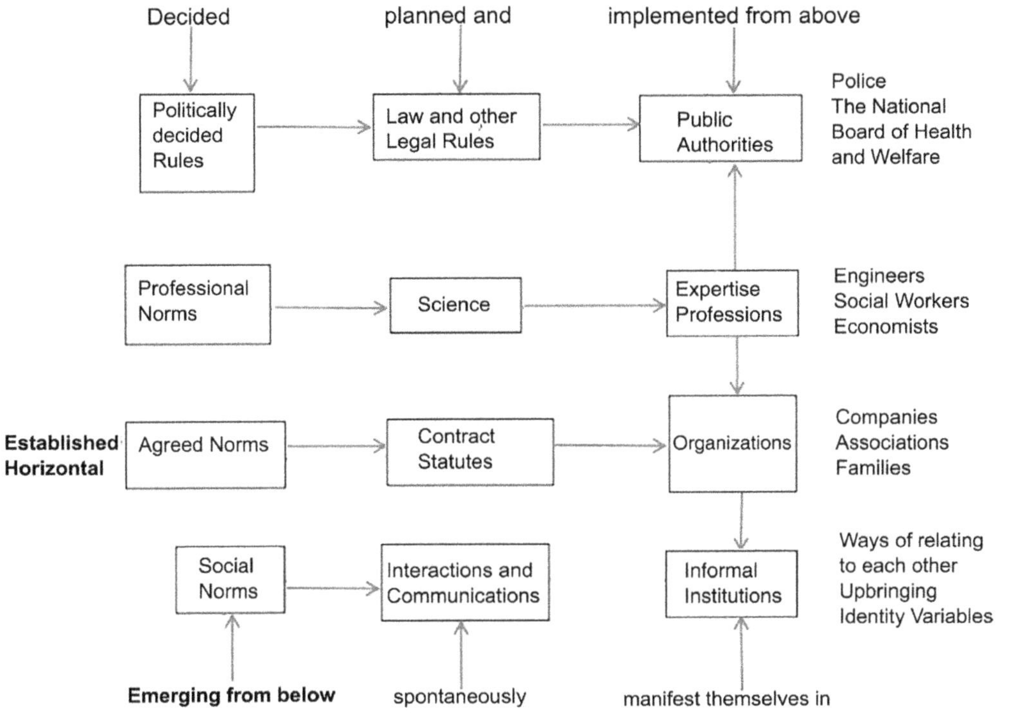

Figure 1.1 Types of norms and institutions.

4. Law and the pathology of society

'Pathology' (medieval Latin pathologi'a, the patho-and-lodging) means the study of the causes and development of diseases, primarily based on changes in the building of cells, tissues and organs. Pathology involves the scientific study of disease processes. It is tempting to use the term also in social contexts.

Durkheim studied the incidence of suicide as an expression of pathological conditions in the societal body that affect people's behaviour.[30] According to Durkheim, a low degree of social control can be associated with something he referred to as 'anomie', which roughly means the same as resolution or chaos. Anomie was at that time considered a consequence of a modern society undergoing major changes and proliferating processes of urbanisation, which could (can) lead to ambiguous norms and values among society's individuals. As such, this lack of clarity can cause an imbalance and backlash in the form of deviant behaviour. There is thus a connection between illness in society and among human relations. Today, there are many indicators of the same kind of anomie.[31]

An organisation in the form of an authority or a company thus has a formal structure that makes it legitimate to speak of an organisation. This organisational life is characterised in

30 *Suicide* (French: *Le Suicide*) is a book written in 1897 by Émile Durkheim. It was the first methodological study of a social fact in the context of society. Ostensibly a case study of suicide, it is a unique publication for its time that provided an example of how a sociological monograph should be written.

31 See for Swedish circumstances, Regeringens Missbruksutredning, SOU 2011:35. *Today, mental illness* accounts for 40% of all sick leave in Sweden.

part by its formal structure. The content of an activity is filled, however, by social and professional norms that are mainly unspoken and more or less taken for granted. As soon as people come together, some kind of lasting relationship arises through what we have described in terms of social institutions, i.e. conventions about how we should act. This is something that Berger-Luckmann says can be described as a necessary consequence of the lack of instincts as a guide for human action.[32] Berger–Luckmann considers that institutions emerge in the 'instinct empty room' in order to compensate for human weaknesses in various respects in comparison with animals. Animals are already programmed by their instincts for social community. People assimilate this ability through the upbringing and socialisation they experience during their formative years, their *primary socialisation*, and through the socialisation they participate in as adults through education and professional life, their *secondary socialisation*.

This gives us a situation where we have reason to expect an element of informal social institutions within a formal organisation. To understand how the organisation works therefore requires both knowledge of formal structures and tasks, on the one hand, and the interference of social institutions on the other. An additional requirement is the knowledge of how form and content interact, especially regarding what will be the weighted outcome. The problem with such situations may be that there is no longer congruence between 'the common interest' and 'self-interest'. In public organisations, there is no comparable expectation to follow the rules and act in the common interest, so it is legitimate to ask why people follow and obey rules. Sometimes, employees prioritise their own (self-)interest, potentially hampering the organisation's ability to pursue its public task.[33] The most problematic of these situations is corruption, i.e. when civil servants or private-sector employees demand bribes.[34] In many parts of the world, this is a devastating phenomenon that impedes societal development.[35]

In both public and private organisations, there is also an additional category of norms that come into play, namely, professional norms. This is something that the literature of organisation theory primarily addresses in terms of management strategies, which have been developed in private-sector organisations. Private-sector management strategies can be compared with bureaucratic public administration traditions in public organisations: while management strategies are all about efficiency in the implementation of the management's functions, bureaucracy is about legal certainty and predictability in the fulfilment of the bureaucracy's functions. Management strategies are primarily aimed at meeting the demands of the organisation and its owners for profitability, a kind of inner motive, while bureaucratic accountability to the rule of law is dictated by the demands of predictability and uniformity of treatment of similar cases. This is therefore mainly based on external demands. This does not mean that bureaucracy cannot be used to facilitate the organisation's internal operations: a bureaucratic approach facilitates the everyday management of various tasks. Everyone knows what he or she should do, which makes the work easier and smoother.[36] But if this goes too far, it might have a negative impact

32 Berger & Luckmann, *The social construction of reality* [Elektronisk resurs].

33 One example is Karsten Åström's study of parallel norm creation processes, where much of the application of the legal rules in a social welfare authority was coloured by the employees' self-interest of creating convenient rules that were easy to follow, Åström, Karsten, *Socialtjänstlagstiftningen i politik och förvaltning: en studie av parallella normbildningsprocesser*. Akademisk avhandling, Lund University Press, Lund, 1988.

34 See e.g. Jain, Arvind K. (ed.), *The political economy of corruption*, Routledge, London, 2001.

35 Since 2002, the World Bank has collected data about corruption in the world from face-to-face interviews with top managers and business owners in over 155,000 companies in 148 economies. See www.enterprisesurveys.org/methodology, September 2016.

36 Ibid.

on the external interest of predictability. There is always a kind of balance between the formal internal application of rules and principles and external outcomes in substance. It is not always a given that the strict formal application is the one that gives the fairest or most predictable outcome.[37]

Professional norms are, however, not only about management: they can also be about economy and technology. As mentioned above, they can also be about education, social work, city planning, environmental protection and so on. Professional norms are a question of the translation and operation of scientific knowledge in different fields to induce normative consequences about how best to act in different situations, given the organisation's mission. Professional norms are as frequent and important in private organisations, especially companies, as in public authorities. Normativity is formed in these situations when the organisation's mission is combined with knowledge from such scientific fields as economy and business administration, social work, chemistry, physics and medicine. Since both schools of economy and business administration and institutes for technology can provide more ready-made normative solutions, they are also regarded as most valuable sciences, providing knowledge that can be transferred more or less directly into practice. Economics has a standardised opinion about what creates normativity in relation to fulfilling material needs and defines it in terms of self-interest. With this as a presupposition, economists go a long way towards recommending professional solutions. Since technology is related and subordinated to the laws of nature, civil engineering has to adjust to the normative principles of nature. The foundation for this is provided by natural science, in a process that has taken place primarily in relation to an exploitation of nature for fulfilling human needs and only more recently about protecting the environment and/or looking for sustainable technical solutions.[38]

As a consequence of normativity's dependence on systemic conditions, i.e. the so-called 'objective' structural relations in the systems mankind has created in relation to human needs, there is a risk that these conditions form a normativity that takes over the preferences and contents of the various different laws, rules and norms we have been talking about. Jürgen Habermas has addressed this difference between System and Lifeworld in terms of the systems colonising and distorting individuals' lifeworld.[39] For instance, there is a strong interdependency between the circulation of goods and the economic system. Economic growth is regarded as a must: if it fails, we may end up facing societal illness in terms of recession. This also affects other systems: when the fiscal power for and of the State decreases, the political system's ambition to uphold a welfare state is threatened. Projecting this logic, social problems related to unemployment and social insecurity arise, a pathological tendency in the present situation for post-industrial states: it is where we are today, all over Europe, in the United States and in Japan.[40]

This dependence on the circulation of goods creates an atmosphere based on the notion that anything goes. Competition leads to large-scale units of production and distribution, using fierce methods to fight for market shares. In this struggle for more of the same, the benefits for consumers are more and more pushed aside, creating a counter-reaction where Small and Medium-Sized Enterprises are promoted by building on better quality and better

37 Lawmaking as process. A general model of lawmaking processes (H Hydén, K Åström, A Piasecka). In Трансформацiя полiтики в право. 2006.

38 Abraham, M.A. (red.), *Sustainability science and engineering: defining principles*, Elsevier, Amsterdam, 2006.

39 Habermas, Jürgen, *Lifeworld and system: a critique of functionalist reason*, Beacon, Boston, MA, 1989.

40 Castells, Manuel, *The information age: economy, society and culture*, Vol. 1, Blackwell, Malden, MA, 1996.

techniques.[41] Another consequence of the dependence on economic growth via the circulation of goods is the external effect of production processes on individuals and on nature. Although these have long been well known, they are still unsolved, indicating that we tend to close our eyes, since we regard ourselves as so dependent on economic development. It is only recently that these issues have been taken seriously as something that is happening, as climate change has become insidious and, thus, become visible to all of us, even if not all accept the truth. When the circulation of goods in society goes faster and faster, the planet's temperature rises; yet society, unlike the human body, is not equipped with a thermostat. This makes this pathological tendency increasingly problematic for mankind, both as individuals – after all, we are dependent on our collective behaviour – and on a societal scale.

5. The life cycle of society

Another parallel between the human organism and human society that has an impact on the normativity is that both have a limited life cycle. A human being is born, grows up, matures and dies. The same goes for society: it is initiated, expands, becomes stabilised and dies before finally withering away to be replaced by another form of society. This cyclical way of looking at societal development occurs in many disciplines. Some of the most influential work is related to Immanuel Wallerstein and his theory about World Systems.[42] A strong proponent of this perspective within economic theory is Nikolai Kondratiev (1892–1938),[43] who spoke about cycles of about 60 years between boom and depression. These business cycles are called Kondratiev waves. In history, the Annales School has adopted similar ideas of recurrent events,[44] among other things using the concept of 'the history of mentalities'. By mentality, they mean ideas that are not necessarily conscious, but are shared within a collective and change slowly. Perhaps the most prominent member of the Annales School, Fernand Braudel, divided historical time into different rhythms, coining the expression *la longue durée*,[45] which refers to the analysis of trends in a long term perspective as a study of continuities and discontinuities, where society is regarded as a totality of economic, social and mental patterns.[46]

It seems as if the world opens up for each new leap in development, i.e. in the transition from one system of society to another, from one wave to the next. In the transition from the handicraft/agrarian society to industrial society, the differences between city and countryside were evened out. During the handicraft/agrarian society, a city's walls determined the frame within which production and purchasing were allowed to take place. After a while, the space became too constricted and via a technological leap, the transformation of primary energy into secondary energy sources, the gulf between the city and the countryside

41 Groen, Aard (red.), *New technology-based firms in the new millennium*. Vol. 9 [Elektronisk resurs], Emerald, Bingley, 2012.

42 Wallerstein, Immanuel Maurice, *World-systems analysis: an introduction*, Duke University Press, Durham, NC, 2004.

43 Barnett, Vincent, *Kondratiev and the dynamics of economic development: long cycles and industrial growth in historical context*, New York: St. Martin's Press, 1998.

44 Clark, Stuart (red.), *The Annales School*. Vol. 3, Fernand Braudel, New York: Routledge; first edition, 1999.

45 Braudel, Fernand, Civilization and capitalism: 15th-18th century. Vol. 1, *The structures of everyday life: the limits of the possible*, [New ed.], Collins, London, 1981.

46 My own understanding of societal development in terms of waves is inspired by the expert on future studies Anders Ewerman, see Ewerman, Anders, Marknaden 1000 år: fem eror i Europa, Ewerman Business Intelligence, Stockholm, 1996 and Ewerman, Anders, Civilisationens DNA: västerlandets historia 4000 f.Kr.-2000 e.Kr., Ewerman Business Intelligence, Stockholm, 2007, Normative Transitions.

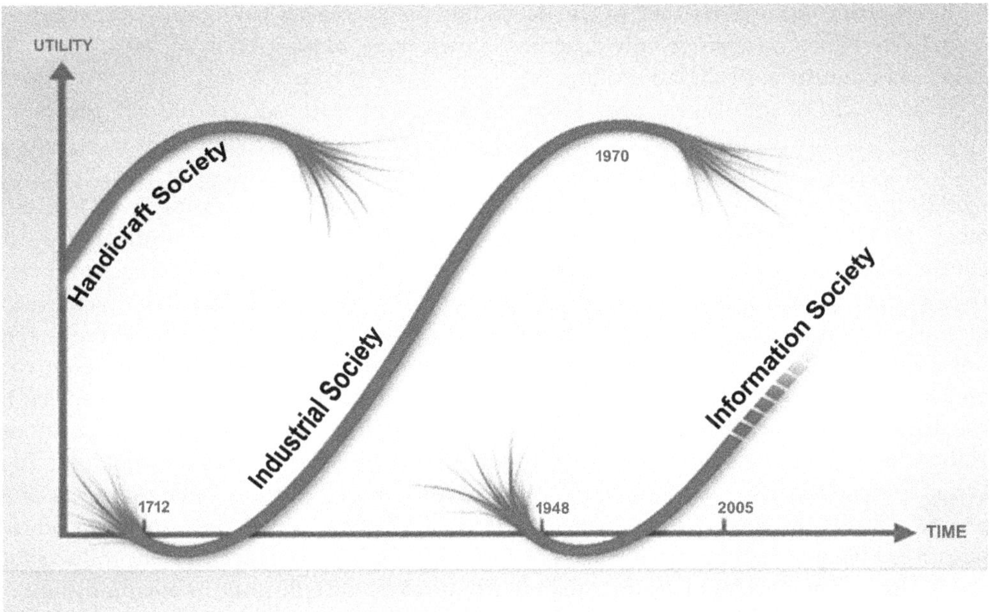

Figure 1.2 Types of normative transitions.

was reduced, the city walls were torn down and the flow of trade was set free. In return, the nation state emerged and, with it, a larger arena for production and trade. We are presently witnessing the latest leap, as the nation state weakens under the impact of today's new information technology, whereby boundaries between countries cease to be barriers for peoples' and companies' domiciles. Digital technology gives rise to new economic approaches that open up the world. This technological leap has now enabled us to tear down the remaining few walls that hinder humans from interaction across national state borders (Figure 1.2).

When industrial society's utility curve begins to descend, the prerequisites for politics change radically. From having been concerned with distribution, the focus will gradually come to rest on crisis management. Politics will acquire the task of trying to reconcile criticisms emerging from people's negative expectations, shifting from being distinguished as the art of the possible to the art of the insufficient. In order to solve an impossible equation, politicians use law to smoothen out social inequalities and calm tensions so that cracks in the market economy – built on the idea of the invisible hand – do not become visible. This is when the legal form of intervention prevails.[47]

What are the normative implications following on this transition?

The time of dramatic change between an old and overly mature industrial society and the digital society that more and more takes over can, for the sake of simplicity, be described as a transition society, what some scholars call a postmodern society.[48] Within this society,

47 Hydén, Håkan, Towards a theory of law and societal development, in Wahlgren, Peter, ed., *Scandinavian studies in law*, Vol. 60, Stockholm: Jure Law Books, 2014.

48 The ambivalence the transition society gives rise to reflected in social sciences. There are two leading theorists of the postmodern society. One is Jean Baudrillard, who believed that modern society was characterised by production, while the postmodern come to be characterised by simulation and a kind of implosion in the signs

contradictions appear between the old and the new: tensions arise between people who live with different conceptions of the world, depending on where they have localised themselves cognitively, which, in turn, mainly depends on their material position in society, if they are engaged in industrial or digital production.

Every system of society describes a type of wave, where the society is born, grows up and matures, only to reach a culmination, die out and finally decompose, leaving only a trace in peoples' memories. Industrial society reached its culmination in the developed world's industrial countries, the Organisation for Economic Co-operation and Development (OECD) countries, in the beginning of the 1970s. Since then, productivity has continued to increase until recent times, when the financial crisis set the scene for recession, but the benefit of the societal system had subsided long ago, as industrial society can no longer grant us more benefits. It is this circumstance that leads to financial crises and unstable situations in the stock market. There are no healthy alternatives. Admittedly, the benefits are unevenly distributed, but the injustice is structural and can only be solved if we abandon our present system and find a new way to live, produce and distribute goods and services. This development follows a logic that applies to all systems, which reach a certain potential, then eventually become counterproductive. Monopolies – both state and private – that have grown strong during the large-scale phase of industrial society produce negative consumer value today instead of providing us with constantly better products for lower prices. The development for the better that takes place during these circumstances is an effect of the giants, although everything is beginning to be challenged by small and medium-sized companies, as mentioned above, which are driven by the aspiration to find new solutions, whilst the established companies struggle to keep old solutions that give them advantages.

In this chapter, I have defined concepts as normativity in general[49] and different types of norms: law and legal norms, rules, social and professional norms. What we have learnt from equivalent shifts in history, much as the one we are currently facing, is that societal changes generate normative shifts, not immediately, but eventually. The transition from the large scale to the small scale is a prominent example.[50] Society starts over again from the beginning, where old human needs – which do not change over time – are met in new ways, since the increasing availability of new technologies opens the way to new possibilities. We could use the expression *forward to basics*, one move forward, although on a superficial level it might look as if we were starting all over again. It is in this process that communication becomes important: there are no given answers to what the best solutions are; there is no key to the correct answers. They can only be created by us through communication between people.

The consequence of the transition from one societal organisation to another is that we go from formal governmental regulation and control to less formal supporting systems and

---

and symbols from different media. In today's society, we have therefore lost touch with reality, according to Baudrillard. The second theorist, Jean-Francois Lyotard, believes that science's hierarchical authority over postmodernism is collapsing in a multiplicity of discourses, and that science is no longer entitled to claim the only legitimate truth. The sociologist Zygmunt Bauman has addressed postmodern problems in multiple books. See e.g. Bauman, Zygmunt & Bauman, Lydia, *Culture in a liquid modern world [Electronic]*, Polity, Cambridge, 2011.

49 Banakar, Reza, *Normativity in legal sociology: methodological reflections on law and regulation in late modernity*, Springer, Switzerland, 2015.

50 The shift from stable employments for the individual to more of what is called gig-economy with temporary jobs is only one example. The growth of SMEs is another.

self-regulation, i.e. from law to rules and norms. The new that emerges does so not as a result of centrally made decisions, but by testing various types of social experiments, different ways to live and support oneself. As the old society loses its ability to satisfy human needs, people look for new livelihoods and ways to live their lives, gradually developing new patterns to satisfy human needs. In this way, the normative anatomy of society changes successively in certain periods of history before achieving a stable form with a new constitution that suits its specific societal formation, followed cyclically by the development of new patterns, etc. as indicated in the figure above.

6. Conclusions

I have used the metaphor of the human organism in relation to our understanding of the notion of society. The living organism is dependent on certain operations that can be regarded as rule-based. The body's operations follow a certain pattern based on specialised functions taking place between the organs. As we have seen, there are parallels to society: how a society functions depends on specialised operations taking place between different societal institutions. Rules and norms play a fundamental role for the operations, both of the human body and of society. In both cases, there is an essential distinction between the norms of play and other norms. The norms of play define a society. They play the role of a political constitution for that society.[51]

In this perspective, constitutional rules, in particular, define the political arena and the political system of game rules. They tell us primarily what characterises the political and electoral system in society. In this sense, the constitution has no direct relation to individuals, but comprises primary directives for the State and State organs. Constitutions also tend to contain ideas, attitudes and patterns of behaviour, elaborating on the principle that the authority of government derives from and is limited by a body of fundamental law, especially the relations between government (public authorities) and citizens. These rules may have an impact on how the game is played, but only indirectly.

The social system is even more spontaneous. This is better defined by the criminal legal system. In this sense, the constitution of the social system is defined in the negative: actions within the bounds of criminal law are accepted, often without any further restrictions. In these cases, law is rather distinct in character. We refer here to what can be called duty rules that specify under which conditions the law applies. In legal systems influenced and/or dominated by religion, the law also comes into play in the arena of social relations, as is particularly the case in Muslim countries,[52] although the phenomenon is also present in countries with a strong Christian or Hindu influence: how the social system interacts with the family, divorce and relations between parents and children and between men and women is subject to legal regulations that follow the religious ideology. In many Muslim countries, Sharia law is the guiding principle.[53]

51 Note the dual relation between State and Law. The State enacts laws, while law at the same time defines the State and, via the constitution, regulates when and what the State can regulate by law. See Habermas, Jürgen, *Between facts and norms*: contributions to a discourse theory of law and democracy, Polity, London, 1996.

52 An illuminating and interesting example is the book by Reza Banakar, where he uses driving culture as a kind of indicator of the larger legal culture. Banakar, Reza, 1959-, Driving culture in Iran: law and society on the roads of the Islamic republic, I.B. Tauris, London, 2016.

53 Sharia is the religious law governing the members of the Islamic faith. It is derived from the religious precepts of Islam, particularly the Quran and the Hadith. Sharia is a significant source of legislation in many Muslim countries, some of which, including Saudi Arabia, Sudan, Iran, Iraq, Afghanistan, Pakistan, Brunei, United

A country's legal system forms a more or less coherent system based on certain constitutive rules. All organisation and community formations require some sort of basic rules by which the sovereignty is defined as representing the unit. The nation state forms a more or less arbitrary social community that is defined by such constitutive rules. As the market expands and society undergoes modernisation, the norms of play become relevant in a global perspective.

A discussion about the constitutions of social sub-areas, initiated by Gunter Teubner, recently came to light as not just an issue of functional differentiation on a global scale, but one that had already become virulent in the era of the nation state.[54] It starts with liberal constitutionalism and discusses why the constitutional question was raised in relation only to the state and not to other sectors of society, then goes on to describe how totalitarian regimes have dealt with different sectors of society. Against this background, three models of societal constitutionalism in the welfare state are presented: (1) social state constitutionalism, which attempts to politicise social sectors; (2) economic constitutionalism, which insists on the autonomy of the economic constitution, and (3) neo-corporatist models of societal constitutionalism, which develop constitutions of diverse social sectors, allowing for different rationalities to be co-ordinated.

Another factor that supports the economic system's self-generation is technical development. The World Wide Web is a global interface that has led to a widespread representation of global corporations. The services they offer disrupt traditional economic models and, thereby, also legal models. While this is not the space to elaborate on this, I merely want to point out the role of intermediation platforms: intermediation is the action of matching two types of actors (clients, users, services) in a context, such as banking, where the matching cannot take place without intermediaries. Intermediation platforms enact two-sided markets, where an algorithmically driven virtual agent makes matches between those who offer goods or services and those who consume them. The search engines we all use, for example, intermediate between people producing knowledge (web pages) and people seeking knowledge.[55] The best known platforms are private corporations such as Google, Amazon, Facebook, Apple and Uber (and the like), all platforms that are growing extremely fast. In these cases, law has been supplanted by technological tools, bringing us close to what Lawrence Lessig expressed when he said that "Code is law".[56] In the mentioned context of online platforms, the expression could even be extended to include 'Code is the Constitution'.

My understanding of the problem raised by Teubner is that what we usually mean as constitution is concerned with the establishment and organisation of the political system.

Arab Emirates, Qatar, Yemen and Mauritania, apply a majority or part of the Sharia code. In these countries, Sharia-prescribed punishments, such as beheading, flogging and stoning, continue to be practised judicially or extra-judicially. The concept of crime, judicial process, justice and punishment embodied in Sharia law is different from that of secular law. The differences between Sharia and secular law have led to an ongoing controversy as to whether Sharia is compatible with secular forms of government, human rights, freedom of thought and women's rights. See e.g. *Hajjar, Lisa. 'Religion, state power, and domestic violence in Muslim societies: a framework for comparative analysis'*, Law & Social Inquiry 29 (1): 1–38, 2004.

54 Teubner, Gunther, *Constitutional fragments: societal constitutionalism and globalization*, Oxford University Press, Oxford, 2012.

55 Gasser, Urs and Schulz, Wolfgang, *Governance of online intermediaries: observations from a series of national case studies (February 18, 2015)*. Berkman Center Research Publication No. 2015-5. Available at SSRN: https://ssrn.com/abstract=2566364 or http://dx.doi.org/10.2139/ssrn.2566364

56 Lessig, Lawrence, *Code: version 2.0*, Basic Books, New York, 2006. www.nlc.state.ne.us/epubs/creative commons/Lessig-Codev2.pdf.

The 'political' dimension is not something that grows spontaneously in the same way as the economic system: it has to be constructed after and in relation to power games and negotiations among stakeholders, be they clan leaders, religious leaders or political parties of different kinds. In this respect, the political system is a construction that has to be manifested in some form of document and the constitution fulfils this role. The economic system, on the other hand, is based to a great extent on the self-interest shared among different actors and the common interest 'of playing the (market) game': it is something that grows from the bottom up. The market does require norms of play, but primarily tools for co-operation. These legal means for cooperation have to be defined and agreed upon legally. Property rights, contract, security rights and the concept of legal persons are among the legal pillars of the market economy. The same goes to a certain extent for the social system. It is negatively determined by criminal law telling us what is socially acceptable behaviour and, thereby, indirectly who belongs to the social system. Thus, different parts of society have their own but separate constitution within the normative anatomy of society.

2 A typology of legal cultures

Alberto Febbrajo

1. Introductory remarks

As is often the case with sociological terms, the concept of legal culture is closely interwoven with different theoretical perspectives. This explains why sociologists of law often prefer to use it implicitly.[1]

The aim of this chapter is to suggest a multi-layered definition of legal culture that concentrates on the solution of a basic problem: why legal orders have the ability to change social reality and why they are sometimes not able to do so on the ground of diffused cultural resistances. The concept of legal culture will be represented here as the central element of a circular connection in which legal culture plays the role of a mirror that reflects both the legal image of society and the social image of law. This conceptual crossroad includes empirically observable elements that could explain the role of legal norms in social orders as well as the role of social norms in legal orders. After having discussed some possible specifications of the very general concept of legal culture (par. 2), I will try to illustrate four complementary models of 'reflexive' legal culture, each of them characterised by ideal typical images of legal and social norms in particular moments of the complex functioning of legal orders.[2]

I will focus on (a) a *traditional* model of legal culture that highlights the overwhelming importance of social 'customs' for establishing a deeply rooted identity of the legal order, (b) a *reactive* model of legal culture that underlines the significance of social and legal norms in selecting the possible 'sanctions' imposed by the state's jurisdiction and/or public opinion against deviant behaviours, (c) an *innovative* model of legal culture that concentrates on the reciprocal adjustments of social and legal norms required by a state's legislation that constantly tries to redefine its specific 'purposes' and (d) a *global* model of legal culture that reformulates the relations between legal norms and social norms in an as yet unclear set

1 On the somewhat impressionistic character of the concept of legal culture, cf. Roger Cotterrell, 'The Concept of Legal Culture', in David Nelken (ed.), *Comparing Legal Cultures*, Aldershot: Dartmouth, 1997, 13–32.

2 The four socio-legal models considered here have one point in common: their opposition to a 'normative' model of legal culture characterised by insufficient consideration of social norms. Starting from the same perspective, Teubner speaks of three possible connections between social and legal norms: the production of social norms outside the legal order but in open competition with legal norms; the inclusion of social norms extraneous to the law but implicitly necessary to defining legal decisions; the development of non-legal theories of law that describe the mutual relations of law with its inter-systemic environment. In addition, Teubner suggests a transnational perspective characterised by its heterarchical dimension. (cf. G. Teubner, 'Constitutionalising Policontexturality', *Social and Legal Studies* 19 (2011): 17ff.; Id, *Constitutional Fragments. Societal Constitutionalism in Globalisation*, Oxford: Oxford University Press, 2012).

of transnational 'values' (par. 3). I will then point out the strategic relevance of these typical forms of legal culture when we have to address some of the main theoretical and empirical problems of the sociology of law from different temporal perspectives (par. 4). Finally, I will briefly consider the possible analogies of legal and political cultures in democratic societies (par. 5).

2. Some negative specifications

Before sketching out – from different though not incompatible socio-legal perspectives – four typical models of how legal cultures might reflect social and legal norms, I will briefly consider some negative specifications of the concept of legal culture that could indirectly contribute to the demarcation of its core meaning. Starting from the very general premise that legal cultures cannot be defined on the basis of simple dichotomies, I will touch upon three basic questions.

a) What does the word 'legal' mean in the concept of legal culture?

In order to answer this question, a clear-cut alternative, characterised by a distinction between two typical lenses, is often suggested. The first lens concentrates on an internal and hierarchical image of what is legal; it represents the perspective of legal operators who routinely apply legal norms and are typically interested in making formally correct and undisputable decisions. The second lens concentrates on an external and plural representation of what is legal; it represents the perspective of ordinary people who define their behaviour and construct their personal images of the legal order on the basis of their own attitudes, expectations, opinions and evaluations.[3]

This dual distinction provides useful orientations. Nevertheless, both kinds of legal culture are not only based on the typical perceptions of different actors but also call for further, more specific, articulations.[4]

In fact, a legal culture can be 'internal' or 'external' to a legal order, according to at least three different elements: the *actors* who, as we have seen, might or might not belong to a legal institution, the *criteria* of their decisions, which might or might not be based on arguments relevant to official legal reasoning and the *objects* of their attention, which might or might not be relevant from a legal point of view.[5] In different situations, each of these elements may be internal or external, regardless of the others. So we have a fully 'internal' legal culture if the three main indicators – i.e. the 'actor', the 'object' and the 'criteria' – are all internal to the legal order, as, in the case of a judge who applies formally suitable legal criteria to decide legally relevant objects of conflicts.

3 Cf. L.M. Friedman, 'Legal Culture and Social Development', *Law and Society Review* 4 (1969): 29–44. Friedman's definition of external and internal legal culture refers to the contrast between popular culture and insiders' perception of law. This opposition between lower and higher legal culture is partially connected to our basic distinction between social and legal norms.

4 Legal cultures have also been differentiated by means of the two economic concepts of *supply* and *demand*, referring to their different roles in the production of norms. Cf. Ehrhard Blankenburg, 'Civil Litigation Rates as Indicators for Legal Culture', in D. Nelken (ed.), *Comparing Legal Cultures*, Aldershot: Dartmouth, 1997, 41–68.

5 In the same vein, cf. Bruno Latour, *The Making of Law. On the Ethnography of the Conseil d'Etat*, Cambridge: Polity Press, 2002. According to him, the autonomy of internal legal actors does not mean that the criteria and the objects of their decisions are also internal to the legal order.

Otherwise, a legal culture can be only partially external or internal, according to the different combinations of its internal and external elements. We may suppose, for instance, that an official representative of the legal order, such as a policeman, reacts in the face of legally relevant objects, as certain crimes, under the influence of criteria suggested not so much by written legal norms as of 'external' social norms. We may also imagine that a single actor, such as a simple citizen who is not member of a legal institution, dutifully follows the official criteria of the internal legal culture and spontaneously defends other citizens who would otherwise be victims of criminal acts.

A higher level of differentiation is achieved if the relevant features of legal cultures we have just seen are considered 'more or less' internal or external in specific cases.[6] Thus the researcher has to estimate the real distance of every case from a certain model of legal culture. Analogously, we could, for instance, observe that the religious culture in a certain community is stronger than in other communities if we look at a single variable such as the higher percentage of individuals who attend mass regularly. But the result could be completely different if we consider other indicators such as the percentage of religious marriages, or the commitments to missions of mercy. In this context the use of a plurality of suitable variables is necessary for ascertaining the concrete facets of a legal culture.

b) *What does the word 'culture' mean in the concept of legal culture?*

A very general definition of 'culture' normally combines several indicators characterised by different empirical perspectives. First of all, the main cultural indicators used by anthropologists and easier to observe, are the regular behaviours based on traditional customs. Facing serious difficulties of interpretation, sociologists consider more general cultural perspectives as problem of social control through institutions committed to values shared by a certain group of people. An overview of all these elements generates a differentiated vision of the culture of the group because the more concrete the level of analysis, the easier it is to find inconsistencies between the official legal norms announced within the group and the social norms regularly followed by its individual members.

Does this mean that every legal culture, where words do not correspond to facts, is ideological? The answer obviously depends on the concept of ideology we have in mind. We can speak of an ideology if the distance between official self-representation of law and concrete reality is the product of a conscious choice guided by specific interests. For instance it is possible to consider this lack of realism as ideological if legal professionals share a legal culture more coherent with the interests of their own status than officially admitted, or if they continue to represent law as totally neutral, equal and predictable, despite their different experiences and knowing that this image is completely unrealistic. From an external point of view we could consider ideological the use of law for bypassing law in order to meet concrete and not yet officially regulated expectations. But in both cases, it is not always possible to approach the problem from a simple "yes or no" perspective.

Generally speaking, the automatic identification of a legal culture with a sort of ideology seems to be an oversimplification.[7] Legal culture as such does not necessarily produce

6 Alberto Febbrajo, 'Cultura giuridica. Contenuto e funzioni di un concetto', in A. Febbrajo, A. La Spina, M. Raiteri (eds.), *Cultura giuridica e politiche pubbliche in Italia*, Milano: Giuffrè, 2006, XI–LXIII.

7 Cf. W. Kaupen, *Die Hüter von Recht und Ordnung, Die soziale Herkunft, Erziehung und Ausbildung der deutschen Juristen. Eine soziologische Analyse*, Neuwied-Berlin: Luchterhand, 1969. The problem touched upon by Kaupen is culturally circular: are judges who tend to be excessively formalist following the socialisation processes of their own institution or their original psychological aptitude to become defenders of law and order?

'ideological' images of law defended for personal interests by someone who knows that they are unreal. We have to separate the diffused image of an 'ideal' law from the image of an ideological law. Every kind of culture has to face a gap between self-representations and reality, between paper norms and norms in action. This means that legal cultures could be considered 'excessively formal' if they underestimate the influence of social norms, or 'excessively material' if they do not recognise the relevance of legal norms.

Furthermore legal cultures are basically connected to a not only normative but also cognitive approach that concretely suggests different combinations of legal and social norms in different situations. In this context it should not be forgotten that if we observe law through the lenses of our own legal culture, it is extremely difficult to maintain the necessary detachment from the different images of the legal order in which we are embedded[8]. As it is difficult for hikers to perceive the transition from plains to hills during a hike, so it is difficult for individuals to perceive where the borders lie in our society between the legal and social norms they apply in their daily lives. Legal norms have constantly to learn from social norms while society has constantly to adjust to the legal order.[9]

Here a question arises: can a sociologist, who also has the role of a social actor in his society, succeed in the apparently impossible task of observing and being observed?[10]

Every sociologist who wants to keep the necessary distance from the object of his/her research and to gain a better insight into it has to practise an accurate control over the knowledge acquired as an actor and as an observer of different social actors. The sociologist has to use a sort of mirror of other mirrors in order to observe himself as an 'observer'. [11] In this case, far from being an ideology, legal culture could be considered as a factor that can explain, and, in turn, requires explanation, as an instrument for a self-critical, approach.[12]

c) Is the concept of legal culture necessarily limited by state borders?

One of the most interesting applications of the concept of legal culture is comparison.[13] But with reference to which spatial borders can a homogeneous legal culture be identified?

8 For collecting more data about the legal culture of a specific group of people the empirical instrument of the interview is normally used. In this case, the interview of a legal actor is often exposed to concrete risks of misrepresentation since the actor could prefer to strike a pose in order to give the sociologist a trustworthy image of himself and, indirectly, of his own legal culture.

9 A legal culture that corrects itself while translating social knowledge into new norms was recently discussed under different headings. A model of legal culture capable of learning was in particular designed with the label of "responsive law" (P. Nonet and P. Selznick, *Law and Society in Transition*, New York: Harper & Row, 1978), and "reflexive law" (G. Teubner, 'Substantive and Reflexive Elements in Modern Law', *Law and Society Review* 17 (1983): 239–285).

10 The apparent impossibility of combining action and observation is represented in literary terms by L. Pirandello, *One, No One and One Hundred Thousand*, New York: Marsilio 1992, 13, when he describes his sudden encounter in a street with his image reflected in a mirror: "When I stood before a mirror, a kind of arrest took place inside me; all spontaneity vanished, my every movement seemed artificial, an imitation".

11 The internal approach to law seems to be a sort of selfie, where the same person is both photographer and photographed. But the intriguing side of this new mania appears to be more narcissistic than ideological.

12 As a matter of fact, it is equally dangerous to know too much or too little about a given object. If, for instance, a judge is writing a book on judges, the author requires a sophisticated methodological filter for assuring a reliable interpretation.

13 G. A. Caldeira, 'The Legal Cultures of Europe', *Law & Society Review* 30 (1996): 55 ff.; P. Legrand, 'European Legal Systems are not Converging', *ICLQ* 45 (1996): 57 ff.; D. Nelken (ed.), *Comparing Legal Cultures*, Aldershot: Dartmouth, 1997; M. van Hoeke and M. Warrington, 'Legal Cultures, Legal Paradigms and Legal Doctrine: Towards a New Model for Comparative Law', *ICLQ* 47 (1998): 495 ff.; C. Varga (ed.), *Comparative Legal Cultures*, Budapest: Szent Istvan Tarsulat, 2012.

The state, considered as a political and sociological entity, is limited by visible borders, and we may suppose that legal cultures within its territory are all oriented to the same legal order, albeit from different perspectives. Yet it should be noted that, although the normal use of the concept of society often presumes the dimension of a state (French society, Italian society, etc.), state's borders are nothing more than the accidental result of historical events and are not necessarily linked to corresponding legal cultures.

Consequently, the demarcation that 'rigidly' defines the contents of a cultural identity at national level often takes the form of a 'stereotype'.[14] As a matter of fact, the borders that circumscribe the state are not always culturally relevant for the purpose of defining the area of a sociological comparison. They can be somewhat unreliable, or even misleading, when it comes to detecting homogeneous cultural entities.[15] People who live in adjacent valleys separated by a watershed that designates the state's border have far more social norms in common with one another than with the people who live in the capital cities of their respective states. On the other side, different states that have a common past and share many social norms may reciprocally maintain strong cultural links and similar legal cultures.[16]

In general, legal cultures could be stabilised independently of state borders[17] also by geographical factors (as in the case of an island culturally separated from a larger state), linguistic factors (as in the case of post-colonial states) and so on. The cultural juxtaposition between what is inside and what is outside the borders of a state must be replaced by more flexible, albeit less evident, factors of demarcation, such as the presence of a convergent cultural background.[18]

In a nutshell, the three negative qualifications discussed above show how difficult it is for a sociologist to draw culturally meaningful borders in relation to the complex concept of legal culture. They underline different strategies of inclusion, observation and delimitation. The concept of legal culture could be thus defined using: (a) more articulated social intersections instead of simple internal/external alternatives based on institutionalised roles, (b) more articulated levels of observation instead of ideological criteria of interpretations

14 A good example of a national stereotype adopted as a normative advice by a multinational company was the label of a bottle of Cinzano vermouth, whose German wording recommended: to be served at a temperature between x and y degrees, while in Italian it suggested: to be served neither warm nor cold. The premise was clearly that the thorough precision of the norm was generally more appreciated by customers in one social context than in the other.

15 When Weber speaks of the "destiny" of nations in his comparative studies, he is clearly considering not the formal borders of states but, at ideal typical level, the cultural mission of representatives of the great methodological divide between common law and statutory law, in Great Britain and in Continental Europe (cf. M. Rheinstein (ed.), *Max Weber on Law in Economy and Society*, Cambridge: Harvard University Press, 1966, 284. On this aspect of Weber's work: A. Febbrajo, 'Dall'unità alla pluralità del diritto', in P. Rossi (ed.), *Ripensare Max Weber*, Rome: Accademia Nazionale dei Lincei, 2015, 171–192).

16 A similar case recently became evident in Europe with the admission in the EU of "post-communist" countries after a phase of transition. Cf. J. Priban, 'Constituting the Heterarchy of European Constitutionalism in EU's New Member States', in A. Febbrajo and W Sadurski (eds.), *Central and Eastern Europe after Transition. Towards a New Socio-Legal Semantics*, Farnham: Ashgate, 2010, 13–34.

17 Authors who analyse legal cultures as instruments for sociolegal comparisons of different states underline the diffusion of stereotypes also at a non-national level ("Crossing the road in Trento in North Italy is a much safer enterprise than doing so in Naples" in D. Nelken, 'Comparative Sociology of Law', in R. Banakar and M. Travers (eds.), *Law and Social Theory*, Oxford and Portland: Hart, 2013, 350).

18 What is decisive is not physical but cultural proximity. The production of different social norms can be observed not only in different cities, or parts of the same city, but in different generations: the closest example is the profoundly divergent legal cultures that often coexist in the same family.

and (c) more articulated spatial delimitations of cultural points of reference instead of historically established national borders.

In any case, legal cultures are the result of applications of a dual code but have to refer to further specifications. In order to reach more concrete points of reference, we would rather speak of a reflexive reiteration of distinctions in order to define typical legal cultures.[19] This procedure creates a set of alternatives, which paves the way for a classification of legal cultures closer to social situations.

3. Towards a reflexive definition of legal culture

For decades, sociologists of law have defined their specific field of study as the reciprocal relations between law and society.[20] This complex subject matter, whatever theoretical approaches it may require, presupposes the use of the very concept of legal culture. Without analysing the contents of legal culture based on the mutual relations of social and legal norms, sociology of law would not be able to follow the continuous normative interplay from society to law and vice versa.[21]

Indeed, as the main components of legal cultures, 'social' and 'legal' norms share the common task of guiding the lives of human beings but with distinct and complementary ambitions. It is thus necessary to reflect on legal cultures, avoiding the illusion of an absolute predominance of legal norms presupposed by the formal model of legal culture. It is possible to imagine a primitive society regulated exclusively by social norms but not a modern society regulated without a combination of legal *and* social norms.[22] Also in modern societies social norms are at least quantitatively far more widespread and recognised than legal norms; they are the second leg of the more easily changeable legal norms and their task is basically subsidiary, i.e. meant to regulate what legal norms cannot regulate in a manner acceptable to the actors concerned.

Legal norms are formally imposed top-down through state organisations and should be oriented to a difficult engineering of interpersonal relations, whereas social norms emerge autonomously bottom-up and are generally oriented to the stabilisation of already-tested customs. Legal norms, formulated in a technical language, are normally connected to rapid change, whereas social norms, mostly unwritten, are generally discerned through direct observation of the behaviour of others and tend to be less changeable; legal norms, formulated in technical language and, known by a limited number of professionals, are the

19 In these cases, mathematicians speak of complex processes of "discretisation", which could be formalised by variable combinations of borders. Cf. Benoit B. Mandelbrot, *The Fractal Geometry of Nature*, Freeman, 1977.

20 This widely accepted definition (cf. R. Treves and G. van Loon (eds.), *Norms and Actions, National Reports on Sociology of Law*, Dordrecht: Springer, 1998) opens up two possible fields of research: the mutual relations between legal norms and social reality and the mutual relations between social and legal norms. I prefer to develop the latter perspective here, not least because social reality appears to be a *normatively* ordered reality, which would not exist if it were not *constituted* by social norms (on the distinction between "regulative rules" and "constitutive rules", see John R. Searle, *Speech Acts*, London: Cambridge University Press, 1969, 50).

21 A pluralistic concept of legal culture acknowledges that social norms are visible even at the highest level of a constitution. Cf. A. Febbrajo, 'Constitutionalism and Legal Pluralism', in A. Febbrajo and G. Corsi (eds.), *Sociology of Constitutions: A Paradoxical Perspective*, London-New York: Routledge, 2016, 68–98.

22 Primitive thinking survives to the present day in various forms, in our mind and in our actions. Cf. Pierre Clastres, *Society against the State*, Oxford: Basil Blackwell, 1977; Leopold J. Pospisil, *Anthropology of Law: A Comparative Theory*, New York-London: Harper and Row, 1971; C. Geertz, *The Interpretation of Cultures. Selected Essays*, New York: Basic Books, 1973; Sally Falk Moore, *Law as Process. An Anthropological Approach*, Oxford: Oxford University Press, 1978, Norbert Rouland, *Anthropologie Juridique*, Paris: PUF, 1988.

institutionalised product of the process of separation of law from the rest of society, whereas social norms constitute – also in contemporary legal orders – the pervasive and unforgotten legacy of less differentiated societies. This is particularly evident for a 'living law', where - as in the case of family law - 'unofficial' norms are often closer to the daily life than the 'legal' ones.[23]

Some basic questions arise in this context: what is it that ultimately ensures unity and consistency to the different legal and social instruments used for regulating societies? How is it possible to combine legal and social norms in given circumstances and interpret them in the most convenient and acceptable way? Which kind of 'meta-norms', resulting both from the legal interpretation of social norms and from the social perception of legal norms, influence human beings in their constant oscillation between social and legal norms?[24]

An overall instrument for answering these questions can be found in a comprehensive and pluralistic concept of legal culture, able to reflect the different representations of law produced by heterogeneous combinations of social and legal norms.[25] In this context every model of legal culture is reflexive for at least two reasons: because, as we have seen, it has to be applied concretely through reiteration of distinctions (first level of reflexivity), and because it is basically the product of self – referential forms of normativity that are cognitively adjusting single norms to given situations (second level of reflexivity). In this way, different legal cultures may refer directly or indirectly to different forms of normativity and vice versa.

I will indicate here a series of *typical* models of legal culture characterised by different intersections of social and legal norms respectively oriented to specific aspects of the functioning of legal systems: the stabilisation of traditional *customs*, the selection of defensive *sanctions*, the variation of legislative *purposes* and the re-orientation of universal *values*. The typology suggested here is thus based on a double – systemic and cultural – perspective and tries to reflect fundamental aspects of the life of legal orders.

a) Traditional legal culture

A long-established legal order appears to be overwhelmingly oriented to a legal culture based on models of behaviour and way of thinking originally produced by traditional norms. A tradition is normally generated by deeply embedded social norms that appear to be best suited to a certain group of social actors, especially in those sectors that are more culturally distant from the state.[26]

The classic example of a plurality of individuals, who are unified by social norms and traditional beliefs, is a 'community' supported by durable cultural relations among its

23 In this context, legal and social norms could be represented by means of several conceptual couples, i.e. not only "internal–external" but also "endogenous"–"exogenous", "institutionalised"–"not institutionalised".

24 The combination of social and legal norms in meta-norms influenced by different cultural factors (as, for instance, by moral choices or by utilitarian calculations) can be analysed in the realm of law using the complex model of *social game*. See the pioneering contributions of Max Weber, 'Stammler and the Materialist Conception of History', in H. H. Bruun and S. Whimster (eds.), *Collected Methodological Writings*, London-New York: Routledge, 203–226.

25 Cf. Adam Podgorecki and Maria Los, *Multi-dimensional Sociology*, London: Routledge & Kegan Paul, 1979.

26 The distance of spontaneous social orders from official legal orders was one of the historical leitmotif of Ehrlich's sociology of law (E. Ehrlich, *Fundamental Principles of the Sociology of Law*, New York: Russell & Russell, 1962).

members. It is normally held together by the internal cohesion of a legal culture based on the widespread perception that the community is more than the sum of its single members.[27]

Traditional legal culture typically shows a closer connection with social norms than with legal norms. In this context, a new legal norm is weaker than an established social norm. What is functionally at stake here is first of all the cultural stability of the legal order. Traditional legal cultures are not easily changeable; they stabilise, through social experience and gradual processes of 'trial and error', a set of norms adequate to the cultural identity of a given community.[28] This attributes a stable authority to social norms and justifies their continuous influence upon the production of legal norms.[29]

This does not mean that legal and social norms are exempt from conflicts. Social norms often ignore legal norms that are perceived as too distant from the profound beliefs of a traditional community while legal norms that are incompatible with social norms, may induce human beings to respond not only with acquiescence, half-obedience or covert compromises, but also with open refusals and rebellion.

The original sense of togetherness and solidarity, typical of local communities, is not left behind completely in modern societies. Many grey areas can be observed where the traditional normative structures of the community partially survive in spite of increasing official regulations. The model of community to which this legal culture is connected has several meaningful articulations still influential in a modern society, such as peer groups, social networks, organisations, religious communities and minorities with common historical and linguistic backgrounds. Each of these forms of associations could represent traditional customs and specific legal cultures even in the larger state's community.

b) Reactive legal culture

A further model of legal culture, connected to a different combination of legal and social norms, is developed when a legal order has to face deviant behaviour. In the case of an open infringement of a legal norm that is not considered as a mere paper law, the legal order and its operators are 'obliged' to react with official sanctions in order to confirm the validity of the infringed norms and support the potential reactions of normal individuals. Should no official reaction be forthcoming, a sanction of second order has to be applied against the operator responsible for having avoided reacting with the due sanctions. The mutual relations between official reactions of the first or second order and social reactions are sensitive detectors of the level of vitality of internal or external legal culture and of the level of legitimacy of the legal order.[30]

Originally, the defence against deviance came into being before the official introduction of a state-regulated court proceeding. Since then, however, priority was gradually attributed not only to social norms, as in the previous model of legal culture, but also to legal norms, seen as the safest instrument for protecting individuals against deviant behaviours,

27 Ferdinand Tönnies, *Fundamental Concepts of Sociology*, New York: American Book Company 1940. For studying this type of legal culture sociolegal and anthropological perspectives are basically complementary.

28 This is the fundamental reason of the strength of "living law" also in modern societies.

29 Cf. the well-known hypothesis of the development of law and society from the more traditional *status* to the more flexible *contract* (Cf Henry J. S. Maine, *Ancient Law: Its Connections with the Early History of Society and Its Relation to Modern Ideas*, London: John Murray, 1861).

30 Cf. Ehrlich, *Fundamental Principles of the Sociology of Law*, cit., 121.

and deviant behaviours against excessive reactions on the part of the legal order or of single individuals.[31]

The decisive relevance of legal norms for labelling some behaviours as officially deviant and imposing legal sanctions does not exclude the possibility that social norms are still important for defining both the positive sanctions, or rewards, by which a society and its subgroups mould their members into conformity, and the collateral consequences of legal punishments, that are often accompanied by a loss of public image.[32]

In this context the role of legal norms is regulated minutely by the state's jurisdiction and by selective court proceedings. Judges, guided by an internal legal culture, have to furnish an official definition of the object of the proceedings and have to follow the basic 'script' of the procedure in accordance with the legal norms that rigidly define its formalities and deadlines.

Apparently, this leaves little room for mantaining a flexible border between what is lawful and what is unlawful. Yet, even within court proceedings, legal norms are often interpreted in differentiated ways.[33]

As a matter of fact, in order to avoid open conflicts with pre-existing social norms, court proceedings reduce the possibility that reactions to deviant behaviours automatically follow the indications of legal norms.[34] Informal procedures can skip legal norms or adjust them to socially relevant interests if these have been ignored or not explicitly considered by legal norms, or by requests of public opinion.[35] On a case by case basis, sociologists of law can define to what extent the procedural 'game' of the court proceeding remains sufficiently fair, and which interpretations of legal norms are suggested by extra-legal norms.

The structured control of legal norms by other legal norms is open to different outcomes, and a happy ending can be expected by the individuals involved with an acceptable level of risk. Consequently, the so-called 'certainty of law' has to be replaced pragmatically by a 'bearable uncertainty', reflected by a legal culture that is not always interested in having recourse to the courts.[36]

31 The principle, originally based on social norms, that he who commits an error must pay proportionally ("an eye for an eye, a tooth for a tooth") has gradually developed a much more sophisticated balance between deviant behaviour and legal sanctions, which takes the interests of the victims into consideration (H. Strang, *Repair or Revenge. Victims and Restorative Justice*, Oxford: Clarendon Press, 2002).

32 This has been underlined by different strands of "legal realism". See T. Geiger, *Vorstudien zu einer Soziologie des Rechts*, Neuwied am Rhein: Lucherhand 1964; L. Loevinger, 'Jurimetrics: Science and Prediction in the Field of Law', *Minnesota Law Review* 46 (1961): 255–275.

33 In the juridical praxis "conditional programmes" such as 'in the presence of fact X, code Y legal. In the presence of fact Z, code Y illegal'(see N. Luhmann, *Law as Social System*, Oxford: Oxford University Press, 2004, p, 19) are neutral procedures. On the basis of a flexible approach, administrative procedures should be, in principle, even more automatic and neutral. But both, from a socio-legal perspective, are ideal-typical abstractions and are not able to ensure a completely neutral – under given circumstances unjust- procedure (*summum jus, summa iniuria*).

34 On the ambiguous role of the judiciary between legal and social norms, cf. C. Guarnieri and P. Pederzoli, *The Power of Judges*, Oxford: Oxford University Press, 2002.

35 Unclear legal norms, or extensive legal delays, could increase preferences for mediation and informal justice. Cf., from a general perspective, Richard L. Abel (ed.), *The Politics of Informal Justice*, New York: Academic Press, 1982; K. Zweigert and H. Kotz, *An Introduction to Comparative Law*, Oxford: Oxford University Press 1987.

36 Like every social game, court proceedings are also legitimated not only for the certainty of their procedure but also for the uncertainty of their outcome, perceived to be neutral because nobody knows it in advance, as in a fair game (N. Luhmann, *Legitimation durch Verfahren*, Frankfurt a.M.: Suhrkamp, 1983).

This physiological uncertainty raises a further question: how can general criteria be found outside court proceedings to achieve a preliminary and wider convergence of legal and social norms? The answer might be: through the innovative character of a state's legislation and its legal culture.

c) Innovative legal culture

An additional way of considering the role of legal cultures focuses neither on social traditions nor on the state's jurisdiction, but on the state's legislation. Especially in differentiated societies, a functionally innovative legislation is an essential condition for maintaining the flexibility of legal orders and, at the same time, the basic convergence of legal and social norms. Every legal system has to perceive whether legislation is compatible or incompatible with social expectations, and whether its manifest functions are fitting the consequences produced by official norms.[37]

Legal norms must be neither too close to, nor too far from, social norms that are largely accepted in the daily relations of the average citizen. In the first case, legal norms would be almost useless because their contents would substantially correspond to what has already happened; in the second case, legal norms would be unattainable because their purposes would exceed the possibilities of change defined by established social norms. When people act, react and decide in everyday life, they accept new legal norms not only because of the higher authority of the state but also because these norms are supported by social norms that may incorporate extra-legal orientations (for instance, to religion, politics, economics, science).

From a legal point of view, paying taxes is generally represented as one of the most important duties of every citizen, while from a social point of view, it could be perceived as one of the essential pre-conditions for a loyal relationship of every single member with the community. Influenced by a socially widespread sense of justice, however, public opinion could also concede that the full payment of the prescribed amount of taxes entails socially negative consequences, in particular situations not yet considered by general legislation.[38] On the other hand, acts of discrimination that are still compatible with legal norms may, in given situations, provoke a widespread sense of solidarity with the victims and, in the long term, also influence a legislative intervention with the potential to fill this gap.[39] In other words social norms provide a sort of 'alarm system' for reducing or absorbing the impact of socially unsustainable legislation.[40]

The functional approach adopted by general social systems theory has pointed out that the differentiation of specific social systems based on their own criteria of rationality is not

37 This means that a politically responsible legislator has to take the risk of a purpose-specific programme i.e. the risk that "the future present will not be what is assumed to be the present future". Cf. Luhmann, *Law as a Social System*, p. 199.

38 A socially widespread sense of justice is often oriented to common sense evaluations of the advantages obtained and the costs sustained in different social systems by the application of legal norms. Cf. R. Masters and M. Gruter (eds.), *The Sense of Justice. Biological Foundations of Law*, Newbury Park, CA: Sage, 1999.

39 Howard Zehr, *The Little Book of Restorative Justice*, Intercourse, PA: Good Books, 2002.

40 I prefer here to define 'social norms' as norms that are produced in a society by anonymous traditions independent of the state, and 'extralegal norms' as those social norms that are culturally embedded in social systems different from the legal system. In the first case, the basic question is how social norms are generated; in the second, it is where they are coming from.

producing a rigid distinction internal vs. external.[41] In every system, including the legal system, the stimuli coming from the external complexity of the environment call for more internal complexity. Normative institutions are thus depicted not as basically repressive but as instruments for reducing to an acceptable level the number of alternatives of behaviours and decisions offered by an over-complex environment.[42] This most comprehensive function of legal systems, i.e. the reduction of external complexity through social and legal norms, is generally supported by inter-systemic relations.

Legal systems are closely connected to political systems because they provide the legitimacy that the legal system requires. Furthermore, legal systems are closely connected to economic systems because both contribute to the enlargement of foreseeable social relations. The norm of the norms, i.e. the constitution, is from this perspective one of the most important instruments for connecting legal systems with political systems. An essential inter-systemic function of the constitution is rejecting legally inconsistent law and enhancing a politically better law.[43] This draws up a political map of legally anchored rights and duties compatible with the functioning of both systems.

d) Global legal culture

The phenomenon of globalisation, based on real or potential economic and political worldwide connections, crosses state boundaries more or less explicitly. What is at stake here is the cultural extensibility of a valid legal order in a dimension where population, territory and sovereignty assume potentially transnational accents. The emerging model of a global legal culture raises several questions: is the current specification of what is social and legal adequate to the wider horizon created above the state? How can new views of law – in particular, those emerging from the 'societal constitutions' of transnational entities – be combined in a consistent legal culture?[44]

Sociology of law cannot afford to ignore these challenges to the dynamics of legal cultures. The main problem here is connected to an increasing normative heterogeneity, which could give more scope to transnational conflicts between legal authorities. In this framework, global channels of digital communications play an important role even if they are often working at levels far removed from direct personal experiences.[45] They, on the one side, exert a profound influence on the construction of collective memories and, on the other, are inspired by a global call for humanity.

41 On systemic differentiations with flexible external borders, see, for instance, N. Luhmann, 'The Coding of the Legal System', in G. Teubner and A. Febbrajo (eds.), *State, Law and Economy as Autopoietic System. Regulation and Autonomy in a New Perspective*, European Yearbook in the Sociology of Law, Milano: Giuffré, 145 ff.

42 N. Luhmann, *A Sociological Theory of Law*, London: Routledge & Kegan Paul, 1972; Id., *Risk. A Sociological Theory*, Berlin: de Gruyter, 1993.

43 It is no coincidence that the constitution has been described as an inter-systemic instrument of "structural coupling", in particular, as the most legal part of the political system and as the most political part of the legal system. Cf. N. Luhmann, 'Operational Closure and Structural Coupling: The Differentiation of the Legal System', *Cardozo Law Review* 13 (1992): 1419–1441.

44 A general presentation of the concept of 'societal constitution' in G. Teubner, *Constitutional Fragments: Societal Constitutionalism and Globalisation*, Oxford: Oxford University Press, 2012.

45 Actually, some age groups seem to be more exposed to the influence of the media and to the difficulties in distinguishing between real and virtual dimensions Cf on the constitutive character of the media N. Luhmann, *The Reality of the Mass Media*, Stanford, CA: Stanford University Press, 2000.

This communicative perspective consolidates new actors, criteria and contents of legal cultures and explains the increasing importance, for the harmonisation of different legal orders, of the most abstract normative level: that of values.[46] Thanks to their broader range of interpretations, abstract values are capable of outlining a virtual model of legal culture that is not limited by the state's borders and its norms. This higher level of generalisation of values limits potential divergences and direct confrontations with less abstract normative levels. It facilitates an inflation of values, which multiplies general compatibilities, supports trans-constitutional horizons and overcomes concrete difficulties of substantial harmonisation, allowing for extremely heterogeneous and, sometimes, only symbolic interpretations.[47] A widespread 'optimism of values' can be affirmed by legal cultures without indicating the social costs of values and their limits of compatibility with other societal restraints.[48]

One possible limit of this process of increasing abstraction is that legally and/or socially oriented values have often 'zero sum' relations, also in a transnational context. It is thus impossible to ensure their parallel and generalised growth. When, for instance, the area occupied by norms concerning personal security increases, the area reserved for a defence of the freedom of individuals has to be reduced, and vice versa.

The global model, because of its higher level of abstraction, is able to absorb the models of legal culture we have seen in so far as their characteristic elements are inserted into a transnational perspective: local traditions could become stronger in weaker states; juridical praxis appears less certain because of the decline of formal hierarchies; national legislations, especially in periods of global crises, have to expand their own purposes dramatically, yet with limited expectations of success.[49]

Summarising, the typical connections between social and legal norms suggested by the different models of legal culture outlined here, respectively address complementary normative perspectives which have to be (a) remembered, since they are rooted in customs; (b) applied, since they are valid for judges; (c) renewed, since they are changeable for legislators; and (d) harmonised, since they are produced outside a state-centred hierarchy.

The main conceptual connections used for defining these different models of legal culture can be represented schematically as follows (Table 2.1):

Table 2.1 Four models of legal cultures

Type of Reflexivity	*Instrument*	*Perspective*	*Main Alternative*	*Point of Reference*
Traditional	Customs	Stabilisation	Centre/Periphery	Local Community
Reactive	Sanctions	Selection	Lawful/Unlawful	Jurisdiction
Innovative	Purposes	Variation	Compatible/Incompatible	Legislation
Global	Values	Generalization	Virtual/Concrete	Transnational Horizon

46 Nowadays, the increasing importance of values seems to have little in common with a revival of natural law. Whereas natural law is still a significant attempt to reach a comprehensive harmonisation of legal norms, the current interpretation of values seems to basically rely on implicitly regional (in Europe mostly Eurocentric) horizons.

47 M. Neves, *Transconstitutionalism*, Oxford: Hart, 2013.

48 On the social costs of implementing legal values and a self-critical control of their concrete possibility to be translated into reality Eric A. Posner, *Law and Social Norms*, Harvard: Harvard University Press, 2000.

49 P. F. Kjaer, G. Teubner and A. Febbrajo (eds.), *The Financial Crisis in Constitutional Perspective. The Dark Side of Functional Differentiation*, Oxford-Portland: Hart, 2011.

Furthermore, we have to underline that in this typology of legal cultures, some basic requirements for the functioning of every social system come to the fore. Traditions are based on the *stabilisation* of customary relations among social actors in a local community; reactions against unlawful behaviours are based on the *selection* of possible sanctions; innovations are based on cognitively adjusted *variation* of the inter-systemic purposes of legislation; finally, global legal culture appears to be based on the disorder of values and the virtual *generalisations* produced by their high level of abstraction.

4. Some implications of legal cultures

The complementarity of these typical models of legal cultures is essential for the functioning of legal orders. According to a pluralistic approach to the concept of legal culture, these typical models diminish the relevance of written law, expand the normative power of society and contribute to a less rigid balance between social and legal norms.

They show that law: (a) has a subsidiary role, in so far as it may be more or less successfully integrated or even replaced by spontaneous reiteration of already tested social schemes of action; (b) is defended against deviant behaviours not only by the conditional programmes of judicial decisions but also by diffused and efficient social sanctions; (c) is oriented not only to the purpose-specific programmes of legislation but also to the convergence of socially relevant extra-legal criteria and (d) is inclined to accept mutually compatible social norms and abstract values from the world society even if the single state is no longer able to exercise a hierarchical control of the concrete situations.

The complementarity of these models of legal culture opens up a large field of possible concretisations. In particular, it entails a direct reference to different temporal orientations and to some of the major fields of research of socio-legal studies.

A traditional legal culture refers to the sources of a state's law, which are typically oriented to the *past*. Here, the central problem to be considered is that of the *genesis* of law, which is basically seen as the result of a gradual process of legal institutionalisation of social customs. In this context, an important point of reference is one of the oldest fields of socio-legal research, which includes studies concerning different types of Knowledge and Opinion about Law (KOL). It can be particularly useful for the reconstruction in a certain community of the established legal cultures that influence the origin of the official legal norms.[50]

A reactive legal culture underlines how social and legal sanctions against *present* cases of deviance and illegality are important for the control of the real force of legal cultures. In this context, the central problem to be considered is that of the *effectiveness* of juridical sanctions because every explicit violation offers an opportunity to check the resilience of legal norms, as well as the vitality of the legal culture they reflect.[51] Of particular relevance here is the contribution offered by the well-established strand of research of legal professions.[52] Studying these roles, which appear to be 'interstitial' between legal and social norms, this field of research analyses how their work could actually pursue the task of defining the contents

50 Cf. A. Podgorecki, W. Kaupen, J. van Houtte, P. Vinke and B. Kutchinski, *Knowledge and Opinion about Law*, London: M. Robertson, 1973.

51 The reaction to unlawful behaviours is a decisive factor; in the absence of violations, even the official norm remains invisible from a realistic point of view. See Theodor Geiger, 'The Social Order', in R. Mayntz (ed.), *On Social Order and Mass Society. Selected Papers*, Chicago-London: University of Chicago Press, 1969, 39–80.

52 This field of research was extensively present in the classical sociology of law. Cf. R. Abel and P. S. C. Lewis (eds.), *Lawyers in Society. An Overview*, Berkley/Los Angeles/London: University of California Press, 1995. *Law and Social Theory*

of legal decisions according to criteria based on both internal and external legal cultures.[53] Related paths of research called Alternative Disputes Resolution Processes (ADR) and Access to Justice are also important. Starting from a 'normative scepticism', these researches underline the different perceptions of the process and the different obstacles that make in particular civil procedure inaccessible to a large proportion of law consumers.[54]

An innovative legal culture focuses attention on the different ways in which legal orders try to develop *future*-oriented perspectives[55] and check how legal norms could become essential factors of 'social engineering'.[56] The central problem here is the *change* of law that takes the possible conditions of a variation of legal norms and of their successful impact on social reality into consideration. In this context, implemented by mutual adjustments of legal and extra-legal norms, an important contribution has been developed by the strand of research called Critical Legal Studies (CLS) that concentrates on the reconstruction of the major inter-systemic relations of law. In this framework, a critical analysis of the distributive function of law in terms of money and power shows that the formal purposes of law could produce illusions being *de facto* incompatible with the functional requirements of political and economic systems.[57]

Finally, a global legal culture imposed on legal institutions by the perceived emergence of a meta-legal order[58] crosses the boundaries of nation states and develops an as-yet unclear influence of international courts that defy the power of states. This cross-cultural set of connections above established legal orders[59] supports the controversial emergence of the potentially universal field of *human rights*. In the absence of global hierarchies, the transnational dialogue not only among judges but also among public opinions[60] is here characterised by heterogeneous inputs, short-term illuminations and shocking information disseminated globally by wide-ranging channels of communication. What emerges is thus a sort of atemporal *hyper-present*, so conscious of the force of its novelty as to be tempted to forget the past and give up imagining a far-reaching future.[61]

These conceptual connections may be represented as follows (Table 2.2):

53 Max Weber, *M. Weber on Law in Economy and Society*, Cambridge, MA: Harvard University Press, 1966, 198–223.

54 In this context, the legal culture concerning the real perception of civil procedures is the result of a circular relation featuring three interacting elements: social needs, legal response and real impact. Cf. M. Cappelletti, 'Alternative Dispute Resolution Processes within the Framework of the World-Wide Access-to-Justice Movement', *The Modern Law Review* 56 (1993): 282 ff.

55 A. Febbrajo, 'Come regolare il futuro della società. L'eterna sfida del diritto', Revista Direito Mackenzie, 11 (2017)

56 A. Podgorecki, J. Alexander and R. Shields, *Social Engineering*, Montreal: McGill Queens Press, 1986.

57 D. Kennedy, 'Law-and-Economics from the Perspective of Critical Legal Studies', in P. P. Newman (ed.), *The New Palgrave Dictionary of Economics and Law*, London: MacMillan, 1998, 465–474. R. Mangabeira Unger, *The Critical Legal Studies Movement*, Cambridge, MA: Harvard University Press, 1986.

58 The global predominance of economic interests, brought about by the greater ability of money to circulate without limits of space, constitutes a crucial challenge for a trans-national perspective, especially in periods of crisis, when the reduced normative control through established legal and social norms are particularly evident. Cf. A. Febbrajo, 'The Failure of Regulatory Institutions – A Conceptual Framework', in P. F. Kjaer, G. Teubner and A. Febbrajo (eds.), *The Financial Crisis in Constitutional Perspective. The Dark Side of Functional Differentiation*, Oxford-Portland: Hart, 2011, 269–302.

59 Cf. F. Newman and D. Weissbrodt, *International Human Rights*, Cincinnati: Anderson, 1990; N. Luhmann, 'Grundwerte als Zivilreligion: Zur wissenschaftlichen Karriere eines Themas', in *Archivio di Filosofia*, Roma: Istituto di Studi Filosofici, 1978, 51–71.

60 On a constitutional dialogue outside a state's borders, cf. P. W. Hogg and A. Bushell, 'The Charter Dialogue between Courts and Legislatures', *Osgoode Hall Law Journal* 35 (1997): 75–124; Miguel P. Maduro, 'Contrapunctual Law: Europe's Constitutional Pluralism in Action', in N. Walker (ed.), *Sovereignty in Transition*, Oxford: Hart Publishing, 2003, 501–537.

61 Cf. N. Chomsky and E. Herman, *Manufacturing Consent: The Political Economy of the Mass Media*, New York: Pantheon, 1988.

Table 2.2 Possible applications of reflexive legal cultures

Type of Reflexivity	*Temporal Dimension*	*Main Problem*	*Main Field of Research*
Traditional	Past	Genesis of Law	KOL
Reactive	Present	Effectiveness of Law	Legal Professions Access to Justice
Innovative	Future	Change of Law	CLS
Global	Hyper-present	Heterarchy of Law	Human Rights

Summarising, the typical models of traditional, reactive, innovative and global legal culture bring together several socio-legal contributions. These are oriented to different cultural aspects, not only legally but also politically relevant, that is, respectively, to a culture of identity, a culture of defence, a culture of hope and, finally, a culture of dialogue.

5. Concluding remarks

The classification of legal cultures proposed here could easily be extended to political cultures. In general, given the political relevance of legal cultures and the legal relevance of political cultures, the legal system appears as an important support for the functioning of political systems and vice versa. A legal system can only be legitimised by political systems and a political system can only become operative in a given society through the complex machine of the legal system and the influence of its legal cultures.[62]

If we look at the democratic procedure as a complex strategy for channelling both legal and political risks,[63] the periodical evaluations of a political élite carried out by normal citizens take the form of a legally institutionalised tool for interpreting the otherwise mysterious 'will of the people'. It seems to be the result of a constantly changing combination not only of social and legal norms but also of legal and political culture.

This is particularly evident when we consider the key concept of 'participation', which is one of the most significant expressions of the common dimension of political and legal cultures. One question could be raised here: what kind of 'participation' would be better suited to producing and disseminating new types of legal cultures in the political system and new types of political cultures in the legal system?[64]

Given the complexity of its functions, the concept of participation ensures several typical connections between political and legal cultures. We could, for instance, speak of *identifying* participation, when political and legal cultures converge to defend a legal and political heritage; of *competitive* participation, when legal and political cultures converge to support a political actor in a political competition; of *creative* participation, when legal and political cultures converge to create the conditions to a campaign focusing on emerging, not yet legally regulated, issues; and of *messianic* participation, when legal and political cultures

62 Luhmann, *Law as a Social System*.

63 The strength of democracy lies in its so to say a-temporal dimension, given its possibility to decide without eliminating the discarded possibilities of decision. Cf. N. Luhmann, *The Future of Democracy*, Thesis Eleven, Sage Publication, 1990, 46–53; Id. *Risk. A Sociological Theory*, New York, Routledge 2017; Id. *Legitimation durch Verfahren*, Neuwied-Berlin, Luchterhand, 1969. G. Sartori, *The Theory of Democracy Revisited*, Vol. 2, Chatham, NJ: Chatham House Publishers, 1987.

64 C. Crouch, *Post-democracy*, Cambridge: Polity Press, 2005; B. de Sousa Santos, *A Dificil Democracia. Reinventar as Esquerdas*, Sao Paulo: Boitempo, 2016. Recent EU experience shows that the sum of national democracies is able to produce not a meta-democracy, but more likely a new form of oligarchy.

converge to enlarge their scope beyond the state in view of globally relevant issues as environmental problems.

In this context, the use of political culture as an element that has to be integrated by legal culture suggests a series of functional symmetries: the role played by a community in stabilising the identity of a legal culture corresponds to the role played by political parties for defining as collective organisations a certain political culture; the role played by a judicial process in selecting legal decisions corresponds to the role played by institutionalised political procedures for regulating confrontations in the political arena; the role played by legislation in the continuous variation of its legal purposes corresponds to the role played by political programmes for allowing their continuous adjustment; the role played by a transnational legal culture oriented to global values corresponds to a new version of the political concept of 'commonweal', expanded beyond the borders of a single state.

Especially in periods of crisis, legal and political cultures appear to be complementary in terms of criticising legal decisions from a political perspective and/or defining new public policies on the basis of legal instruments. It is impossible to go into the parallelisms of legal and political cultures here. I can only underline that the functional 'couplings' of legal and political lenses currently constitute one of the major challenges to socio-legal studies. In a wider and still opaque perspective, they teach us that the observation of law requires the mutual reflection not only of legal and political cultures but also of other kinds of extralegal cultures, such as religious and economic cultures.

3 Pluripoiesis of law and the kaleidoscope of legal cultures[1]

Pedro Rubim Borges Fortes

1. Introductory remarks

The point of departure of this chapter is the perception that the traditional tenets of Niklas Luhmann's systemic theory of law, in particular, concepts like structural coupling, autopoiesis and self-referential coding, could be enlarged by a new set of conceptualisations such as structural grouping, pluripoiesis and fusion of multiple normative elements. The sociology of law based on Luhmann's thesis, that autopoietic law is cognitively open and normatively closed, that constitutions comprise the dual articulation between law and politics and that law is the single normative element for the coding of legal systems, needs to be closely and empirically scrutinised nowadays. As a matter of fact, observation of the contemporary constitutional state implies an articulation of multiple legal cultures and provides a fusion of law not only with politics but also with economics and religion.

In this chapter, I will concentrate on a significant example as a case study: the Brazilian constitution, which, in my opinion, should not be considered merely as a structural coupling between law and politics.[2] After all, it seems that the Brazilian constitutional structure articulates law, politics, economics, religion, science, etc. simultaneously. In other words, an observer should analyse the Brazilian constitution as an instance not of ***structural coupling*** but of ***structural grouping*** – or, in more provocative terms, of ***structural polygamy***. The Brazilian constitution is a much more complex structure that articulates multiple systems at once in a grouping or in polygamous fashion.[3] In this chapter, I will explore this insight in relation to its compatibility with the work of Niklas Luhmann.

Second, I aim to provide an account of legal culture as a kaleidoscope. This is intimately connected with my first point. Instead of drawing on univocal ideas on law, contemporary observers of the legal system are influenced by plurivocal ideas. Therefore, legal culture should accommodate multiple perspectives on legal phenomena. Communications about what is legal/illegal are proclaimed more and more with reference to the economic analysis of law, conflict theory, legal ideologies, technological evidence and developmental discourse.

1 A preliminary version of this chapter was presented at a workshop on Sociology of Constitutions organised by Alberto Febbrajo and Germano Schwartz in Fermo in the summer of 2016, and I am grateful to the participants for their relevant feedback. Likewise, I am indebted to Denis Galligan and Alberto Febbrajo for their commentaries on a mature draft, which significantly improved the text. Any errors are all mine.

2 Niklas Luhmann, *Law as a Social System* (OUP 2004), pp. 403–405.

3 See Germano Schwartz, *Constituicões Civis e Regulacão: Autopoiese e Teoria Constitucional*, Anais (Conpedi 2009); Id., O Processo de Diferenciacão Funcional dos Direitos Fundamentais e a Necessária Conexão entre as Práticas Sociais e a Normatividade, in Felipe Dutra Asensi e Daniel Giotti de Paula (editors), *Tratado de Direito Constitucional: Constituicão no Século XXI*, volume 2 (Elsevier 2014).

I suggest that the evolution of law has produced a trend of normative fusion in the legal system that may be perceived by observing structural groupings. As part of my argument, I analyse select aspects of transversal rationality, critical systems theory and constitutional fragmentation. I also consider the hypothesis of a complex articulation of structural groupings that generates the fusion of multiple normative elements observed as a *pluripoietic system*, constituted by a plurality of self-referenced and hetero-referenced coded communications. Drawing on the evolutionary insights from system's theory, I argue that orthodox defences of Niklas Luhmann's concepts ignore the necessity of empirical observation of actual legal systems and the possibility of future systemic developments that affect the structure of the legal system and how the observer observes the law.

In addition to these introductory remarks, Section 2 investigates the hypothesis of structural grouping. Section 3 explains the kaleidoscope of legal culture and the hypothesis of a *pluripoietic system*, constituted by a fusion of self-referenced and hetero-referenced coded communications. Section 4 contains some conclusive remarks.

2. From structural coupling to structural grouping

Niklas Luhmann advocated the operative closure of law, arguing that "only the legal system itself can effect its closure, reproduce its operations, and define its boundaries".[4] In his view of law as a social system, Luhmann explains that the legal system is programmed through a particular coded communication that proclaims what is 'legal' and 'illegal' according to a network of recursive normative operations.[5] A chain of self-referential internal communications within the legal system produces normative statements following a binary scheme that decides what is 'legal' or 'illegal', operating in a normatively closed way.[6] If legal/illegal is characterised as a normative communication resulting from the internal operations of the legal system, law operates in a circular fashion because the legal structures determine their character as part and parcel of the legal system also by proclaiming what is legal/illegal.[7] Borrowing the terminology used by the biologist Maturana,[8] Luhmann considers the legal system to be autopoietic, operating within itself to specify its operations as legal through self-reference and differentiation with the environment.[9] In this sense, 'autopoiesis' means that a system can generate its own operations only by means of the network of its own operations'.[10] Therefore, this operational closure of systems implies the need for internal formation of the legal structures, while the system's very own operations generate these structures through self-organisation.[11]

However, the legal system is related to the environment and to other systems operating with cognitive openness and systemic interconnection.[12] The concept of structural

4 Luhmann, *Law as a Social System*, p. 100.
5 Ibid., pp. 98–99.
6 Ibid., p. 106.
7 Ibid., p. 86.
8 Humberto Maturana, Autopoieses, Structural Coupling, and Cognition: A History of These and Other Notions in the Biology of Cognition. *Cybernetics & Human Knowing*, 9, 3–4 (2002), pp. 5–34; Humberto Maturana, The Organization of the Living: A Theory of The Living Organization. *International Journal of Man-Machine Studies*, 7 (1975), pp. 313–332.
9 Luhmann, *Law as a Social System*, p. 90.
10 Niklas Luhmann, *Introduction to Systems Theory* (Polity Press 2013), p. 76.
11 Ibid., p. 70.
12 See the various case studies collected in Alberto Febbrajo and Gorm Harste (editors), *Law and Intersystemic: Understanding 'Structural Coupling'* (Ashgate 2013).

coupling explains these relations between systems and their environment.[13] Luhmann explains that systems are selective and it is important to observe what is included and excluded because these structural couplings simultaneously filter and trigger external influences in a system's internal operations.[14] Particularly regarding the legal system, Luhmann analyses the coupling between law and economics and between law and politics. In his view, the legal recognition of interests as legally protected/unprotected results from an operational structure built inside the legal system as a station for reception and transmission of economic information.[15] The constitutive relationship between economy and law is clear in the observation of such institutions as property and contract.[16] Property is a transaction, but the economic system observes it as a profitable investment, whereas the legal system observes the consistency of decisions that legally secure the interests involved in such a transaction.[17] And the institutionalisation of freedom of contract enables broad economic transactions without any limitations being imposed by a restrictive discipline of particular types of contracts.[18]

Analysing the structural coupling between the law and politics, Luhmann emphasises the emergence of the state as the pivotal structure generated by this reciprocal influence between the political system and the legal system.[19] Importantly, the constitution transforms positive law into an instrument for political organisation and turns constitutional law into an instrument for the legal discipline of politics.[20] Interestingly, the constitution has a different meaning in each system, being observed as a supreme statute in the legal system and as an instrument of politics in the political system.[21] Luhmann notes that "the positivisation of law and the democratisation of politics support each other reciprocally and have left a significant mark on both the political system and the legal system of today".[22] And yet, he explains that both systems remain separate, with their own internal operations, communications and coding.[23]

Luhmann normally examines these reciprocal influences between systems by observing structural couples, such as law and politics or law and economics. This hypothesis of structural relationships connecting three, four or more systems simultaneously may therefore sound heterodox at first sight. Perhaps the expression *structural grouping* or *structural polygamy* may also sound unusual for orthodox Luhmannians. However, a close observation of his work suggests that inter-systemic relationships may generate complex structures between multiple interconnected systems. For instance, his analyses of contract and property are not limited to the dual influence of law and economics but also refer to the dimension of political power found in land ownership, public taxation and the implementation of contracts.[24] Additionally, his study of the state constitution is not restricted to the reciprocal

13 Luhmann, *Law as a Social System*, p. 380.

14 Luhmann, *Introduction to Systems Theory*, pp. 85–87. Luhmann, *Law as a Social System*, pp. 382–383. Niklas Luhmann refers to irritations, surprises and disturbances, but Gunther Teubner once explained to me that all these expressions may very well be substituted for influences.

15 Luhmann, *Law as a Social System*, p. 390.

16 Ibid.

17 Ibid., p. 392.

18 Ibid., p. 399.

19 Ibid., p. 404.

20 Ibid.

21 Ibid., p. 410.

22 Ibid., p. 364.

23 Ibid., p. 367.

24 Ibid., pp. 393, 400.

influence between the legal and political systems but also includes economic considerations related to the conditions for the welfare state.[25] In his remarks on the dynamic operations of structural coupling, Luhmann seems to admit the possibility of these multiple structural relationships between more than two systems by stating that "the functioning systems of politics, law, and the economy (others have not been discussed here) exhaust the limits of their possibilities, and their intensive reciprocal irritation ensures the maintenance of sufficient compatibility".[26] It seems that these inter-systemic relationships are not necessarily limited to dual structures but may emerge through the multiple structures I term *structural grouping* or, if you like, *structural polygamy*.

The multiple influences of law, politics and economics on the contemporary constitutional state are very clear. After all, the constitution is simultaneously the supreme law of the land, the fundamental political decision and the institutional framework for the market economy. Additionally, constitutions are no longer observed only as social contracts but more as mechanisms for broad institutional co-ordination and as mission statements for societal development.[27] In his discussion of the financial crisis in a constitutional perspective, Teubner also refers to the economic constitution as the structural articulation of economy, law and politics, explaining that "numerous structural couplings of institutionalised politics and the economy and the law do exist, for example, the taxation system or the lobbying of economic organisations".[28] Teubner refers to these structures as 'trilateral structural couplings',[29] but the expression 'structural groupings' or 'structural polygamy' seems not only to be more precise but also to highlight the complexity of these particular structures. In a nutshell, economic interests are stabilised by the law and are protected by the monopoly of the force of politics.[30] In his defence of trans-constitutionalism, Neves also criticises the limitations of the formulation of structural couplings as a bilateral mechanical articulation between two systems, admitting the entanglement of more than two systems in particular cases, such as taxation, central banking and elections.[31]

Contemporary constitutions also establish the relationship between the church and the state, articulating the separation and connection between the religious system on the one hand and the political, legal and economic systems on the other. Some constitutions establish theocracies without any clear functional differentiation between politics and religion – Islamic states, in particular, have resisted secularisation.[32] But most states separate the function of forming collectively binding decisions from the interpretation of incomprehensible mysteries.[33] In any event, the constitutional state is the structure that articulates these relationships, controlling the religious influences over collectively binding decisions.[34] This structural differentiation establishes a separation between political and religious roles, and

25 Ibid., p. 412.

26 Ibid., p. 422.

27 See generally Denis J. Galligan and Mila Versteeg (editors), *Social and Political Foundations of Constitutions* (CUP 2013).

28 Gunther Teubner, A Constitutional Moment? The Logics of Hitting the Bottom, in Paul Kjaer, Gunther Teubner, and Alberto Febbrajo (editors), *The Financial Crisis in Constitutional Perspective: The Dark Side of Functional Differentiation* (Hart 2011), p. 38.

29 Ibid.

30 Ibid., p. 39.

31 Marcelo Neves, *Transconstitutionalism* (Hart 2013), p. 35.

32 Niklas Luhmann, Society, Meaning, Religion: Based on Self-Reference. *Sociological Analysis*, 46, 1 (1985), p. 15.

33 Ibid., p. 13.

34 Niklas Luhmann, Differentiation of Society. *The Canadian Journal of Sociology*, 2, 1 (1977), p. 35.

the decision to believe or not to believe becomes a matter of private choice.[35] Luhmann suggests that religion gained structural autonomy at the cost of recognising the autonomy of other subsystems by accepting the secularisation of the world.[36] Nonetheless, several examples indicate the enduring influence of religious beliefs over legal, political and economic systems. German law, for example, contains provisions regarding religious taxation, prohibitions against usury and religious education in state schools, revealing Christianity's strong influence on the constitutional state. In addition to this influence on substantive law, economic interests and the national ethos, religion still exercises a strong influence on the constitutional ideology, i.e. on the belief in a repository of aspirations embodied in the constitutional state, such as eternally valid principles, its self-sufficiency for dispute resolution and the completeness and coherence of the constitution.[37] The constitutional state has gone through a process of secularisation but has retained the mystical authority of a civic religion or of a political theology.[38]

The Brazilian constitutional state provides a prodigious example of the multiple influences of law, politics, economics and religion. The constitutional text is the supreme statute, establishing the Brazilian Supreme Court as the guardian of the constitution.[39] Constitutional law is a positive legal instrument not only for the protection of rights and guarantees but also for the discipline of politics and the institutionalisation of the market economy.[40] Moreover, several constitutional clauses regulate the relationship between the church and the state, by protecting religious freedom, exempting the church from taxes and establishing religious education in public schools.[41] Likewise, the Brazilian constitution has become a pivotal instrument of politics, disciplining the relationship between government and opposition, electoral disputes between various political parties and the complex institutional interdependence of executive, legislative and judiciary. For instance, the Brazilian constitution provides legal guidelines for courts to overview presidential impeachment, abuse of power during presidential elections and excessive expenditure in the federal budget.[42] These constitutional norms are political instruments available to the opposition to the presidential government in Brazil. The Brazilian constitution also establishes the institutional framework of the market economy, by protecting private property, freedom of contract, free competition and sustainable development.[43] In summary, the Brazilian constitutional state comprises a complex articulation of multiple structures of the legal, political, economic and religious system that are not captured by the simplified analysis based on the duality of a structural coupling.

35 Luhmann, Society, Meaning, Religion, p. 13.

36 Ibid., p. 14.

37 Roger Cotterrell, *Law, Culture, and Society: Legal Ideas in the Mirror of Social Theory* (Ashgate 2006), p. 89.

38 See Jacques Derrida, *Acts of Religion* (Routledge 2002); Duncan Kennedy, American Constitutionalism as Civil Religion: Notes of an Atheist, *Nova Law Review* 19 (1994–1995), p. 909; Carl Schmitt, *Political Theology: Four Chapters on the Concepts of Sovereignty* (University of Chicago Press 2005); Carl Schmitt, *Political Theology II: The Myth of the Closure of Any Political Theology* (Polity Press 2008). The fact that we can observe the constitutional state with references to the coding of the religious system – belief/disbelief – already provides evidence of this enduring influence of religion over law, politics and also the economy.

39 Article 102 of the Constitution of the Federal Republic of Brazil.

40 Articles 5–130 of the Constitution of the Federal Republic of Brazil.

41 Articles 5, VI; 150, VI, b; and 210, § 1 of the Constitution of the Federal Republic of Brazil.

42 See, for instance, www.theguardian.com/world/2015/oct/08/brazils-president-dilma-rousseff-loses-legal-battle-and-could-face-impeachment (last checked on 11/23/15).

43 Articles 5, XXII–XXVI and XXXVI; 170, IV–VI of the Constitution of the Federal Republic of Brazil.

The analysis of property may clarify this point. The Brazilian constitution guarantees the right to private property but also states that the property must attend its social function and establishes a normative framework for agrarian reform. George Mészáros examined this complex bundle of property rights in the setting of disputes between rural landowners and the movement of landless workers over the course of two decades in several parts of Brazil.[44] His rich empirical study reveals that this constitutional structuring of rural property rights in the Brazilian constitution may not be observed exclusively from a perspective of rights discourse or economic interests because it also generates complex political disputes between government and opposition at the federal, state and municipal level.[45] Additionally, various institutional organs from the executive, the legislative, the judiciary and the attorney general's office participate in the complex operations necessary for producing collectively binding decisions regarding rural property rights.[46] Moreover, observation should also include the religious system because the Catholic Church protects the interests of the landless workers and also influences the advocacy of social movements with the religious revelations of the theology of liberation.[47] In a nutshell, these disputes involve legal norms, economic interests, political disputes and religious beliefs that are part and parcel of the complex discursive practices involved in the decision-making processes regarding rural property rights. Should the legal system incorporate and use economic references in its internal operations of judicial decision-making in these cases? Luhmann seems to be indecisive about this possibility: "It is not clear, however, whether constitutional law, when interpreting the protection of property, must apply the same separate treatment or should not rather advocate a readier opening up to economic reality (regardless of the juridical consequences)".[48]

Another interesting example comes from the adoption of the principle of efficiency as one of the cornerstones of public administration. The Brazilian constitution states that the state shall operate efficiently. An economic principle that requires optimal use of resources, cost and benefit analysis, and the maximisation of value is thus internalised in the structure of the constitutional discourse and communicated throughout the legal and political systems. Luhmann actually expresses scepticism about the viability of the economic analysis of law: "At any rate the separation of the systems prevents the automatic reception of the economic approach into the legal system (despite all the theories of 'economic analysis of law')".[49] Nonetheless, economic influence of the legal system seems inevitable as a consequence of the reference to the principle of efficiency in the Brazilian constitution. In particular, in the case of the system of administration of justice, the National Council of Justice was established in 2004 for the administrative control and professional overview of judicial activities.[50] Legal indicators were adopted for monitoring, measuring and controlling the efficiency of judges in terms of number of sentences, trial length and amount of procedures in a court's dockets.[51] Because the governance of the Brazilian judiciary is determined by

44 George Mészáros, *Social Movements, Law and the Politics of Land Reform: Lessons from Brazil* (Routledge 2013).

45 Ibid.

46 Ibid.

47 Ibid.

48 Luhmann, *Law as a Social System*, p. 400.

49 Ibid.

50 Pedro Rubim Borges Fortes, How Legal Indicators Influence a Justice System and Judicial Behavior: The Brazilian National Council of Justice and 'justice in numbers'. *The Journal of Legal Pluralism and Unofficial Law*, 47, 1 (2015), p. 40.

51 Ibid.

statistical data, mathematical formulae and complex equations, the legal system is strongly influenced by these evaluations of efficiency and inefficiency of its internal operations.[52] Economics inevitably influences the legal and political system, requiring that judges become efficient in exercising their jurisdictional power.[53]

This setting of structural groupings emerges from the complex interplay of multiple societal demands in Brazil that has resulted in a prolix and comprehensive constitutional state. As Denis Galligan and Mila Versteeg put it, "the Brazilian experience adds an interesting twist: although extensive popular engagement resulted in a long, complex and unwieldy text, effective government – and hence a high level of co-ordination – appears to have been achieved".[54] Several other examples of interplays between law, economics, politics and religion may be provided in the Brazilian constitutional context. For instance, consumer protection, environmental policies and healthcare rights depend on complex institutional dynamics related to legal frameworks, political actors, economic interests and belief in the force of law.[55] Neves once suggested that there was a low level of differentiation between law and politics in the peripheral countries of the globe, referring to the Brazilian case as an example of a symbolic or nominal constitution.[56] His critique now seems premature because the Brazilian experience demonstrates the normativity of this constitution and how constitutional law regulates social life, influencing politics, economics and religion, for instance. The Brazilian constitution is not a symbolic fantasy or a disguise but a well-tailored civic dress for the political body.[57] Contrary to Neves's diagnosis, the Brazilian constitution is observed to be an important structural articulation of law, politics, economics and religion – constituting and regulating dimensions of inter-systemic communications regarding legality/illegality, government/opposition, efficiency/inefficiency and belief/disbelief.

3. The kaleidoscope of reflexive legal culture

In recent works, system theorists have departed from orthodox analyses of autopoiesis/structural coupling/self-referential coding – perhaps revealing the limitation of more traditional concepts of Luhmann's work for the study of contemporary socio-legal questions. For instance, Neves escapes from structural coupling to transversal rationality. His point of departure is the idea of a multi-centric modern society, in which various spheres of communication have emerged and a plurality of self-descriptions of society has led to a complex formation of conflicting partial rationalities.[58] This illustration of contemporary world

52 Ibid., pp. 48–53.

53 Interestingly, Marcelo Neves exercised the role of counsellor of the National Council of Justice in Brazil between 2009 and 2011, controlling the efficiency of Brazilian judges in their exercise of jurisdictional power.

54 Denis J. Galligan and Mila Versteeg, Theoretical Perspectives on the Social and Political Foundations of Constitutions, in Denis J. Galligan and Mila Versteeg (editors), *Social and Political Foundations of Constitutions* (CUP 2013), p. 36.

55 See Pedro Rubim Borges Fortes, The Phenomenon of Lucrative Illegality. *Oxford Socio-Legal Review* 1 (2015); Lesley K. McCallister, *Making Law Matter: Environmental Protection & Legal Institutions in Brazil* (Stanford University Press 2008); Germano Schwartz, *Direito à Saúde: Efetivacão em uma Perspective Sistêmica* (Livraria do Advogado 2001).

56 Marcelo Neves, *Verfassung und positivität des Rechts in der peripheren Moderne: Eine Theoretische Betrachtung und eine Interpretation des Falls Brasilien* (Duncker & Humblot 1992).

57 Marcelo Neves borrowed this terminology from Karl Loewenstein, who uses this metaphor of the constitution as a fantasy, a disguise or a well-tailored dress of the political body. See Karl Loewenstein, *Verfassungslehre* (Mohr 1975, 3rd edition).

58 Neves, *Transconstitutionalism*, pp. 18–19.

society is presented as a *unitas multiplex*: "a *unitary* connection of a *plurality* of spheres of communication in competitive and simultaneously complementary relations".[59] This world society produces multiple types of knowledge – religious, pedagogic, legal, political, scientific, economic, etc. – that are selectively filtered by the media for public opinion. Importantly, Neves distinguishes this social knowledge from the specialised knowledge of experts, which is internally constructed and predominates in the different systems of science, education, medicine and economics, for instance.[60] In traditional systems theory, structural couplings promote and filter reciprocal influences between the various autonomous systems, excluding certain influences and facilitating others.[61]

Fischer-Lescano recently also proposed a revision of traditional systems theory, arguing for its re-conceptualisation as critical social theory. In a very provocative essay, Fischer-Lescano seems to accept the criticisms addressed by Jürgen Habermas to Niklas Luhmann that systems theory is not critical-emancipatory, but descriptive and hermetic.[62] Fischer-Lescano imagines Niklas Luhmann in a comfortable VIP Lounge with air conditioning and a glass of champagne in his hand, observing the social struggle for emancipation from the 27th floor, while the critical systems theory has its feet on the ground.[63] Inspired by conflict theorists like Marx, Adorno and Foucault, he proposes an integrated analysis of law, politics and the economy related with the formation of capitalist society.[64] Importantly, the rigid closure of the legal system is also compared to a potential systemic autism.[65] Fischer-Lescano proposes the establishment of structural couplings from heterarchic and polycentric private and public organisations that would ultimately result in more open and democratic societal decision-making processes.[66]

Teubner reformulated his concepts on the subject by theorising about constitutional fragmentation and the phenomenon of the self-constitutionalisation of global orders without a state.[67] Observing the juridification of conflict resolution by transnational regimes – exemplified by international trade with the WTO, the Internet with the ICANN and international football with FIFA[68] – Teubner defends the thesis that constitutions should

59 Ibid., p. 21.

60 Ibid., pp. 22–23.

61 Neves, *Transconstitutionalism*, pp. 26–34. Borrowing insights from Welsch and Lyotard, Neves observes this multi-centric society from the particular standpoint of the heterogeneity of language games, to introduce the concept of transversal rationality as an ability to establish "entanglements that serve as 'bridges of transition' between heterogeneous genres of language". Neves seems concerned with the possibility that "the code of one of the systems is sabotaged by the code of another system, so that the former loses its ability to reproduce consistently" and examines various problematic cases of systemic corruption. However, Neves concludes that these "entanglements that promote transversal rationality contribute above all to exchange and reciprocal learning between experiences with different rationalities, entailing the mutual sharing of complexity pre-ordered by the systems involved and thus comprehensible to the receiver". In other words, Neves concedes that transversal rationality departs from traditional accounts of autopoiesis, structural coupling and self-referential coding, but argues that this interpretative move does not corrupt the systemic structure and the autonomy of the various social systems.

62 Andres Fischer-Lescano, Systemtheorie als Kritische Gesellchaftstheorie, in Marc Amstutz and Andreas Fischer-Lescano (editors), *Kritische Systemtheorie: Zur Evolution einer Normativen Theorie* (Transcript 2013), pp. 14–15.

63 Ibid., p. 16.

64 Ibid., p. 21.

65 Ibid., p. 28.

66 Ibid., p. 36.

67 Gunther Teubner, *Constitutional Fragments: Societal Constitutionalism and Globalization* (OUP 2012), pp. 51–53.

68 Pedro Rubim Borges Fortes, We The Fans: Should International Football Have Its Own Constitution? *Southwestern Journal of International Law*, 21, 1 (2014), p. 63; Pedro Rubim Borges Fortes, The Law Relating to

be disconnected from statehood and decoupled from institutionalised politics and from the medium of power.[69] Constitutional power is not vested in the people in sparse constitutional moments but is identified rather as *communicative potential* – a social energy that remains as a permanent irritation to the constituted power.[70] Additionally, the collective self-established by these constitutional fragments emerges within 'an ongoing process during which its identity changes through a series of reflexive actions, though alternating questions and answers'.[71] He admits his departure from the traditional framework developed by Niklas Luhmann, explaining that the 'theory of autopoietic systems has long broken with the axiom of classical structural functionalism, namely, the imperative of sheer system maintenance'.[72]

It seems problematic to depart from the traditional concepts of Luhmann's systemic theory and suppose that these interpretative moves would not alter the strict internal differentiation of each particular social system. Teubner addresses this point briefly, admitting that social systems are not entirely autonomous and that there are always points of heteronomy,[73] yet this seems to be just a small concession. Teubner insists on the imperative of

Brazilian Sports Fans: An Introduction for a British Audience. *Entertainment and Sports Law Journal*, 11 (2013); Pedro Rubim Borges Fortes, Das Brasilianische Sportfan-Gesetz: Eine Einführung für das deutsche Publikum. *Mitteilungen der Deutsch-Brasilianischen Juristenvereinigung*, 32, 1 (2014); Pedro Rubim Borges Fortes, A Responsabilidade Coletiva de Torcidas Organizadas. *Revista do Ministério Público do Estado do Rio de Janeiro*, 48 (2013), p. 211; Pedro Rubim Borges Fortes, War and Peace among Organized Support Groups: The Challenge of Ensuring Safety in Football Stadiums. *Cadernos FGV Projetos*, 8 (2013), p. 86.

69 Teubner, *Constitutional Fragments*, pp. 51–60.

70 Ibid., pp. 59–66.

71 Teubner, *Constitutional Fragments* (OUP 2012), pp. 66–76. Interestingly, Teubner explains that contemporary global constitutionalism has two basic aims: (1) to break down closed structural couplings between function systems and nation state politics and law; and (2) to enable function-specific communications to be interconnected globally.

72 Teubner, *Constitutional Fragments*, pp. 79–112. This departure from the orthodox approach allows him to observe societal constitutionalism as a balancing act between external intervention and self-direction:

> A 'hybrid constitutionalisation' is required in the sense that in addition to state power, external societal forces – that is, formal legal norms and civil society's counter-power from other contexts (media, public discussion, spontaneous protest, intellectuals, protest movements, NGOs, trade unions, professions, and their organisations) – exert such massive pressure on the expansionist function system so that it will be constrained to build up internal self-limitations that actually work.Massive external interventions from politics, law, and civil society are necessary to contain self-destructive tendencies from political-legal regulation and social influences on systemic dynamics – leading to necessary changes in the arteries responsible for communication and circulation of the 'capillary constitution'. Following his argument, Teubner emphasises the role of various 'reflection-centres' within society as points of application for societal constitutionalism and explains the constitutional processes in terms of double reflexivity: the constitution as a double phenomenon of law and society, being simultaneously a system constitutive of secondary legal norms and generative of social order. Examining the coding of this hybrid constitutionalisation, he explains that there are two different normative codes – 'constitutional/unconstitutional' and 'legal/illegal' – and argues that systems remain autonomous even when there is reciprocal influence of different systems, as in the case of law and economy in the economic constitution. According to Teubner, a reciprocal re-entry of law and economy establishes differentiated constitutional programmes, with different normative meanings in each different context, such that property and contract are constitutional concepts with peculiar uses according to the particular contexts of law and of economy – following the logic of language games. Teubner refers to these differentiated constitutional programmes as "imaginary spaces". Elsewhere, however, he has agreed with the idea that the economic constitution should be conceived as the "trilateral structural coupling of economy, law and politics".

73 Teubner, *Constitutional Fragments*, p. 65.

connectivity of recursive operations and the orientation of the legal system towards one and only one binary code of legal/illegal.[74] However, these points of heteronomous communication could also integrate the internal legal discourse and participate in the internal operations of a legal system. Political, ideological and economic arguments are part of legal discourse and regularly make their way back into the legal system. Empirical observation suggests that contemporary legal discourse has incorporated knowledge from economics, politics, religion and other social systems in their own terms, without necessarily translating this heteronomous knowledge into legal terms. Discussions about economic efficiency, political parties and religious belief may therefore very well result in legal reasoning that communicates their decision-making in hybrid terms – if economically efficient, then legal; if politically correct, then legal; if religiously transcendent, then legal. The recourse to economic, political and religious normative elements in the internal operations of a legal system eliminates the connectivity of recursive operations, but does it necessarily result in systemic corruption, systemic disintegration or any other systemic pathology?[75]

I agree with Teubner, Neves and Fischer-Lescano regarding the inevitability of a multiplicity of social voices: "*homo sapiens, homo faber, homo oecologicus, homo militans, homo oeconomicus, homo politicus, homo sociologicus, homo religiosus, homo psychologicus etc*".[76]

74 Ibid., p. 79.

75 Both Neves and Teubner are quite ambiguous. Sometimes they suggest that the incorporation of normative elements from other social systems in their own terms would lead to the corruption of the legal system, especially through the influence of economic analysis of law for legal interpretation or the abuse of economic power for the democratic rule of law. Teubner is very critical in particular with regard to the incorporation of economic analysis of law:

> Economic constitutionalism, transaction cost theory, the theory of property rights, public choice, the economics of institutions and legal economics are all different strands of one movement that wishes to replace the supposedly stale terms of public interest, justice, and solidarity with the ideal of economic efficiency. The movement speaks with the pathos of a natural law, simultaneously in the name of 'nature' and of 'reason'. The internal rationality of market and organisation is identified with the nature of modern society, which needs to reflect the legal constitution of economics and society. It stylises itself as the result of a paradigm shift that completely replaces older moral-political orientations and, in its claims to exclusivity, tolerates no other paradigm besides itselfTeubner, *Constitutional Fragments*, p. 34For Marcelo Neves, the influence of economic forces may also corrupt the system:
>
> Here the code of one of the systems is sabotaged by the code of another system, so that the former loses its ability to reproduce consistently. Thus, if the code 'having/not having' (economics) corrupts the rules of the democratic game, via the electoral process or taxation, directly sabotaging the code of politics (the democratically constructed difference between government and opposition), systemic corruption will follow if the political system proves unable to react to negative superimposition by the economy with its own criteria and programmes. Neves, *Transconstitutionalism* (Hart 2013), p. 30. Other times they consider inescapable the premise that our lifeworld is constituted by a multi-centric contemporary society and its poly-contexturalism with a pluralism of partial rationalities. Once an observer accepts the possibility of transversal rationality or constitutional fragmentation, legal discourse seems open to multi-vocal normative influences and the influence of interdisciplinary perspectives on the legal system seems inevitable. Both Neves and Teubner also seem to accept the incorporation of multiple sources of knowledge into the operations of the legal system. Neves, *Transconstitutionalism* (Hart 2013), pp. 18–36; Teubner, *Constitutional Fragments*, pp. 162–173. Teubner even praises the 'openness' of law towards society represented by legal pluralism with its potential to bind law to diverse social discourses and become a source of law's tacit knowledge of the social environment. Law may open up to the multiplicity of social discourses and dynamics of civil society. Gunther Teubner, Legal Pluralism as a Form of Structural Coupling, in Alberto Febbrajo and Gorm Harste (editors), *Law and Intersystemic Communication: Understanding 'Structural Coupling'* (Ashgate 2013), pp. 358–360.

76 Andres Fischer-Lescano, Systemtheorie als Kritische Gesellchaftstheorie, in Marc Amstutz and Andreas Fischer-Lescano (editors), *Kritische Systemtheorie: Zur Evolution einer Normativen Theorie* (Transcript 2013), p. 21.

However, observing our contemporary societies empirically, my intuition is contrary to their insistence in preserving autopoiesis, structural coupling and self-reference as part of the conceptual tools for constitutional analysis in systems theory. The multiplicity of socio-legal discourses and of normative sources reflects into legal thinking through a complex kaleidoscope of legal culture. Kaleidoscopes operate on the principle of multiple reflections because several mirrors are placed inside the cylinder at a certain angle to each other. The ultimate image observed by the observer comprises a fusion or a bricolage of multiple elements constituted by the various mirrors inside the kaleidoscope. Likewise, a constitution's multiple normative influences are reflected in the kaleidoscope of legal culture, producing a fusion or a bricolage of multiple elements for the observer. This metaphor of the kaleidoscope of legal culture suggests that contemporary constitutions are constituted by structural groupings of law, politics, economics and religion. Multiple normative influences are incorporated into legal discourse, while the internal operations of legal systems combine heterogeneous elements in the coding that eventually generates a decision on constitutional/unconstitutional.

As an observer of contemporary constitutions, it seems that the question lies beyond the traditional debate between *autopoiesis* (closed self-referential autonomous systems) and *allopoiesis* (opened hetero-referential dependent systems). Contemporary constitutions contain collectively binding decisions covering a wide range of legal, political, economic and religious issues and require continuous reciprocal influence from various systems for their complex plurivocal operations. In this sense, the legal system maintains its own internal legal references and relative autonomy but must incorporate multiple normative elements from the other social systems in order to operate and to solve complex constitutional questions. The Brazilian constitutional state provides a prodigious example: how can we observe the principle of efficiency without knowledge of law, economics and politics? How can we observe the question of the social function of property and the complex social demand for agrarian reform without reflecting on law, economics, politics and religion? How can we observe issues related to consumer protection, environmental policies and healthcare rights without paying attention to legal frameworks, political actors, economic interests and belief in the force of law? In contemporary constitutional analyses, various normative elements are essential for the discursive operations in the legal system that combines multiple references in a fusion of normative horizons.[77] Interestingly, Luhmann himself suggested that the problem of the structural articulation between law and politics could be a matter of demarcation or, perhaps, of fusion.[78] Even if Luhmann and his followers never pursued this alternative path of considering that inter-systemic communications produce a fusion, it fits much better with contemporary constitutional interpretation, which is influenced by hermeneutics and interdisciplinary studies.

It seems that this complex articulation of structural groupings, which generates this fusion of multiple normative elements, could be observed as a *pluripoietic system*,[79] constituted

77 See Hans Georg Gadamer, *Truth and Method* (Continuum Impacts 2004); Ronald Dworkin, *Law's Empire* (Hart 1998); Luhmann, *Introduction to Systems Theory*, pp. 151–152.

78 Niklas Luhmann, The Unity of the Legal System, in Gunther Teubner (editor), *Autopoietic Law – A New Approach to Law and Society* (De Gruyter 1987), p. 13.

79 I am introducing this term as a neologism, borrowing from the contemporary terminology related to cellular reproduction that refers to pluripotency as the power of stem cells to reproduce in various ways. In contrast to the self-referential model defended by Maturana, contemporary biological research indicates the existent of pluripotent, totipotent, and multipotent cells, but scientific investigation has not found any cases of unipotent cells, which would have the capacity to differentiate only into one cell type (following Maturana's model of self-referential reproduction of living cells).

by a plurality of self-referenced and hetero-referenced coded communications. By *pluripoiesis*, I mean the biological development of a system grounded on the phenomenon of *pluripotency*, i.e. the potential of cells to differentiate into a continuum of various types of embryonic stem cells. *Pluripotent* cells have the power to differentiate into any type of germ layers – endoderm, mesoderm or ectoderm, or any of the 200+ cell types found in an adult body.[80] Pluripotent stem cells have specialised landscapes of genetic variations, which are important for maintaining pluripotency.[81] In contrast to the preference for unipotent cells and for self-referential reproduction in the internal operations of systems defended by Maturana, contemporary biological research indicates that pluripotent embryonic stem cells provide an endless source of any cell type for replacement therapies, providing possible cures for many destructive conditions.[82] Importantly, contemporary biology distinguishes between processes of differentiation, dedifferentiation and trans-differentiation of differentiated cells, revealing a new panorama of plasticity of animal cells and their typologies.[83] Some studies reveal the complexity of developmental processes and the delicate balance between pluripotency and differentiation of cells.[84] Interestingly, differentiated cells can be reprogrammed into a pluripotent state by transferring nuclear content or by fusion with embryonic stem cells.[85] One of the important findings related to the discovery of induced pluripotency is the observation that certain transcription factors are determinants of a cell's fate whose 'enforced expression can switch one mature cell type into another'.[86] In a nutshell, contemporary biology reveals a complex setting of pluripotency and differentiation that does not correspond to the simplex distinction between autopoiesis and allopoiesis formulated by Maturana and Varela – and also adopted by systems theorists.[87]

I anticipate that systems theorists may argue that the references to evolutionary biology, autopoiesis, structural coupling and self-referential coding and programmes are metaphorical. According to this argument, even if the scientific research on cellular development were to transform our knowledge of pluripotency, structural complexity and trans-differentiation of differentiated elements, the traditional concepts of Luhmann systems theory could still have a stronger explanatory force that justifies their conservation. Yet, his concepts seem

80 Shoukhrat Mitalipov, Totipotency, Pluripotency and Nuclear Reprogramming. *Advances in Biochemical Engineering/Biotechnology*, 114 (2009), pp. 185–186.

81 Gaoyang Liang and Yi Zhang, Embryonic Stem Cell and Induced Pluripotent Stem Cell: An Epigenetic Perspective. *Cell Research*, 23 (2013), p. 49.

82 Mitalipov, *Totipotency, Pluripotency and Nuclear Reprogramming*, p. 186.

83 Kaoru Sugimoto, Sean P. Gordon, and Elliot M. Meyerowitz, Regeneration in Plants and Animals: Dedifferentiation, Transdifferentiation, or Just Differentiation? *Trends in Cell Biology*, 21, 4 (2011), p. 212.

84 Patrick Western, Foetal Germ Cells: Striking the Balance between Pluripotency and differentiation. *The International Journal of Developmental Biology*, 53 (2009), pp. 393–394.

85 Kazutoshi Takahashi and Shinya Yamanaka, Induction of Pluripotent Stem Cells from Mouse Embryonic and Adult Fibroblast Cultures by Defined Factors. *Cell* 126 (2006), pp. 663–676; Kazutoshi Takahashi, Koji Tanabe, Mari Ohnuki, Megumi Narita, Tomoko Ichisaka, Kiichiro Tomoda, and Shinya Yamanaka, Induction of Pluripotent Stem Cells from Adult Human Fibroblasts by Defined Factors. *Cell* 131 (2007), pp. 861–872; Junying Yu, Maxim A. Vodyanik, Kim Smuga-Otto, Jessica Antosiewicz-Bourget, Jennifer L. Frane, Shulan Tian, Jeff Nie, Gudrun A. Jonsdottir, Victor Ruotti, Ron Stewart, Igor L. Slukvin, James A. Thompson, Induced Pluripotent Stem Cell Lines Derived from Human Somatic Cells. *Science*, 318 (2007).

86 Matthias Stadtfeld and Konrad Hochedlinger, Induced Pluripotency: History, Mechanisms, and Applications. *Genes & Development*, 24 (2010), p. 2239–2263.

87 F.G. Varela, H.R. Maturana, and R. Uribe, Autopoiesis: The Organization of Legal Systems, Its Characterization and a Model. *Cybernetics Forum*, 10 (1981), p. 8; Marcelo Neves, From the Autopoiesis to the Allopoiesis of Law. *Journal of Law and Society*, 28, 2, (2001) pp. 242–264.

to have been aligned with the positivist tradition of a pure theory of law or of a concept of law with separability between law and morality.[88] However, this dogma of a pure theory of law based on a circular process of normativity grounding normativity has been relativized by contemporary legal positivists.[89] It should also be attenuated by contemporary systems theorists for lack of coherence with the empirical observations of contemporary constitutional experience – unless, if I may paraphrase Fischer-Lescano, we would like to imagine ourselves ordering another glass of champagne in a VIP lounge completely detached from experience. With our feet on the ground, we will observe the legal system's internal operations with plurivocal communicative elements – efficient/inefficient; supported/opposed; belief/disbelief – leading to jurisdictional decisions about the constitutionality/unconstitutionality of cases. Nowadays, these communicative elements of the constitution are pluripotent, having the power to generate similar or different communicative elements within the dynamics of inter-systemic communication in accordance with their particular environmental niche.[90] For instance, most decisions handed down by the legal system on the legality/illegality of a merger are based on an economic analysis of the law, while most decisions on electoral issues are grounded in political arguments. Cases of secularism and religious freedom inevitably combine communications of belief/disbelief or transcendence/immanence with legal elements. In other words, environmental niches influence the gravitational force of legal, political, economic or religious influences on the constitutional state and the legal system.

Luhmann would perhaps oppose this proposal of conceptualising the constitution as a *pluripoietic system*, constituted by the structural grouping of law, politics, economics and religion, and with communications generated by a fusion of self-referential and hetero-referential normative elements. A *pluripoietic system* would be relatively autonomous, a possibility that Luhmann entertained and rejected in order to preserve the hardness of the concept of *autopoiesis*, i.e. according to him, a system cannot be just a little *autopoietic* – either it is or it is not *autopoietic*.[91] However, a *pluripoietic system* would not be a hypothesis of mere de-differentiation or – following Bruno Latour – a suggestion that "we have never been modern".[92] On the contrary, it is a hypothesis of high structural complexity of social systems.[93] As Luhmann anticipated, "relations between systems and their environments are becoming more complex to the point where increasing numbers of relatively improbable

88 Hans Kelsen, *The Pure Theory of Law* (Lawbook Exchange 2009); H.L.A. Hart, The Concept of Law (OUP 2012, 3rd edition); H.L.A. Hart, Positivism and the Separation between Law and Morals. *Harvard Law Review*, 71, 4 (1958), p. 593; Hans Kelsen, The Pure Theory of Law and Analytical Jurisprudence, *Harvard Law Review*, 55, 1 (1941), p. 44; Nicola Lacey, *A Life of H.L.A. Hart: The Nightmare and the Noble Dream* (OUP 2006).

89 John Gardner, *Law as a Leap of Faith* (OUP 2014); Julie Dickson, *Evaluation and Legal Theory* (Hart 2003).

90 Because of limitations of space, I cannot explore this insight fully here, but I should simply mention that the concept of niche was very important for Maturana, although it does not seem to receive the same attention from Luhmann:

> The most fundamental result of the dynamics of structural coupling is that a living system is never out of place while living. I call the place that a living system occupies in the realisation of its living, its *niche*. As a consequence of living in the conservation of adaptation in its niche, a living system will always appear knowing how to live in the circumstances in which it lives until it dies: living systems are never out of place, or 'more' or 'less' adapted while living. Maturana, Autopoieses, Structural Coupling, and Cognition, p. 17

91 Luhmann, *Introduction to Systems Theory*, p. 82.

92 Bruno Latour, *We Have Never Been Modern* (Harvard University Press 1993).

93 Luhmann, *Introduction to Systems Theory*, p. 73.

structural couplings are required for their maintenance".[94] But Luhmann insists that social systems must preserve their autopoiesis, as otherwise they will tend to self-destruct.[95] However, examining the same point, Maturana emphasises the plasticity of structures and the systemic capacity to undergo changes and conserve the system's identity.[96] If we take evolutionary perspectives into consideration, structural plasticity would also explain the adaptation of law into a *pluripoietic* system. After all, observers have no reason to imagine that – following Fukuyama – Luhmann also pointed to the end of history with his theory of autopoietic social systems.[97] On the contrary, the kaleidoscope of reflective legal culture provides multiple sources of influence for a society of kaleidoscopic individuals[98] – or, according to Elias, of *homo apertus* and not of *homos clausus.*[99]

Just as pluripotent cells will differentiate into a continuum of various types of embryonic stem cells, constitutional arguments also have the power to differentiate in multiple directions, combining elements from law, economics, politics and religion through a bricolage or a fusion of these various social systems. There is therefore not necessarily any normative closure in a *pluripoietic* system because what *ought to be* lawful/unlawful may be defined by a complex combination of analysis of what *ought to be* efficient/inefficient, supported/opposed and believed/disbelieved. In this context, legal decision-making depends more on the reflective behaviour of kaleidoscopic individuals, who negotiate normative meaning and mediate legal outcomes by communicating their legal, economic, political and religious ideas about law in society. The kaleidoscope of reflective legal culture therefore operates through the principle of multiple reflections because several socio-legal discourses and sources of legal thinking constitute the normative communications of the internal operations of the legal system. Because the legal system is normatively open and does not rely exclusively on a self-referential code of legal/illegal, communications made by the consciousness of individuals may be incorporated into the normative code of the legal system without resulting in its destruction.

4. Concluding remarks

In this chapter, I propose a new hypothesis for observing contemporary constitutional states from a systems theoretical perspective. As I explained, such systems theorists as Neves, Fischer-Lescano and Teubner have departed from the traditional conceptualisation

94 Ibid., p. 95.

95 Ibid., p. 88.

96 Maturana, *Autopoieses, Structural Coupling, and Cognition*, pp. 16–17.

97 Francis Fukuyama, *The End of History and the Last Man* (Penguin 1992). See, for instance, Chris Thornhill, *A Sociology of Constitutions: Constitutions and State Legitimacy in Historical-Sociological Perspective* (CUP 2012).

98 Lawrence Friedman, Law, Lawyers, and Popular Culture. *Yale Law Journal*, 98, 8 (1989), pp. 1585–1586.

> The *legal* individual, like the individual of today's popular culture, is not to be confused with the pale, economic actor of the 19th century, that humourless, God-fearing, hard-working, eager maximiser; rather, the individual of contemporary times is a full-blooded autonomous *person*; an expressive individual, a kaleidoscopic individual, an individual of a million choices of styles, habits, colours, religions, modes of dress, cuisines and sexual preferences; an individual whose rationality, so to speak, goes far beyond 19th century rationality and whose needs and demands as expressed in life and law are greater and more complex.

99 Norbert Elias, *Civilizing Process* (Blackwell 2000); Eric Dunning and Jason Hughs, *Norbert Elias and Modern Sociology* (Bloomsbury 2013).

of autopoiesis, structural coupling and self-referential coding to develop alternative theories based on insights from critical social theory of post-colonial studies, the Frankfurt School and French Post-Structuralism. Nonetheless, transversal rationality, critical system's theory and constitutional fragmentation have retained the core conceptual framework of Luhmann's systemic approach. This chapter revises these traditional concepts by suggesting that we may consider observing the constitutional state as a case of structural grouping between law, politics, economics and religion. And because an observer conducts an empirical observation of the continuous reference to multiple normative elements in the internal operations of the legal system, it seems that any legal claim may have the power to differentiate into multiple normative directions in a *pluripoietic* legal system. Moreover, the kaleidoscope of a reflective legal culture operates through a principle of multiple reflections, framing horizons of normative meaning that will eventually constitute a fusion of horizons – inviting kaleidoscopic individuals to think about law, negotiate normative meaning and communicate their ideas, thoughts and opinions about law in society. Therefore, this chapter engages with the contemporary literature on law as a social system, providing an internal conceptual revision of its basic tenets and calling for an account that corresponds more to contemporary empirical observation of law in society and departs from dogmas based on a pure theory of law or on ideas borrowed from critical legal studies.

4 Towards a global legal culture?

Spaces of law in the transnational constellation

Lasha Bregvadze

1. Introduction

Culture has been conventionally recognised as a factor of unrepeatability, singularity and divergence, representing unique local knowledge. But transnational constellation establishes new global knowledge. Globalisation changes law, legal culture and society; it creates alternative identities for the newly emerged legal orders.

This chapter constitutes an attempt to develop some arguments about the emergence of transnational legal cultures that can be structured as follows:

- Legal culture is in fact a much older concept than claimed in current socio-legal literature and its use can be detected at least in the nineteenth-century literature. Already in the writings of the nineteenth century, the notion of legal culture has been employed as a tool to rethink legal orders beyond the state.
- In late modernity, earlier forms of law beyond the state, universal natural laws, started to be replaced by new forms of culturally innovated legal regimes – international and transnational orders – where the domination of human interests and cultural power over natural force is evident.
- Culture, broadly understood as societal power that can change nature (modern medicine, technology, science, art and the military are functional examples), has become the main source of modern global law – old visions of metaphysical *natural law* have been transformed by *cultural law* on the global level.
- Transnational legal cultures reproduce both unity and diversity: unity on the global level beyond national differences but diversity between functional domains. The identity of legal culture beyond the state is the functional one.
- Systems theory gives an exceptional possibility to rethink the emergence of global cultural processes through transnational interactions, organisations and functional regimes of society, shaping world law in all its fragments.

2. Early conceptions of legal culture

Although in standard manuals or other texts on sociology of law and legal anthropology, the introduction of the concept of legal culture dates back to the stimulating writings of Lawrence M. Friedman,[1] the concept of legal culture is in fact much older (not to mention

1 Lawrence M. Friedman himself transplanted the concept of legal culture into the law and society movement from political science, where the concept of political culture had been established in order to study broad public expectations, demands and attitudes towards the political system and to compare the behavioural patterns

its earlier functional equivalents, like 'spirit of the people' or 'legal consciousness' – *Volksgeist* and *Rechtsbewußtsein*). The use of the concept of legal culture, for example, is documented in 1802, on the page of the German periodical edition: *Critical Archive of Newest Juridical Literature and Judicature.*[2] The term 'legal culture', in its old German spelling *Rechtscultur*, appears in different works but with less defined meaning and minor conceptual clarity.

One of the first comprehensive legal works in German, dedicated to the interaction between law and culture, dates back to 1865: Wilhelm Arnold's "Culture and Life of Law".[3] Although less engaged in terminological clarifications and formation of concepts, Arnold gives an empirical-historical account of interdependence and mutual influence of culture and legal reality. He employs seven distinct spheres that are constitutive for human societies of 'cultivated peoples' and include arts, language, morality, economy, law, state and science (excluding Christian religion, which he thought of as already widespread and celebrated among 'cultivated peoples'). Arnold tries to find internal ties between real experiences and legal development, between life and law, calling his endeavour 'psychology of law'.[4] Although providing no substantial advance for constructing the term of legal culture, the work is significant as one of the first attempts to couple two distinct concepts of law and culture together and bring legal developments close to societal processes, to real social life.

But probably one of the first and conceptually sound uses of the concept of legal culture goes back to a Swiss jurist, Johann Caspar Bluntschli (1808–1881). As a mediator between the historical school and codification movement, trying to bring social dynamics to law, Bluntschli was probably one of the first scholars to use the concept consciously and with conceptual clarity in his writings. As early as 1858, Bluntschli delivered a public lecture dealing with the concept of law. The lecture was published later in the collection of the author's essays, where he states the following:

> The basic merit of the Romans was the formulation of law, of legal culture and the basic merit of the Germans is the protection of moral essence, of legal nature. The purpose of humanity, however, is not to diminish nature through culture, but to refine it and develop it consciously. In this sense, the formation of modern law has a mission to develop the highest legal culture on the basis of a true legal nature.[5]
>
> (Translated by L. Bregvadze)

In this short but meaningful passage, Bluntschli expresses his whole vision about the essence of modern law, its historical ties to the Roman legal rationality and, most importantly, the dualism of nature and culture – the natural and cultural embodiment of law. Long before

---

of different nations. The concept of political culture, as an inspiration for Friedman to adopt such a variable for legal studies, had been introduced in 1963: Almond, Gabriel A. and Verba, Sidney: *The Civic Culture: Political Attitudes and Democracy in Five Nations*, Princeton, NJ: Princeton University Press, 1963 (3rd edition, Newbury Park: Sage Publications, 1989).

2 *Critisches Archiv der neuesten juridischen Litteratur und Rechtspflege*, Band 2, 1802: 385. The archive was edited by Danz, Emelin and Tafinger.

3 Arnold, Wilhelm: *Cultur und Rechtsleben*, Berlin: Dümmler's Verlagsbuchhandlung, 1865.

4 Hofmann, Hasso: "In Europa kann's keine Salomos geben". – Zur Geschichte des Begriffspaars Recht und Kultur", in: *Juristenzeitung*, 64 (1), 2009: 1–10, 2.

5 Bluntschli, Johann Caspar: "Der Rechtsbegriff", in: Bluntschli, Johann Caspar: *Gesammelte kleine Schriften. Erster Band: Aufsätze über Recht und Stat*, Nördlingen: Verlag der C.H. Beck'schen Buchhandlung, 1879: 1–43, 42. Although published in 1879, two public lectures, on which this essay is based, had already been delivered by Bluntschli in 1858. See the note by the author: ibid. p. 1. If not stated otherwise, all the translations from German that follow belong to L. Bregvadze.

establishing the *Institute of International Law*, Bluntschli treats culture as a basic force for shaping law. Culture, for him, is a power of modernity, while nature remains an eternal, transcendental force that regulates mankind. Humanity has no right and cannot in fact oppose natural forces, disregard natural principles through cultural innovations or undermine nature through culture, but it can and must reconstruct, modify and redirect norms. Modern legal rationality has to be based on genuine natural principles, and this will enable legal culture to be celebrated as a highest evolutionary achievement. If the Romans had been decisive in the formulation of basic legal and cultural principles of law, the modern generation (in the case of Bluntschli, the Germans, through the reception of Roman law) has to safeguard these achievements, protecting their moral and natural characteristics. The desired legal culture can be achieved only on natural grounds. Modern law has to base itself on genuine natural processes if it is to be capable of achieving this highest standard. The author stresses the mutual importance of tradition and innovation, of nature and culture, and only sees a possibility of achieving the paramount standard of legal evolution in their meaningful interplay. The result of this developmental path would be establishment of 'the highest legal culture'.

Yet, in concluding passages of the essay, summing up proposed arguments, Bluntschli claims that

> Legal culture, which produces the formulated law, cannot free itself from its basis, legal nature, but has to develop and refine it. In legal nature, priority is given to the human necessity for relationships, but in legal culture, first of all, human freedom is manifested.[6]

In his vision, positive law is spawned through cultural processes and is a product of legal culture, but only on the basis of legal nature. Positive law can only be formulated and enacted on the grounds of legal nature, which underlines any form of legal rationality. For Bluntschli, legal culture is thus a mechanism for producing law, while legal nature is an encompassing force shaping legal evolution. Legal nature, as a ground of any kind of normative manifestation, can only be refined and further developed by legal culture. Legal culture, though articulated by humanity, cannot totally free itself from influences of legal nature, as persons cannot be fully independent from nature. This interplay between natural force and cultural power creates sufficient conditions for legal evolution. Legal nature is defined by the necessity of human co-operation, interaction and relational networks, while legal culture gives priority to human freedom. Only free individuals can interact, co-operate and relate in society. Such a mutual interpenetration of nature and culture creates a scheme for societal evolution. Necessary relations between individuals (nature) have to be co-ordinated by shared rules based on freedom (culture). This short but original definition provided by Bluntschli gives a functional account of both nature and culture, which only together make the processes of legal development successful.

In his extensive treatise on modern international law (first edition 1868), analysing conditions and purposes of war, Bluntschli makes an important reference to the concept of legal culture and states:

> We recognise that there are *natural human rights*, which have to be considered both in times of war and peace and that the legal order of the world and of separate peoples has to be understood in an *eternal historical development* which cannot be stopped and

6 Ibid. 43.

> entirely destroyed through conflict of nations. As it is less likely, after the declaration of a war, that the language and civilisation of nation do not suddenly disappear and fall back into the original cruelty and barbarism, so it is less likely that *legal culture*, an *outcome of centuries of working*, can be terminated at once and replaced by the condition of complete lawlessness. As a war is essentially an *aid to law*, it *cannot deny the legal order which it aims to serve.*[7]

For current commentators on the globalisation of law, this passage might be inspiring in different ways. First of all, Bluntschli speaks about the legal order of world (*Rechtsordnung der Welt*), which has to be shaped in its historical and evolutionary processes and needs to be understood as a continuous and unstoppable component of world society. The world legal order as a universal mechanism of normative regulation cannot be interrupted, marginalised and neglected even in war conditions, as all parties involved in conflict have to respect this order. Human rights, given by nature, represent the most significant manifestation of the world legal order, whose connection to nature once again reveals the superiority and fundamental character of natural rights: although various nations may differ in competing cultural achievements and scientific discoveries and their interaction with nature may end up with diverging levels of progress or regress, and there also might be sound inconsistencies in ideological or societal arrangements, religious or political preferences – all nations have to declare the superiority of natural human rights.

This 'rights consciousness' offered by Bluntschli and its recognition as the main element of the world legal order might bear some similarities with the expansion of modern human rights ideology, the 'human rights culture'[8] that has been declared to be the most important trait of the current global legal discourse. Eternal historical development is another important metaphor used by the author for describing the expansion of natural human rights. Evolutionary processes of law cannot be subordinated even to the destructive forces of war, as the cruellest embodiment of cultural conflict between nations or groups of people. On the contrary, – war itself can be described as an episodic event used within the broad societal evolutionary process for realising prompt changes desired by cultural inconsistencies between involved parties; but after this 'violent communication', the outcomes of 'clash of civilisations' are still shaped and rearranged by evolutionary processes.

The quoted passage also reveals the philosophical teachings of Bluntschli's mentor – Savigny – and can be read as a programmatic motto of cultural legal studies. Legal culture is not a product of sudden social transformations but an outcome of long evolutionary processes, spanning across centuries and being unmanageable through political programmes or technocratic interventions. Evolution of legal culture can only be compared to the development of language. Such a parallel between language and law, signalised by Savigny's teachings about the *Volksgeist*, re-enters Bluntschli's argument and makes it even clearer. This is where the master's ideas reappear in the writings of his follower.

Language and legal culture are two immortal forms of sociality. No war, no destruction or violence, can ever undermine natural processes rooted in societal evolution. Language as a universal medium for communication, as a manifestation of local culture, is capable of reproducing its own components and adapting to complex environments. Just as language cannot be terminated through the destructive forces of war, legal culture is also immortal

7 Bluntschli, Johann Caspar: *Das moderne Völkerrecht der civilisirten Staten als Rechtsbuch dargestellt*, 3. Auflage, Nördlingen: Verlag der C.H. Beck'schen Buchhandlung, 1878: 296.

8 Friedman, Lawrence M.: *Human Rights Culture*, New Orleans, LA: Quid Pro, 2011.

and continues its everlasting existence, even in most undesired and externally dominated environments. Outcomes of war can change some legal enactments, statutes or even political constitutions but will never affect legal culture, which is subordinated only to evolutionary processes. Indeed, war can bring situational, symbolic changes into social structures, but if such changes do not coincide with broad social consciousness, with cultural goals and natural principles of human development, they remain only as episodic restructuration of the environment. It is just an issue of time. All empires and despotic regimes are collapsed at the end of the day. But cultural identities and value aspirations of involved communities remain stable, following a difficult but sustainable path of evolution.

When Bluntschli was writing, war was one of the prevailing forms of violent cross-border communication, involving processes of colonialism, invasion and occupation. Two world wars still had to take place, bringing destructive outcomes for the evolution of world society. Still influenced by 'legal romanticism', Bluntschli tried to formulate the idea of a 'just war'. He saw the sole essential function of war in protection of universally acclaimed world legal order, based on continuous evolutionary processes of legal culture. A just war cannot thus deny the universal legal order embodied in shared cultural values that it is supposed to serve. The only war 'conceivable' is one that tries to oppose cruelty, barbarism and destructive violence directed towards harmonious evolutionary goals. And only those wars can serve universally accepted ideals of legality shared by mankind, which are freed from particular religious, ethnic, ideological or national prerogatives. For Bluntschli, the only war that would be theoretically acceptable is one that serves not as an aid to the legal order of certain national or political entities but to the common interests of the world legal order, shaped by an eternal legal culture. If necessary, only for the purpose of securing universally protected global legal ideals might there be a war, which cannot oppose what it has to protect – natural human rights celebrated in a legal order of the world, protected by shared legal culture that can never be replaced by lawlessness. It is here easy to discover the features of global values, standards and aspiration necessary for the formation of world legal order in one of the first conceptions of legal culture.

3. Systems theoretical reformulation of the concept of world legal culture

While systems theory of law is much criticized for lack of 'local knowledge' of law, in reality it can provide effective mechanisms for observation and description of both local and global cultural processes. Luhmann studied the processes of evolving legal culture on the world-societal level even before many legal sociologists: when they were still developing the notion of legal culture grounded on national or ethnic characteristics, he predicted and diagnosed the increasing emergence of global cultural flows shaping law in world society. Before the autopoietic turn in his theory, prior shifting to functional structuralism, while he was still engaged with the classical systems theory informed by Parsons's structural functionalism, Luhmann was already constructing the paradigms of global society, which would also include cultural domains on the world level. In a short monograph published in 1974 – "Legal System and Legal Doctrine", which is based on a series of public lectures delivered at different research institutions (in Karlsruhe, Hamburg and Berlin) and is devoted to the problem of consequence orientation in legal decisions Luhmann, discussing important outcomes of industrialisation and differentiation of functional rationalities, mentions the emergence of an encompassing independent legal culture on the level of world society. While complaining about the lack of reflexive capacity of jurisprudence and criticising critical perspectives (with a sort of second order critique) he concentrates attention on unstructured and inconsistent approaches and admits that modern society requires more complex modes of description and techniques for decision-making. Evolution of modern society is characterised not only by the emergence of differentiated system of law but also by evolving legal culture at the world level:

> And above all the importance of autonomous legal culture on the level of gradually consolidating world society does not allow its underestimation.[9]

The fact that as early as 1974, Luhmann mentions the emergence of self-sufficient legal culture on the world-societal level, highlights the importance of cultural transformation and coevolution of structural and cultural forces for shaping society. Although left without further elaboration, evolving 'world legal culture' can be seen not only as a description of reality but also as a terminological experiment preparing grounds for the formulation of Luhmann's later concept of *Weltrecht* – world law.

In September 1994, Luhmann delivered an address to the fifteenth national conference of lawyers in Brazil entitled "Ethics in International Relations".[10] The text is fundamental in many respects. Alongside with proposing an approach to international ethics, Luhmann formulates his concept of emerging 'world law' and mentions world-societal legal culture, which is spread beyond national boundaries. After providing arguments about difficulties to conceive the essence of ethics in international relations, he claims:

> Such rather sociological analyses of emerging world-societal legal culture must be of interest also for jurists. Jurists however are not confronted directly with these problems, but only to the extent suggested by their national legal system and its valid law.[11]

World-societal legal culture (*weltgesellschaftliche Rechtskultur*), emerging on the global level beyond national configuration is a challenge for dogmatic jurists who are focusing solely on official jurisdictions. Instead, only sociological analysis can give a broad picture that captures cultural dynamics, spreading across political boundaries of national legal orders. In Luhmann's theory, state is a form of segmental differentiation reintroduced – within the functionally differentiated system of politics – as self-description of the politics; it is a form of secondary, territorial differentiation of the world political system. State can be described merely as a local address of political communications. Dogmatic jurists, instead of focusing solely on national jurisdictions and principles of formal validity of law, have thus to broaden their perspectives and to conceive the emergence of an alternative legal reality on the world scale.

All legal communications, including national legal jurisdictions, belong to the functionally differentiated system of law. They comprise totality of legal communications, which are identified through the binary code legal/illegal. But this code does shape various communications beyond the national boundaries and at the level of emerging transnational legal orders.

9 Luhmann, Niklas: *Rechtsystem und Rechtsdogmatik*, Stuttgart: Verlag W. Kohlhammer, 1974: 10. The sentence is followed by reference to his article – "World Society" (Luhmann, Niklas: "Die Weltgesellschaft", in: *Archiv für Rechts- und Sozialphilosophie*, 57, 1971: 1–35), however containing no elaboration on the concept of globalising (legal) culture.

10 The text has been published in Portuguese (1995), German (1999) and Georgian (2014).

11 Luhmann, Niklas: "Ethik in internationalen Beziehungen", in: *Soziale Welt*, 50 (3), 1999: 247–254, 251.

Thus, law is more than the will of the state, it belongs to a global society where the emergence of global law is supported, maintained, restructured and redirected by the force of world-societal legal culture. Only sociological observations on law can adequately describe and analyse such processes. Jurists focused on internal dynamics of state law are limited only to the self-reflection, internal observation of the legal system, which has nothing to do with external, objective, scientific observations of law from the environment – the system of science. Jurists have to share sociological observations on the legal system in order to discover world-societal legal culture. In fact, sociologists can see what jurists cannot see![12]

According to Luhmann, functional differentiation began in Europe. This is where functional rationalities started to emerge and developed mechanisms for self-description and self-organisation. But current world society, due to regional specificities and variation in mechanisms of inclusion and exclusion, is a turbulent space. There are parts of world society where functional differentiation based on autopoiesis is threatened by the processes of allopoiesis.[13] For Luhmann, the legal culture, developed in Europe since the eleventh century, might have some difficulties in spreading worldwide since local forms of differentiation and the level of systemic freedom might be divergent due to asymmetries of functional evolution. The worldwide spread of legal culture, supporting establishment of international ethics, is the mechanism that ensures social change. Without cultural changes, there can be no structural transformations. Luhmann admits:

> If one observes the current world-societal relations under this standpoint, then, sociologically speaking, it is not at all self-evident that the legal culture developed in Europe since the eleventh century is practicable worldwide. But it will be dependent on it whether the transfer of proto-juridical developments in the sphere of international ethics is resulted in applicable, justiciable law.[14]

Thus, these are cultural forces bringing new structural transformations on the world level. If there is sufficient cultural power mobilised for desired societal changes, the goal will be attained. Such a vision of sociocultural coevolution is indeed inclusive, containing both cultural and structural variables. To maintain a change that could be valid and applicable on the world level, the spread of corresponding culture is necessary. Global ethical standards and establishment of applicable international ethics is unthinkable for Luhmann without due cultural spread worldwide.

Also in his major work on law considered as a functional subsystem of world society – *Das Recht der Gesellschaft* – Luhmann cannot avoid mentioning the emergence of worldwide legal culture:

> In relation to comparative law one can observe a rudimentary development of a global legal culture that allows for a wide range of differences but which is nevertheless committed to its own (legal) standards and which rejects any interference from outside.[15]

12 Luhmann, Niklas: "Ich sehe was, was Du nicht siehst", in: Luhmann, Niklas: *Soziologische Aufklärung. Band 5: Konstruktivistische Perspektiven*, Opladen: Westdeutscher Verlag, 1990: 228–234.

13 Neves, Marcelo: *Verfassung und Positivität des Rechts in der peripheren Moderne. Eine theoretische Betrachtung und eine Interpretation des Falls Brasilien*, Berlin: Duncker & Humblot, 1992. Neves, Marcelo: "From Autopoiesis to Allopoiesis of Law", in: *Journal of Law and Society*, 28 (2), 2001: 242–264.

14 Luhmann, Niklas: "Ethik in internationalen Beziehungen", in: *Soziale Welt*, 50 (3), 1999: 247–254, 252.

15 Luhmann, Niklas: *Law as a Social System* (Translated by Klaus A. Ziegert), Oxford: Oxford University Press, 2004: 56–57.

Klaus A. Ziegert uses in his translation the term 'global legal culture'. However, in the original text, Luhmann uses the term *weltweite Rechtskultur* – worldwide legal culture.[16] This difference might be important for conceptual clarity because the concept is still under construction and is conceived differently by different authors. Worldwide legal culture for Luhmann represents an emerging phenomenon beyond the national influences. It contains differences and divergent worldviews while rejecting any intervention from the environment. Worldwide legal culture spreads its standards and maintains own boundaries which deserves further elaboration in systems theory of law. Such a broad elaboration of world-societal, worldwide, global legal culture by Luhmann does indeed demonstrate his unrealised attention towards cultural studies of law. At least such a stereotypical blame that his theory pays no attention to cultural dynamics of law and maintains an idea of extreme isolation must be considered a false accusation, based on selective interpretation of his work.

Autopoietic social systems theory has been employed by Gunther Teubner to observe emerging processes of transnational regulatory regimes beyond the state. The book edited by Teubner – *Global Law without the State*[17] – has become a standard reference work for any academic engagement with global legal processes. In his acclaimed essay from this collection,[18] Teubner uses the paradigm of "living law" as developed by Eugen Ehrlich and with its combination to systems theory, provides an original observation of norm-formation beyond the state. This hybrid approach – of a classical perspective for describing contemporary social transformation – allows Teubner to present an original view on the emergence of global law based on non-state, societal dynamics. Modern society described by Luhmann as a functionally differentiated totality of communications, has freed itself from the state domination and managed to restructure politics as one of the subsystems among other functional rationalities. Politics lost its superior position due to polycentric globalisation processes. Accordingly, for Teubner, new world law is not the politically produced mechanism of regulation but instead the multiplicity of social communications, which according to binary coding and individual function, allows a counterfactual maintenance of normative expectations.

Teubner constructs an alternative concept of legal pluralism, based not on the idea of competing legal layers in post-colonial societies, where the local 'customary' law had been marginalised by imposed models of 'rational legality', but describing plural legal processes at the transnational level, where political or colonial powers have no possibility to dictate own prerogatives. On the transnational level, legal pluralism is achieved by the coexistence of various forms of living law, stemming from different social associations – professional standard-setting bodies, multinational organisations and functionally differentiated regimes that govern Internet, sports, technologies and commerce. Global legal pluralism as defined by systems theory, stresses the influence of 'privately produced law', a world law of transnational private regimes. Global normative orders are produced not within the centre of the legal system (courts as dominant rule-making agencies within the nation state) but in the periphery – at the borders of the legal subsystem with other functionally differentiated subsystems of world society, through diverse forms of structural couplings. Modern global law is a peripheral law – stemming not from the national judicial practices but from intersection of functional boundaries in world society.

16 Luhmann, Niklas: *Das Recht der Gesellschaft*, Frankfurt: Suhrkamp, 1993: 13–14.

17 Teubner, Gunther (ed.): *Global Law without a State*, Aldershot: Dartmouth, 1997.

18 Teubner, Gunther: "Global Bukowina: Legal Pluralism in the World Society", in: Teubner, Gunther: *Global Law without a State*, Aldershot: Dartmouth, 1997: 3–28.

In another stimulating essay, Teubner proposes an innovative idea about the dual constitution of societal subsystems.[19] The role of private actors and processes beyond public politics is increasing in the conditions of globalisation:

> The focus of law-making is shifting to private regimes, that is, to binding agreements among global players, to private market regulation through multinational enterprises, internal rule-making in international organizations, inter-organizational negotiating systems, and worldwide standardization processes.[20]

The main problem of current globalisation discourse lies in the reductionism – every theory tries to reduce the causes of globalisation on one certain functional process among many others – economic, political, religious, legal, military or scientific. The condition and reality of world society is unique in the sense that it is gradually globalised through all of its subsystems and is thus transformed into a global unity, fragmented in different functional rationalities. But as Teubner observes, functional subsystems are also internally differentiated into organised and spontaneous sectors. The same applies also to the legal subsystem, which is characterised by organised but also increasingly spontaneous ordering. Distinction between centre and periphery of the legal system has been maintained in the sense of organised and spontaneous spheres of rule creation – courts and legislation on the one hand and usages and social norms on the other; or formal structures as organisers of 'legal centralism' and unpredicted societal dynamics as facilitator of 'self-regulating spontaneity'. The same processes can be detected on the transnational level – dual constitution of multiple private legal regimes. "Dualism of formally organised rationality and informal spontaneity" – this is the formula capturing the hybrid structure of globally expanding normative regimes.

Internal differentiation of functional subsystem into organised and spontaneous sectors provokes the question: what is the substance of spontaneity within the system boundaries? What does it consist of? How can it be described as a system component having no certain shape, no meaningful essence or defined unit? And this is the point where the idea of cultural diffusion in the subsystems can productively be used without the threat of destroying the theoretical unity of systemic semantics: systems consist of organised structures *and* spontaneous cultures. These are the cultural powers coming from society, carrying societal beliefs, expectations, attitudes, demands and values that shape the legal cultures of organised structures and initiate unpredictable changes in the system components. Systems consist only of functional social communications – being of organised or spontaneous character. Organised structure with stabile institutional components and spontaneous culture with unplannable societal dynamics are the spheres enabling societal evolution in the conditions of their productive interplay and interpenetration. Formal and informal elements of systemic identity make the boundaries of subsystems more inclusive while containing both structural and cultural premises of functionality. Culture as a learning mechanism – maintaining cognitive openness of the system through spontaneous processes supporting the adaptability to the complex environment – is indeed a progressive force for protection against conservative and organised structural stability. Social structures do have to change – in accordance with broad societal evolutionary processes– and these changes can

19 Teubner, Gunther: "Global Private Regimes: Neo-Spontaneous Law and Dual Constitution of Autonomous Spheres?", in: Ladeur, Karl-Heinz (ed.): *Public Governance in the Age of Globalization,* Aldershot: Ashgate, 2004: 71–87.

20 Ibid. 74.

creatively be brought by spontaneous cultural flows, leading to new transformations due to coevolutionary processes in the transnational constellation.

As pluralistic are the various regulatory regimes on the transnational level, as many cultural processes can be observed beyond their normative structures. Those cultural factors have initiated, coordinated and maintained the emergence of structural entities. While cultural prerogatives and impulses change, conditioned by broad societal dynamics, also the change of organised legal structures is to be anticipated. Once featuring particularity, culture is transformed into an encompassing societal power being capable of initiating structural changes of global normative regimes. Indeed, cultural differences have not lost their significance already on the global level – between different functional orders and regulatory mechanisms. Once used to indicate and stimulate national and ethnic differences, now transnationalised legal cultures are diffused within fragmented private regimes of world society. *Multiplicity of national cultures is replaced by the plurality of cultural domains focused on societal functions. Legal culture safeguards on the global level the functional identity of the respective normative order. National, regional, local or ethnic identities are replaced on the global level by transnational functional identities, which are reproduced, reinforced and reorganised by global cultural power processes, beyond the state differences.*

Transnational legal cultures are focused both on unity and diversity. *Unity in the sense of overcoming national boundaries of 'old culture' and difference in the sense of safeguarding global functional identities of normative orders – this would be the formula of 'new cultures' on the transnational level.* Transnational cultures create functional distinction, reproducing further distinctions, 'difference which makes a difference'.

4. The locations of transnational legal cultures

If the emergence of transnational legal cultures is an empirical fact, where these phenomena can be detected in the process of shaping structural elements of global law beyond the state? National legal cultures have been used as units for comparison while searching for similarities and differences rooted in traditional legal sources, peculiar modes of argumentation and broad societal behaviours towards national legal systems, but what about stateless transnational space where no traditions and characteristics connected with national identity can be found? Where are the locations of transnational legal cultures?[21]

The answer to this question, probably supported by dogmatic jurists and potentially obsessed with methodological nationalism, is to be found in systems theory by focusing on various system-building processes: as transnational law is a genuine type of societal law, transnational legal culture has to be observed in connection with different types of social systems – interactions, organisations and functional regimes of society,[22] evolving and developing beyond the state, on transnational level. Globalisation processes allow the spread of transnational legal interactions and 'communications about law in interaction systems' on the global level. Multinational enterprises and emergent types of transnational organisations increasingly become part of the global societal dynamics through reproducing binding decisions beyond control mechanisms of the state. Transnational regimes differentiated as multiple functional sectors of a global society reconstruct fragmented unity of world

21 To misquote Bhabha, Homi K.: *The Location of Culture*, London: Routledge, 1994.

22 Luhmann, Niklas: "Interaktion, Organisation, Gesellschaft", in: Niklas Luhmann: *Soziologische Aufklärung. Band 2: Aufsätze zur Theorie der Gesellschaft*, 4. Auflage, Opladen: Westdeutscher Verlag, 1991: 9–20. Although Luhmann does not apply the given three types of social systems to transnational level in this study.

law while reproducing legal communications mediated through the binary code of legal/illegal.[23] All the mentioned types of social systems are the spaces shaped by transnational cultural flows on the global level. Indeed, current societal developments permit to observe and describe the transnationalisation of different forms of social systems. But what about concrete examples of cultural power driving evolutionary processes of social systems in a transnational constellation? How can culture be diffused within different types social systems on the transnational level? And what will happen with the 'unity' of the social systems theory itself after such transformative modification and 'cultural installations'?

In fact, such an interpretation does not threaten the established conceptual boundaries and semantic structure of the systems theory but derives from its own flexibility. Luhmann's writings have left some space for formulation of cultural diffusion within different types of social systems. This theoretical innovation can lead to distinguishing between culture of functional subsystems, organisational culture and culture of interaction.

It is appropriate to start from the societal level of system building. Legal culture as a societal power on the transnational level was already discussed extensively quoting from Luhmann's original work on emergence of world-societal, global legal culture that transcends national boundaries and creates a global framework for legal evolution. Accordingly, it is evident that alongside a functionally differentiated legal subsystem, there emerges also a world-societal legal culture, "committed to its own (legal) standards and which rejects any interference from outside".

Organisation, as a social system producing its own culture that has nothing to do with the classic notion of national cultural traits, is an established research theme in systems theory. Luhmann's own work on 'Organisation and Decision' contains multiple references to the notion of organisational culture. But in his later work, he also openly admits big organisations as sources of law, as producers of legal communications in the sense of internal organisational order. Certainly, this process is to be monitored and stabilised by organisational culture. Accepting organisations as sources of 'privately produced law' makes his theoretical construction even more flexible. Luhmann writes:

> In a frequent, quite indirect[24] connection with contract law, various new forms of privately produced law prosper. Above all, this can be seen in the internal law of organizations, and also in law created as a result of provisional collective agreements between interest groups and other big organizations, market-specific interpretations of general regulations, the law of general terms and conditions of trade, and others.[25]

Thus, law is produced not only in the functional subsystem of society but also in an organisation, which is a separate type of social system. Organisations are equipped with organisational culture – an important power mechanism present in Luhmann's theory. In his posthumously published monograph dedicated to organisation as a social system, he describes organisations as entities being dependent on membership and reproducing

23 On the fragmentation of global law: Fischer-Lescano, Andreas and Teubner, Gunther: *Regime-Kollisionen: Zur Fragmentierung des globalen Rechts*, Frankfurt: Suhrkamp, 2006.

24 At this place Luhmann in his original text uses the word "indirekt" (which in English can only be transnated as "indirect"), but in the English edition of the work the word has been translated as "direct", probably just a mechanical error; in the present quotation this error has been corrected.

25 Luhmann, Niklas: *Law as a Social System* (Translated from German by Klaus A. Ziegert), Oxford: Oxford University Press, 2004: 293, and right after this passage Luhmann refers to Teubner's work.

their own internal structures through decisions. Here Luhmann devotes special attention to describing the essence of organisational culture.[26] Culture of organisation reflects on such processes as organisational development, formal/informal control mechanisms, networking, using of trust, structural flexibility and other constitutive mechanisms of organisational self-regulation. Some of these mechanisms stabilise normative expectations in organisations, predominantly for organisation members, and thus produce alternative legal mechanisms beyond the state. Such norm-producing processes are overwhelmingly co-ordinated by internal organisational culture. But when organisations evolve on the global scale, when their activities transcend national boundaries, no doubt we have to do with truly transnational organisations. Organisational systems produce transnational normative orders through close cultural revision and inspection. Accordingly, organisational culture on the transnational level is a reality that can be observed and interpreted empirically employing systems-theoretical concepts and logic.

But what about interactions as social spaces shaped by cultural dynamics? Can there be an interactional culture? Is there any possibility of theorising about culture of interactions? Can interactions like 'simple social systems' influence the formation of cultural dynamics? Are interactions, on the other hand, influenced by culture? Do 'interactions interact' with cultural premises and processes?

When Luhmann developed the concept of interaction, the interacting was predominantly possible on the basis of personal presence: face-to-face interactions (not to include one-dimensional communications via written, printed or TV/radio media). However, new forms of communication media in the sense of computer culture and interactions in cyberspace challenge the necessity of physical presence as an exclusive condition for face-to-face interactions in the same space. Technological innovations and worldwide spread of Internet provoke emergence of new interaction types being increasingly of a transnational nature. Online dispute resolution, as an 'alternative' to ADR itself, enables 'electronic identities' to bring their cases to online portal and achieve, through Internet interaction, desired outcomes without 'physical presence' in the 'courtroom'. Such new forms of transnational, transboundary, transphysical interactions produce new culture and challenge old reductive approaches to human communication between persons present in a certain situation. If also new global law is possible without state, new forms of transnational interaction are possible without traditional notions of presence and face-to-face communication.

Interactions as episodic communications make the whole society possible through the meaning communicated in the interaction process. In this respect, interactions about law are of crucial importance for the societal evolution of legal system. Luhmann himself dedicated a special study to the possibility of communication about law in interaction systems.[27] In fact, many anthropological studies are devoted to discovering the local knowledge of law, studying 'elementary' legal communications that do maintain the function of law on the local level. Changing customary legal orders are nothing else but products of interactional law – spontaneous normative decisions involving physically present communicators that articulate with self-made rules and even rules about rules (primary and secondary norms on the level of spontaneous legal interactions!). This interactional law resolves disputes that could be solved in a different way involving different actors with

26 Luhmann, Niklas: *Organisation und Entscheidung*, 2. Auflage, Wiesbaden: VS Verlag, 2006: 240.

27 Luhmann, Niklas: "Kommunikation über Recht in Interaktionssystemen", in: Luhmann, Niklas: *Ausdifferenzierung des Rechts: Beiträge zur Rechtssoziologie und Rechtstheorie*, Frankfurt: Suhrkamp, 1981: 35–52.

different interests and positions in society (hence the contingency of law on the interaction level). And if not only communication about law but also articulation with law and spontaneous creation of norms is possible through interactions, what will protect its spread beyond the national boundaries? Nothing at all – taking into consideration the very worldwide accessibility of current communicative devices! This might be the reason why international arbitration chambers and alternative dispute resolution instruments for transnational cases involve so many interactions while creating 'living law' on the global level – spontaneous, informal, unorganised mechanisms for dispute settlement achieved via bargaining and negotiations (also forms of interaction on their own). If spontaneous customary law shapes local communities, so what protects the use of such mechanisms for episodic regulation in transnational interactions? Especially, is it not reasonable to rethink the possibility of interactional legal culture when such spontaneous self-regulation does not pretend to have a power of precedent and will be arranged employing divergent conditions and outcomes in other interactions? Does not this demonstrate the very contingent character of spontaneous legal ordering? Some empirical studies prove that legal certainty is increasingly secured on the global level via the spread of transborder legal interactions.[28]

But even if formation of spontaneous orders through interactions is possible, how can interactions interplay with culture? Is there something like a culture of interactions? The positive answer of Luhmann is based on an extensive essay dedicated to ethics, which he treats as the reflection theory of morality. Here Luhmann mentions two times the concept of *Interaktionskultur.*[29] The notion of culture of interaction is used by other authors, supporting this innovative phenomenon.[30] Some important concepts and constitutive elements of the systems theory are still under construction (for example, protest movements as a new type of increasingly differentiated social systems).[31] It is up to the development of societal structures and research strategy directed to their study how the concept of interactional culture will be employed and refined, not just as an original metaphor but as a concrete term, describing social reality.

Indeed, interaction as an independent form of social system is a less elaborated type of communicative formation in Luhmann's work, comparing with studies about (world) society and organisation. Accepting interaction as an 'elementary', 'simple' social system, but, at the same time, as a constitutive part of sociological observations, Luhmann stresses the unique importance given to this type of sociality. However, culture of interactions as a less developed concept compared to organisational culture and culture of society, might leave some sort of uncertainty, provoking further misunderstandings. But the use of this concept by Luhmann

28 Dezalay, Yves and Garth, Bryant G.: *Dealing in Virtue: International Commercial Arbitration and the Construction of a Transnational Legal Order*, Chicago, IL: University of Chicago Press, 1996; Gessner, Volkmar: "Global Legal Interaction and Legal Cultures", in: *Ratio Juris*, 7 (2), 1994: 132–145.

29 Luhmann, Niklas: "Ethik als Reflexionstheorie der Moral", in: Luhmann, Niklas: *Gesellschaftsstruktur und Semantik. Studien zur Wissenssoziologie der modernen Gesellschaft. Band 3*, Frankfurt: Suhrkamp, 1989: 358–447, 415.

30 Feldmann, Klaus: *Soziologie Kompakt. Eine Einführung*, 4. Auflage, Wiesbaden: VS Verlag, 2006: 229.

31 Luhmann, Niklas: *Die Gesellschaft der Gesellschaft*, Frankfurt: Suhrkamp, 1997: 847–865. For Luhmann, protest movements are not organisations, while they do not organise decisions, but instead – motives, commitments, connections. But neither can they be considered as interactions, although interactions constitute indispensable part of protest movements, demonstrating their unity and growth. Instead, protest movements have to be treated as an emerging independent type of social systems. Ibid. 850–851. Emerging culture of (global) protest movements could be a potential research topic for further considerations.

legitimises its elaboration in the theory of social systems. Luhmann could have suggested a different notion of interaction had he witnessed the dominating forms of online social networks, 'new relationships' that are marginalising old forms of 'simple social systems'.[32]

If new forms of legal communication emerge at the transnational level, be it an episodic interaction, rule building in organisation or functional regime of world society, the invisible presence of culture is inevitable – culture is everywhere; it shapes social systems and enables societal evolution. On the other hand, cultural premises diffused in different types of social systems are constitutive components of structural unity – they are forms that maintain system identity on the spontaneous, unorganised bases, distinguished from the organised structures. Mechanisms of cultural stabilisation and identity-building on the transnational level have often an unorganised, spontaneous, informal character. As culture is diffused in social systems through its symbolic power and as it maintains evolution and strengthens identity of social systems, locations of transnational legal cultures are to be seen in transnational interactions, organisations and society.

5. Nature vs. culture: transnational legal regimes as cultural creations?

'Agriculture' might be the right phenomenon describing one of the fundamental dichotomies of modernity – nature and culture. Paradoxically, it is at the same time necessary but also somehow impossible to make a sharp divide between nature and culture: it is human activity that transforms the nature as an embodiment of encompassing life; and this transformation itself is based on human nature, the dominating force that drives human activities. Agricultural interventions entail threat to the evolution of nature through uncontrollable and 'unnatural' human activities, as genetic manipulation, artificial interventions into flora and fauna, arbitrary cultural transformation of the environment that might be dangerous for societal dynamics. Industrial systems of production constantly change natural landscapes, reserving no 'right' to nature for 'self-determination' – natural processes are turned into objects by modern 'rational' actors. Culture transforms nature in the modern world, and the same processes can be detected in the legal system – culturally produced law has transformed natural law, innovation has replaced tradition with its positive and negative consequences. If in early modernity it was a condition of social emancipation to fight for freedom from imposed 'natural' orders and to use cultural achievements in this fight, in late modernity, cultural domination over the natural processes entails threats for broad societal evolution and the idea of life itself.

While providing his account on legal culture, Ralf Michaels claims: "given that culture has traditionally been defined in opposition to nature, since the downfall of natural law, all law must necessarily be cultural".[33] It is difficult to share this opinion about "all law" being cultural, taking into consideration that principles derived from natural law and transformed into modern discourse on natural rights still serve as a foundation of any human legal order. But processes of transnational norm-creation and application beyond the state are indeed the right spheres where the 'cultivation' and intervention of legal rationality into multiple functional realms of world society can be explored. The importance of immanent natural

32 Luhmann, Niklas: "Einfache Sozialsysteme", in: Luhmann, Niklas: *Soziologische Aufklärung. Band 2: Aufsätze zur Theorie der Gesellschaft*, 4. Auflage, Opladen: Westdeutscher Verlag, 1991: 21–38.

33 Michaels, Ralf: "Legal Culture", in: Basedow, Jürgen et al. (eds.): *The Max Planck Encyclopedia of European Private Law*, Oxford: Oxford University Press, 2012: 1059–1063, 1060.

law accumulated beyond the state rationality is steadily replaced in the modern world by the multiplicity of normative orders of world society, operating not as natural principles derived from theology, reason or humanity but as flexible and reflexive modes of steering demanded by scientific, economic, military, technological, medical, organisational advancements and new standards achieved by cultural evolution. After increase of cultural growth and domination of technocratic processes over the natural principles, natural life has lost control over evolutionary dynamics, exposing social systems to arbitrary self-expansion that endangers 'environment'. In industrialised modern world, nature is considered of reduced social significance and is often conceived as a totality of resources to be exploited. Unpredictable and turbulent processes of evolution alongside technological advancements bring destructive outcomes to nature. If everything goes this way, re-emergence of natural law thinking is inevitable: in this uncontrollable condition, the marginalised idea of natural law might still evolve and re enter into modern rationality to play the most important role for protecting natural rights and promoting the idea of humanism. Increasing domination of regime-specific prerogatives in the lifeworld might bring the necessity to reduce expansive tendencies of culturally manipulated law for the sake of societal evolution. This could revive the marginalised idea of natural law, which has never disappeared from the landscape of legal life but has remained in the shadow of modernity.

On the other hand, established order needs to be open – at least on cognitive level – for remaining adequate to social transformations and sensitive to cultural determinants. Possibility of deviation represents a mechanism for evolution. Natural law had to be refined during the centuries and where the transformation and adaptation was impossible, necessary steps towards deviation needed to be taken for the sake of legal evolution. Deviation from established natural legal order was always culturally motivated. Such deviations incorporated societal demands and priorities as necessary aspects for legal change. While analysing legal evolution in the old Europe from the standpoint of the Roman legal institutions, where the distinction between natural law (which also included animals) and the law of nations (valid for human beings) was introduced, Luhmann claims:

> This detour via the animal world is significant in relation to the practice of argumentation, because it started a tradition that was maintained well into modern times of justifying deviations from the quasi-animalistic natural law: marriage as a deviation from the natural drive to reproduction, slavery as a deviation from natural freedom, property as a deviation from natural collective ownership, in short: culture as a deviation from natural law.[34]

For Luhmann, modernity is the period when deviation from natural law was fully justified. Although certain deviations from natural order might oppose established propositions of universally accepted natural law – freedom as a natural right vs. slavery as a negative 'cultural' invention– natural law as an eternal force will prove the inadequacy of some unbearable deviations. It follows that natural principles still matter while being rejected for the sake of cultural deviation. Such 'unnatural' orders can exist only temporarily under the domination of a certain structural imposition that is subject to correction during a wide sociocultural evolution. "Culture as a deviation from natural law" – this statement can serve as a formula for legal evolution: there is no advancement without deviation, even in

34 Luhmann, Niklas: *Law as a Social System* (Translated from German by Klaus A. Ziegert), Oxford: Oxford University Press, 2004: 431–432.

the wrong direction. This passage from Luhmann's work also demonstrates that culture as a deviation from nature is not always consistent with ideas of natural rights and freedoms. Broad evolutionary processes have to re-stabilise contingent deviations by reconsidering natural principles. There can be no cultural progress without natural stability.

Problem caused by underestimation of the role of culture to remake an encompassing nature is evident. Evolutionary processes are increasingly shaped by 'unnatural' pathologies. Cultural power causing natural destructions through uncontrollable human development in the risk society is evident. Asymmetries in evolutionary processes are well illustrated by increasing expansion of partial functional rationalities that dominate the external environment (both in systemic and natural understanding): growth of consumerism, increasing industrialisation, excess of juridification, spread of religious fundamentalism, violent militarisation, medical and genetic experimentalism, fetishism of sports, addiction to social networks, daily scandals by mass media – all these are processes that dominate modernity. They can be described as first signs of demolition of functional differentiation, leading to pathological evolution of world society. Heterarchy of world society conceived as a horizontal evolution of functional rationalities is threatened to be undermined by partial hierarchies of certain domains. Forcefully expanding social sectors try to colonise the totality of environment through increasing (anti-)cultural power of specific communication medium.

Indeed, power of culture has been underestimated even within cultural discourses, including the 'law as culture' movement. Discourses that try to bring interdisciplinary visions and inform with broad perspectives, in fact, serve radical reductionism and reproduce only partial outlooks. Prevailing cultural studies of law are focused on a very limited perception of culture, for instance, on artistic activities, embodied in literature, cinema and architecture. Cultural studies of legal evolution focusing on law *as* literature or law *in* literature, law as captured in cinema or fiction, illustrate just episodic features of the broad cultural power of law that shapes all spheres of human activities directed towards nature. In contrast to conventional 'law as culture' studies, the wide notion of culture as a totality of diffused societal power has to be employed. Modernity as a cultural project, in comparison with archaic societies, dominated by natural forces, suggests a difference of structural asymmetries. Culture understood in the sense of 'cultivation' of societal power embodied in different functional rationalities might bring justice to realistic description of turbulent sociocultural evolution. Equilibrium between nature and culture can secure heterarchical arrangement of world society and oppose pathological tendencies of partial systemic dominance established by hierarchic structures.

Nature understood as a force sustaining stability, and culture conceived as a power directed to social change and innovation, explain well the formula of systems-theoretical evolution, postulated as 'dynamic stability'. Only through a meaningful interplay of nature and culture can the functional differentiation be maintained, which would also limit pathological tendencies of certain functional rationalities. Functional differentiation can accept emergence of new legal regimes on the transnational level as an outcome of cultural processes, until these regimes do not violate 'functional freedom' of the other orders and subsystems. As soon as 'functional equilibrium' is undermined, certain systemic problems will emerge in various societal sectors, signalising threats to sociocultural evolution (financial crisis, inflation, political instability, military putsch, ecological threats, religious clashes, ethnic cleansings, epidemic diseases, legal inefficiency and many other pathological tendencies).

While conceiving nature as an eternal force and culture as a societal power, it has to be stressed that for the social systems theory, nature is the mirror, giving to social systems an example of self-reproduction. Autopoiesis of social systems is the mode of self-reproduction borrowed from nature, imitated from life. Even if the autopoiesis of social systems might be endangered through the breakdown of functional differentiation and even if allopoiesis replaces functional freedom of subsystems, such destructive processes are unthinkable for nature as long as life maintains self-reproducing cycles of the living systems. Autopoiesis of nature has no beginning and no end; it will continue as long as life lives, which means even longer than 'language speaks' or 'communication communicates'.

6. 'Transnational legal cultures' instead of 'global legal culture'?

In sum, the idea of *transnational legal cultures* seems to be more appropriate for exploring multidimensional processes of legal globalisation than the homogenous concept of 'global legal culture'. Transnationalisation of legal cultures sounds less idealistic and more realistic. It also allows rethinking internal fragmentation of transnational law into regime cultures and, most importantly, presupposes cultural sensitivity and spontaneous ordering beyond (and not above) nation states or global polity. Accordingly, transnational legal cultures can be conceived as the multiplicity of values, expectations, needs, beliefs and attitudes communicated in world society and directed to the world legal system, based on cultural inclusion and openness. This idea eliminates every attempt to speculate about cultural exclusion or closure. The very notion of transnational legal cultures presupposes pluralism and rejects monism.

Functional difference seen as a realm of transnational legal cultures stresses the importance of functionality as a sole identity of cultural spaces beyond the state. Neither nation nor politics, or even geographic location, but the very social function defines culture on the global level. Transnational business, market regulation, Internet, human rights, commerce, sports, global healthcare, tourism, scientific innovations and many other activities are the functional domains provoking global normative regulation and new, post-national forms of dispute resolution. Functional structures of globality are shaped and reconfigured by invisible cultural forces that lie behind visible constructions. Latent culture reproduces manifest functional regimes and orders. Organised structural units are rearranged by spontaneous cultural power on the transnational level. The multiplicity of functional realms of culture reproduces the fragmented unity of transnational legal cultures. Alongside the mentioned functional realms, transnational organisations and interactions are important carriers of cultural flows beyond the state.

Transnationalisation of normative regimes is an empirical fact in world society. Theoretical constructions observing and analysing such evolutionary processes are, however, mostly ignorant of cultural change. The re-emergence of global legal discourse and necessity to rethink law beyond national constellation is not an ironic turn of history after the demise of classical natural legal thought but a challenge posed by modernity due to self-expanding cultural transformations. The forgotten dichotomy between nature and culture has a major role to play for differentiating between *natural law* and *cultural law*, between law of the humanity and transnational legal regimes. Classical legal narratives and conventional modes of steering have constantly been adopted and remade by cultural innovations. Modern active individuals, capable of transnational interactions and organisation-building, gaining inclusion into performances of functional subsystems, constantly provoke emergence of new types of societal communications. Interactions, organisations and society are exposed to cultural transformations. Specific types of modern law beyond the state – *lex sportiva, lex electronica, lex digitalis, lex constructionis,* internal regulatory mechanisms of multinational organisations and transnational interactions are new carriers of legal rationality, created by culture.

Transnational legal regimes are not universal laws but very particular functional domains of normativity, capable of extending over national boundaries and suggesting global standards only within their 'margins of functionality'. Employing the mechanisms of self-amendment and self-regulation, such standards, rules and norms are under constant review within those domains and subject to change due to cultural demands, expectations, values and attitudes. If there is global living law, it is mediated, reconstructed and maintained by the living legal culture of transnational sectors. There can be law without the state, but there is no law without culture.

5 Competing mirrors

Law's blind spots in philosophical and social-scientific review

Anton Schütz

There is doubtlessly no more audacious venture in matters of social and legal studies today than that of construing one coherent theoretical framework out of the concept of *legal culture*, on the one hand, and on the theory of *social systems*, on the other hand. Legal culture is posited, or posits itself, as an indefinite totality, in other words, as a concept that is both oceanically wide and ecumenically all-inclusive. Any inquiry into legal culture, any observation of it, is bound to take place right *within* legal culture. The study of legal culture, thus, enriches legal culture from the inside, which, one might say, is not entirely unproblematic in epistemological terms. No sharper contrast to this attitude can be thought of than that of social systems theory. Every claim to which *social systems* theory gives rise, including the very notion of system and environment, is predicated on drawing a distinction. Only by clarifying what is counted in and what is counted out, modern society will function in the way in which systems theory claims it does; it is also only at this condition that observation and communication become possible.

Luhmann's ultimate distinction among systems that use meaning for their exchanges is between consciousness-related psychic systems and communication-related social systems. Social phenomenology itself knows of a similar divide: *Lebenswelt*, it has been admitted since long, fails to cover the integrity of social existence, as it is ever more generally admitted that 'official' life, today often shaped by technological and economical dispositives, plays a role of equivalent importance. But which side do we need to choose? The answer will be both, and the reader will be presented with some of the reasons that exclude any fundamentalist one-sidedness on this point. De-differentiating the distances between function systems, abolishing the zones of indifference that allow differentiated systems to co-evolve, is part and parcel of a portfolio of strategies that currently ventures to revoke the process of de-despotisation of the public domain, a powerfully social life-modifying process that has been going on for centuries (or millennia, depending on historians). On the other hand, rejecting the effort of taking stock of the social/legal happening, that is, of legal culture in its totality, is an obscurantist move in its own right. What is needed, instead, is a reciprocal guidance *by and of both* models, a continuous comparative weighing, a sustained study of their complex interplay and the mirror images to which it gives rise. Indeed, it will turn out that playing at once on both keyboards is of the essence of each. In what follows, I shall juxtapose and correlate two views about modern law and society, and the writing of two contemporary thinkers, each of which is fully committed to an enterprise, one of the genealogy of Western law, its effects and sleights of hand, the other of the conditions of maintaining its problem-solving capacities.

I.

While *duty* is a theme common to the philosopher Agamben and the lawyer Teubner, their relevant arguments hover uncertainly at the limit between difference and indifference: the one genealogises the *officium*, disowning its legitimacy, the other constitutionalises duty, thereby officialising hitherto unseen forms of politics. This is more than just an improbable and discreet replay of the old-European-institutional form of a *conflict of the faculties*. Without as much as a recognition, let alone an encounter with the other, each conception offers a contribution, not to bridging but to gauging and 'expressing' their distance. By putting both in a common loop, one gains access to a schizo-analysis of Western sense-making, a Rosetta stone equivalent for the two groups of political languages that are around today, those based on the active duty of constitutionalist lawyering as a 'coping-enabling' device, and those related to the philosophical motives of undoing, inoperativeness and *destituent* (rather than constituent) *power*. Teubner's contributions to both private law regimes and neo-constitutionalism no longer work on systems theoretical premises alone: the empirical focus on fragmentation and its collateral consequences, has outgrown the theoretical focus on social differentiation. Agamben, for his part, has submitted the traditional philosophical avant-garde to an ambitious reshuffle: by its compassing reconstruction of the European past, his nine volume *Homo Sacer* has deflated early Foucaultian 'historical discontinuities' (which were a way of looking in an analogously subversive fashion into historical materialism). These mutual affinities, however, boil down to not much under the onslaught of the divide of *procedural legitimacy* and *speculative philosophy*. Giving in to the immemorial Western temptation of staging oneself as unobserved observer (cf. 1 *Cor.* 2,15 on "judging everything while not being judged by anyone"), *Homo Sacer* is written from the Benjaminian position of a traveller sitting with his back to the engine, on a journey from Antiquity through Western Christianism and scientific post-Christianism and its global pseudo-universalisation. The travel leads through a corridor defined by *form of life* and formless *bare life*. Instead, Teubner's post-systemism's forward-looking view relates to the limits of the possible, and insights and techniques for crisis-management.

On the legal side, the debate has centred for long on the problematic knot between law's virtual omnipresence, the 'natural' penchant (or alternatively: the default setting) of all relations to transubstantiate over time into *legal* relations, and the legal order's factual monopoly-over-law, i.e. the delusively obvious-looking fact that there is no law outside of the legal order – the highly contingent and significant fact *which alone* allows judges to officiate in law's name. But the spiral-shaped relation between being and operation that undergirds both the political-philosophical shaping of life and the legal shaping of procedure and constitution, results in more commonality than either side admits. The salient feature here as there is their intimate non-coincidence. Law of course *denies this: its own conception* of its 'oneness' is Dworkin's "integrity". Law's multiple *operations are immediately identical* (or so the principle has it) with law's *being unique*. Law, in this sense, is monolithic (= "like an indivisible block of stone") in its being, but 'mono-tropic' (= turned towards oneness, i.e., literally speaking, "universal") in its operations. In contrast, the equally intricate relation of form-of-life and bare life favours the Two over the One. This is because it assumes the imminent end of law-ordered times – a counterfactual assumption, as historical events, including the 14th century Franciscan experience, seem to prove beyond reasonable doubt. Remains the oscillation between being *and* operation, the Moebius-loop-like arrangement of the One/Two, the slant to the overall limited affordable inherent in overall management.

The split is nothing new. If the past fifty years of legal theory have seen a wealth of self-centred and confidently modern architectures of law, they have also seen a growing distance from the very idea of a unified legal theory – including as an object that fits into the *concept of a concept*. The comfortable image of a legal system endowed with self-identity has been replaced by a series of monstrously poly-cephalic or acephalous images in Gunther Teubner's inquiries into the genesis, effects, lessons and procedural implications of legal fragmentation,[1] collisions of diverging legal regimes,[2] and indeed, the anthropological and virtue-theoretical conditions of the flourishing of legal as well as economical systems.[3] Much rather than that of an internally coherent *one*, Teubner's portrayal of law shares features with Augustine's portrayal of mankind as *massa perditionis* : a heap of undefinably floating decision-plankton, exposed to external forces with no defences apart from its own routines – apart from what might be termed, with a Luhmannian-Foucaultian expression, the 'discipline of auto-reference'. Agamben portrays legal institutions as decision-making machinery. Validity is trump: it counts irrespective of content, irrespective even of the agent whose procedural success it guarantees. Agamben's genealogy of this core-feature of legal positivity skips Bentham and Austin, Hobbes and even the medieval glossators. He traces the institutional invention known as *positivity* or (since Luhmann) as *legitimacy-by-procedure* all the way to Augustine's anti-donatist doctrine – to the theory of conventional efficacy according to which *if correctly performed* the action is efficacious. Validity is *ex opere operato*, so teaches early fifth century sacramental theory[4], well before modern positivism. Rather parallel to Agamben's genealogical finding, Teubner forestages the unresolvable *aporia* – and the resulting vocation, promise, vow and duty (*officium* – for the legal system, of developing in itself the conditions of what he calls *justice as a transcendence formula*.[5] Teubner thereby adds a philosophical turn to Luhmann's slimmer notion of a *contingency formula*. The duty Teubner enjoins on any and every permanent social organisation (including the Church, nation states, multinationals), is to shoulder the cross of the effects, the adverse unintended effects especially, of *its own earlier choices*. As long as *any* effects are intended, unintended effects cannot be avoided. Whence the need of managing collateral accidents and damages, and of heeding, for each organization or system, the necessity of relativizing its own driving imperatives. In order to realize its mission, the legal order needs to orientate itself referring to its own earlier interventions. In that sense, Teubner claims that *the law* (Recht) must encounter *its law* (Gesetz).

1 Gunther Teubner, Andreas Fischer-Lescano, Regime-Collisions: The Vain Search for Legal Unity in the Fragmentation of Global Law, in 25 *Michigan Journal of International Law* (2004), 999–1046; Gunther Teubner, Peter Korth, *Two Kinds of Legal Pluralism: Collision of Transnational Regimes in the Double Fragmentation of World Society*, in Margaret Young, ed., *Regime Interaction in International Law: Facing Fragmentation*, Oxford (Oxford University Press) 2010; Gunther Teubner, *Constitutional Fragments, Societal Constitutionalism and Globalization*, Oxford (Oxford University Press) 2012.

2 Gunther Teubner, *Altera Pars Audiatur: Law in the Collision of Discourses*, in Richard Rawlings, ed., *Law, Society and Economy*, Oxford (Oxford University Press) 1997, pp. 149–176.

3 Gunther Teubner, Michael Hutter, *Homo Oeconomicus and Homo Juridicus – Communicative Fictions?*, in Theodor Baums, Klaus J. Hopt and Norbert Horn, eds., *Corporations, Capital Markets and Business in the Law*, Dordrecht (Kluwer Law International) 2000, pp. 569–584.

4 Giorgio Agamben, *The Signature of All Things: On Method*, New York (Zone) 2009; Giorgio Agamben, *Opus Dei: An Archaeology of Duty*, Stanford (Stanford University Press) 2013.

5 Gunther Teubner, Self-Subversive Justice: Contingency or Transcendence Formula of Law, in 72 *The Modern Law Review* (2009), 1–23.

II.

Teubner illustrates this need by summoning Kafka's parable *Before the law*, promoted, despite or because of its shortness, among lawyers looking for literary references, to a rank that today outshines the long-time relevant classics *Michael Kohlhaas*, *Bleak House* and *The Merchant of Venice*. It stages a *man from the country* and describes his encounter with the law. In the first *Homo Sacer* volume, Agamben had himself had a look into the philosophical and legal-theoretical interpretations of the parable, finding that they supplemented the tale with the specific mood of tragedy, grief or misery that generally passes for *kafkaesque* among non-readers of Kafka. Deleting decades of tragic – sometimes tragicomically uninformed – readings, he replaced the *kulturkritisch* take of academic interpreters wailing about the passively endured fate of this unfortunate victim of the law with its opposite: the man from the country shows an exhilarating resistance to the *suck* that the law imposes on all those whom it succeeds in subjecting to its fascination and its power.[6] Teubner's reading of the parable, on the other hand, referring explicitly to Agamben's, supplements it with a refinement, a textual discovery that had not surfaced so far. This is the *Glanz* ('shine', 'reflected light'), the inextuinguishable gleam which, whether penetrating or weak, the man perceives breaking from inside of the law.

The eyes of the man from the country grasp the law's glowing presence only in the last moment of the long part of his lifetime that he has spent waiting at the gate of the law, if not of his life. Could it be the case that Agamben's and Teubner's divergence about what constitutes the tale's salient point is ultimately motivated by their appraisal of the proliferation *of lawyerly communications and legal routines in all walkways of life* that has characterized modernity? Is *juridification,* understood as socialised humankind's self-investment in ever more legal rule, what is at stake? Not in the limited, technical sense in which the word 'Verrechtlichung' has emerged a century ago in Germany (in labour relations) but in the sense of the overall significance of juridification, or legalisation: as 'anthropogenetic inflection' (Agamben)? The questions are, then, whether *there is* an outside of the law (cf. poet W. Biermann's older question: Is there life *before* death?). Or whether, to the contrary, the specific normative form called and practiced as law, needs to be understood, not simply as one of its aspects, but as something that is in the cards for any future humankind. Against this, Agamben mints his own philosophical juridification-*irredentism.* His refusal to recognize is directed not centrally against the Rule-of-law but against what might be called the King-Midas-touch-of-law: suppose a legal King Midas *transforming into law whatever he touches, even, and in particular, where his intervention intends to protect against this transformation.* The argument against the extension of law has a price, payable in the currency of *aporia* – Agamben pays it by suggesting the self-exception from law inherent in the "right to have no right" claimed by the hyper-lawyerly argument of a 14th century Franciscan.

That such an argument will make a lawyer impatient is unsurprising; not for reason of professional self-preference or patriotism: simply, concrete legal situations in need to be dealt with, have little to gain from visions of law-free anthropology. At the historical juncture to which we are inoperably connected as its historical inmates, the legal order has had since long to sacrifice its philosophical (and theological) scruples. It can be helped, let alone its trajectory inflected, only from the inside, by a radical self-referentialisation of its effective performances.

6 Giorgio Agamben, *Homo Sacer: Sovereign Power and Bare Life*, Meridian (Crossing Aesthetics) 1998, ch. 4.

As a consequence, mirror-like, two opposed 'civilizing missions' animate juridifying law and anti-juridifying philosophy. The former refers back to Derrida's *aporia* and deconstruction, enriching its possibilistic wager by a licence of impossibilistic deficit spending, an anagogic supplement that allows to 'overcome' the limitation to functions and consequences (Luhmann: "*Funktionen und Folgen*"). The *managementally possible* transforms judgements into measures: the law is promoted to a state of licit exception without discernible stop-rule. In contrast to this is the anti-juridifying position re-describing these remedial interventions critically as managemental-cum-economic bias. Critical of self-reference: of processes and operations that result in ever further processes and operations, of remedies that raise the need of ever further remedies, of the chronicle of unending recursive loops thus foretold.

What is striking about this divide is that it is best rendered, not by what is actually argued by either side but by the gestures and attitudes framing these arguments. Everything looks as if we were confronted with two modes of relating to the world, whose respective reasons and motives barely indicate their fundamental heterogeneity. The divergence of the two views is more original than either side's 'point' would indicate. Its ramifications touch *the level at which one does that which one does* (cf. Wittgenstein: "Words are deeds"). We should therefore consider the possibility that behind and within what we tend to ascribe to each of the two positions involved, what is at stake are deep layers of sedimented traditions or injunctions. Teubner's remarks on Agamben's 'Manichean' position are a case in point.[7]

Manicheanism is a theme likely to come up wherever we find strongly polarized views on legitimacy (or any other legal-cum-genealogical claim). Manicheanism is a blurred matter; in our context, suffice it to say that it is located in the region of the bipolar tension of creation and redemption. As it is well known, Manicheans are suspected to cultivate an exaggerated split between fact and value. Yet, as it is equally well known, anti-Manicheans are constantly at risk of reproducing Manicheanism as a collateral consequence, precisely, of their battle against Manicheanism. Getting used to a bipolar order imposes its toll: no matter what one does or wishes, one has to move within its field of forces. If law features today a split dividing being and operation, entity and actuality, the notion that there is nothing between them, that apart from their split itself, there is no other 'mediation', is Manichaean. To consider law ontologically, as a being, is also to consider it as an integrating part of an existing social order, a region placed within an institutional (id)entity, part of the equipment of the world into which human beings are born and which they leave once the 'run of their life'

7 Teubner's critique of Agamben's take on « Before the Law » contends that Agamben has nothing to offer to make sense of the « shine » (Glanz) that the dying man from the country sees breaking from inside the law (« Das Recht... », pp. 12f., 16). Kafka leaves it cunningly open whether the « shine » is not due to the failure of the dying man's diminishing eyesight, and whether it is thus not (as in a well-known Freudian case) the *glance* of the legal subject that is ultimately responsible for the *Glanz* of the law. For Teubner, salvation lies in the unconcealed aporia and freely admitted incapacity of the legal order (*Recht*) to be up to its task. The confrontation with law (*Gesetz*) serves as a *mirror*, a screen, a surface of inscription, of the legal order's own shortcomings. These shortcomings cannot be helped or avoided structurally or once and for good. They can be helped in the long run – by means of resolutely entering the gate of the law and subjecting the law to future (especially constitutionalist) negotiations. In this way, for Teubner, the possibility of justice (*Gerechtigkeit*) would become possible – possible qua impossible, according to a well-known phrase of the philosopher Derrida (and the lawyer Teubner, speaking on behalf of the legal order, subscribes to Derrida), then combining it to legal configurations such as constitutionalism and proceduralism. The « Manicheism », on the other hand, with which Teubner charges Agamben, would consist in sticking to one's hope for a coming community while continuing to keep a safe distance to the King-Midas-powers of law, by spending and even ending one's life without entering through the gate of the law, unaffected by the claim that « everyone strives to reach the law ».

(referring to the Roman origins of the term 'curriculum') has been accomplished. Considered as an actuality, law appears as a set, a series of result-obtaining operations, operations and procedures-in-progress that give rise to ever more of the same. Law, in this view, is not a reality but rather an 'effectuality', originating as it does not in any thing (*res*), but in an *effectus* (German: *Wirklichkeit*, from *wirken*: "to have effects").[8] If it is correct that the law is both being and operation, then such a doubly determined law cannot help confronting its observer with a bipolar situation, an oscillation between unmediated poles, much as in the case of the famous *Kippbilder* or pivoting images that the eye deciphers as either duck or rabbit, but never as anything 'in-between'.

Within the Western tradition, the Manichean wager features one of the poles of just such a bipolar setting. From the valley of institutionalisation, organisation, etc. with its virgin forest of untreatable divides, we need to discover a way out to find the toolbox helping, not to 'solve' the problem of the underlying split, but to unblock it provisionally and procedurally by means of cunning, life-enabling supplements and devices. In law, the 'twelfth camel' that favours a settlement of an otherwise blocked legal dispute about dividing a succession involving eleven camels,[9] is a case in point. The claim of a third hypostasis of the Holy Trinity in first millennium theology, which favours the overcoming of theological polarisations between the Son (and the theology of redemption) and the Father (and the theology of creation),[10] is another one. It all depends on how such a twelfth or third position is conceived, as a way of cutting a path out of the fascination with the two field-constituting poles. Juridification stabilises: it can give access to more, and to more unforeseen evolutions than the merely erudite task of a genealogical or archaeological description or re-description of the poles at issue. Thus, what is generated is not a system or an agency of ever-continued, ever self-continuing recursive operations, nor an operating *Third* (or *Twelfth*) as in the case of the cunning help of breaking out of a blockage inherent in the *Two* (or the *Eleven*), but simply an observer position. Heidegger's *Verwinden* ('getting round', rather than 'overcome'/*Überwinden*) mirrors a common situation in law, where 'overcoming law' is not an option. The meandering rivers of societal evolution, says Paul Veyne, create improbable proximities between configurations distant by centuries or millennia; the antecedents from Church history referred to in Agamben, especially in his *Theological genealogy of economy and government*, the importance therein of the emergence of Trinitarian theology, and most specifically, the theological discussions in 3rd to 5th century Eastern Church, offer numerous relevant examples.[11] Circumscribing the inner-Trinitarian attributes of the Father and the Son has started, quite simply, as a matter of *constative exactness*, or in other words, of correctly portraying the effective shape of their 'household'-like relation according to the *bipolar* (Old/New Testament) *canon of Christianity*. The suitable technique for these discussions to gain historical attention is to lift them from the *constative* level to

8 Odo Casel, *Beiträge zu römischen Orationen*, in XI *Jahrbuch für Liturgiewissenschaft* (1931), 38ff; cf. the reference to Casel in Giorgio Agamben, *Opus Dei: An Archaeology of Duty*, op. cit.

9 Cf. Gunther Teubner, Alienating Justice: On the Social Surplus Value of the Twelfth Camel, in David Nelken and Jirí Pribán, eds., *Law's New Boundaries: Consequences of Legal Autopoiesis*, Ashgate (Aldershot) 2001, pp. 21–44.

10 Giorgio Agamben, *The Kingdom and the Glory: For a Theological Genealogy of Economy and Government*, Stanford (Stanford University Press), 2011.

11 Ibid.

that of a *performative or illocutionary strategy*.[12] Performative speech claims to produce new facts (constative speech claims to merely document 'what's the case'). The question, for instance, whether one was for or against the extension, to the saviour-Son, of the creator-Father's fundamental privilege of having no beginning in time (of being *anarchos*, from *arché*, meaning 'power', 'command' and 'authority', and also 'origin' and 'beginning')[13] – as linked to performative, political stakes of an order still to be established, though it passed itself off as a mere matter of 'truth', of innocent 'constative correctness'.

III.

More generally, what appeared through millennia to be merely constative claims to validity tend to reveal themselves in retrospect as performative deeds and strategies. *Sitz im Leben* ("site within [social] life") the methodological war-cry of early 20th century Biblical scholarship at its best, summarizes the idea that, in order to gain access to the *meaning* of a socially decisive text, we need to construe its role within social life at the moment when it was 'in the making'. The warring schools in the Trinitarian and pre-Trinitarian battles that were to result in the Nicaean creed, require us to be attentive to the question, not only of the correctness of the *claims to validity* they formulated (constative dimension) but also of the *campaigns they heralded* (performative dimension).

Both the constative and the performative dimensions present objective *Sachprobleme*, whether solvable or less so, that inhabit the legal region at a certain social juncture of the space-time continuum. Their role in the historical and evolutionary dynamic of law as a site of actions and operations, always at least potentially transformative, need to be 'carried'. Foucault, Agamben observes, has not been able to work out the point of convergence between the two aspects of knowledge/power.[14] In the history of Western law, where *operation and being are both at stake*, emerges an overall amphibious landscape – an evolutionary *Eigendynamik* of specific operative systems, networks and recursivities that compounds gestures and truth claims, constative and performative elements, transforming

12 Schematically, a constative utterance refers to a claim to knowledge – which can be true or false, accurate or erroneous, as the case might be, but which in any event is *being-related* – the constative utterance competes for correctly representing a being, mostly because its claim to correctness involves a claim to mastery and to legitimate power, which are always over beings – at least within the post-13th century Western Archaeology of power (cf. Gwenaelle Aubry, Ousia energeia and actus purus essendi. From Aristotle to Aquinas: Some Groundwork for an Archaeology of Power, in 77 *Tijdschrift voor Filosofie* (2015), 827–854). Performative utterances, on the contrary, are not competing for truth or correctness; they aim at creating, at accomplishing a new fact, at giving rise to a situation that changes the parameters of possible action for all those involved. Innovations may or not be triggered by a constative utterance; a performative utterance qua performative intends its operative success; the very performative strategy is designated to operate an innovation rather than to represent a being. Empirically, both occur at once: Whenever points are being made, arguments are being argued, constative and performative elements are involved simultaneously. The historian catches, even if possibly 'red-handed', the action in the moment in which it is performed; even so, a historian contented to limit herself to operations that are operated, evolutions or innovation that are triggered (or completed), boils down to an organizer of official institutional celebrations. In his Inaugural (1888), William Maitland qualified such an attitude both as *orthodox and* as the legitimate attitude for a lawyer. A lawyer, he says, « must be orthodox otherwise he is no lawyer » Yet, « an orthodox history seems to me a contradiction in terms »; finally, « a mixture of legal dogma and legal history is in general an unsatisfactory compound ».

13 Giorgio Agamben, *The Kingdom and the Glory*, cit., 74f., referring to Arius (Ep. ad Alexandrum) and Gregory Nazianzen (Oration XLII).

14 Giorgio Agamben, *Homo Sacer: Sovereign Power and Bare Life*, Torino (Einaudi) 1995, 13f.

mobilized *attention* into effective autopoietic self-continuation. In Western history, each generation has inhabited some such bipolar 'landscape', however different its site and furniture. Within it, smoothly integrated closed systems, sites of successful self-management, without it, no-man's-lands, deserts and other no-go-areas located between those closed and indifferent insides. While systems and post-systems theorists concentrate their attention upon the first, the archaeological and 'anthropogenetic' inquiries practiced by Foucault and Agamben focus on their outside/remainder: *social fabric*, rather than *system*. Overlaps exist; they are located in the zone of management, covering the sub-political range of coping with the fate of discrete entities independently from the standards that apply to public, political life. Whether one puts being or becoming at the core of a philosophically inspired history, or whether one privileges social-scientific inquiry, the object to be investigated is no longer *being* : instead, it is a compound of *being and operation*.

If the bipolar structure of the Western legal tradition has generated divided 'ways of world-making', the question is how the tension itself can be described and identified. This is the point at which 'the Western tradition' comes in as a study topic in its own right. For reasons that are just as impossible to justify in normative terms as it would be to deny their effectiveness in historico-sociological terms, this tradition had structured like none other the genesis of the social world, Western and global. The theological tension of creation and redemption can thus be deciphered as giving rise to a question that is unambiguously (if unadmittedly) *political*, relating to the build-up of institutions and the meta-managerial "essences" of communities. The overwhelming modern secular victory of *operation* over *being* that singles out Western type societies is a repetition of an earlier victory on the field of religious narratives and redemption-theology. It characterises the God of Western-Christian theology far more distinctively than does its ontological, creative component. Whereas creation is 'ex nihilo', unmonitored, uncontrolled, due to pure divine action beyond human reach, operativity is exercised by someone human, open to transitive knowledge and communicable understanding. Secularly speaking, only a house (oikos, *oikia*), not a state (*polis*), is open to methodical inquiry: only *oikonomia*/management, not politics/power.

As the result of a history that is far too winded, long and self-contradictory to fit under the procrustean term of *secularisation*, redemptive theology has resulted in an optimism theological or post-theological: in the immemorial if unfounded trust that every social entity 'normally' includes in its very fabric the chance of realizing and continuing its own self. Springing from this upbeat account of chances of action, Christian narratives of redemption, as well as modern agendas of self-redemption, stipulate an equally upbeat account of a pre-established correspondence of words and acts. Arguments and decisions, beyond that which they confess, profess or argue, always also reveal the act, or *fait accompli*, that they intend. The suggestive formula "Words are deeds" points to a certain *preference for operations* that singles out the household aspect of the Western-Christian theology of redemption; yet, at the same time, it lays the foundations of the modern secular-inner-worldly 'religion' of speech efficiency, and of the absolute secular faith in the preordained givenness, under all conditions, of sufficient means of intervention in the hands of political power.[15] Words are purposive means; arguments owe much of their communicative popularity to the common assumption that they will trigger their own realisation. The anagogical, upwards-guiding drive provides Western institutional forms, Church(es), Empires and, later, states, with their

15 On the genesis of the Western *differentia specifica* as to its superior faith in the *power of political power*, see Marinos Diamantides and Anton Schütz, *Political Theology: Demystifying the Universal*, Edinburgh (Edinburgh University Press) 2017.

distinctive talent. What was needed is a monotheism[16] inclusive of an 'after-creation service', supplementing God's creator-God identity with the identity of a redeemer-God – a perennial duty of administering, governing, saving created and fallen humankind. Jesus Christ's theological-cum-historical endowment as second divine figure of the Christian Trinity is that of an *oikonomos* of the creation, a *manager* of divine economy.[17] Trinitarian theology fused Christ's redemptive action, his death on the cross, with the omnipotence of the author of the creation; it thereby enlists the paradigm of housekeeping, management and economy, and gives rise to the odd field of *managerial theology*. However unwittingly and unwillingly, mostly also in perfectly secular guise, management thus becomes the site of *imitatio Christi*.

The narrative of Christ's self-sacrifice on the cross constitutes, replaced in the context of classical antiquity, a narrative elaboration of the motive of the housekeeping slave who labours at looking after, and repairing the damages caused to, the estate of his absentee landlord for which he is held responsible. Yet this Christian development of duty should not lead to inconsiderate claims of an 'older rights'-based monopolistic claim in favour of Christianism over other religions. Nothing discredits the argument for 'incomparability', more than the absence of a base for comparison.[18] Duty is not a Christian *invention*: campaigns in favour of 'lifelong service', such as the Rousseau- and Kant-quoted *vitam impendere vero* (the imperative of dedicating one's life to the true), go back to Juvenal, a pagan Roman poet of the first-second century CE. Teubner himself, supremely receptive to difficult NT passages (e.g. his reference to the astonishing periscope on Justice *John*, 16, 10), ultimately prefers the help of modern secular literary heroes (cf. Heinrich von Kleist's) and occasionally a mythological intercessor like Sisyphus.[19] Agamben and Teubner are both aware that distinctions such as religion/the secular, inside-religion/outside-religion, etc., have been largely and interestedly overstated. God's becoming-man, his redeeming death on the cross, have revolutionized the history of power and institutions; this in no way precludes us from relating it to secular narratives and contexts or vice versa. The themes of acting or operating within a given situation, of withstanding crises, of outlasting acute environmental pressure, of providing a specific community or population with life-saving help, are integrating part of Christian redemption theology within as without 'religion'. Christ's saving, sacrificial death epitomises a measure of divine management in the creational household (*oikonomia tou theou*/'economy of God'), a successful, imitable deed of life-saving. The Son's saving, continuation-enabling passion and redemption includes a message of supplementing and actualising creation and election, plus a religion-independent one of coping with upcoming contingency.

The narrative of redemption focuses on a household. To keep it afloat, the saviour-*oikonomos* subjects himself unconditionally to the restraints of the 'situation at hand' (this secular lookalike of fallen creation). This looks as if it were at the opposite of the great european claim to sublime or high politics, of the great European acro-political ambition

16 For a thoughtful and radical critique of current uses of « monotheism » see Rémy Brague, *Du dieu des chrétiens et d'un ou deux autres*, Paris (Flammarion) 2008.

17 See, for early Christian texts and further literature, Agamben, *The Kingdom and the Glory*, cit., cap. 2; also, Marie-José Mondzain, *Image, Icône, Economie: les sources byzantines de l'imaginaire byzantin*, Paris (Seuil) 1996, 40ff.

18 For a history of the methodologico-theologico-political objections to comparison cf. Jonathan Z. Smith, *Drudgery Divine: On the Comparison of Early Christianities and the Religions of Late Antiquity*, London (School of Oriental and African Studies) 1990.

19 Cf. Teubner, *Self-Subversive Justice*, 1–23.

of politics understood as sovereignly unconstrained, thus truth self-assertive true speech. In practical terms, the innovation underlying the theology of the sacrificial filial fixing of the needy fatherly creation after the Fall is a 'deal' that displaces the point of gravity at once from creation to household, from sovereignty to self-subjection, from being to operation and 'coping'. Operation acquires a new standing, with a plot written in the language, well known to the early 21st century, of crisis management. Created humankind is caught in its collateral consequences; the redemptive Son, not involved in it, takes all unforeseen epigenetic ramifications of the initial creative act, all the sins of this created world, upon himself. The socio-politico-legal meaning of the dogma of the Trinity lies in this economic/saving measure. The period spanning from the Neronian persecution until the dogma of the Trinity hosts a unique theological learning process fated to transform the commitment of the 'Jesus-people' into that of 'Christians', and to give rise to Empire, its government, its masses, much as, after a further learning process, one point five millennia later, a similar learning process will enjoin them to become atheists, in order to remain faithful to the core Christian message: that of an emancipation from superstition.[20] Divinity divides in two, Father and Son – with a third position, the Spirit, as an enabling and hedging device destined to avoid, precisely, the abysmal perspective of a Manichean duel.[21] To save the helpless glorious Father's creation is the Son's Duty ('deal', 'job', 'task', 'mission'). Only the smallest part of this Christian *art of governing/managing* belongs to what is today identified as *religion*. In contrast, *time* plays a key role: the bounded mean-time between two divine interventions, one creating, one corrective-managerial. Redemption can take place *after* creation only, as a corrective supplementary measure to correct, save, repair, sustain. After having created it as its generous glorious creator-father, God redeems it as his own self-sacrificing, miserable son.

Lurianic kabbalah knows of a creator whose generosity leads him to retract ever further from creation, assigning ever more space to created humanity.[22] Allah, for his part, is not going down this road. Instead, he remains most merciful,[23] and the world he had created, an unending series of his continuing miracles; managing the unforeseen consequences of the latter, is a lesser concern. The powerless and merely dutiful aspect of a redeeming God, abandoning his life to fulfil the responsibility that he imposes upon himself by creation, is the core and the hapax of the Christian narrative.

IV.

Complex issues in history do not, William Maitland told the public of his Cambridge Inaugural in 1888, receive the same treatment as complex cases in law.[24] Legal cases will be decided upon by competent officials, and the decision they take, the 'solving of the case', will be valid and definite. Historians, on the other hand, though equally professionals of qualified choices, *never decide*, having no access to the surplus-value of triggering *res iudicata*. Maitland locates the split in the *officium iudicis* of the old-European legal tradition: only a judge, by dint of her formal *officium*, is authorised to judge – to wield an operative

20 Cf. Serge Margel, *Superstition: l'anthropologie du religieux en terre de chrétienté*, Paris (Galilée) 2005.

21 On this and related secular aspects of (Western) Trinitology, cf. Diamantides, Schütz, *Political Theology*, 2017.

22 On *tsim-tsum* (divine self-contraction) in Kabbalah thought, see Gershom Scholem, *On the Mystical Shape of the Godhead*, New York (Schocken Books) 1991, p. 83.

23 Cf. Franz Rosenzweig, *Der Stern der Erlösung*, Freiburg (Universitätsbibliothek) 2002, p. 185.

24 Frederic William Maitland, *Why the History of English Law Is Not Written* (Inaugural Lecture), 1888, *Collected Papers, vol. I*, Cambridge (Cambridge University Press) 1911, p. 488ff.

competence with well-defined effects attaching to its performance, guaranteed in advance by the compassing agency, the legal order. To the extent that it invests any judge's decision with the character of 'res iudicata', the power held by the judge is effectively some sort of official magic. Historians are deprived of any 'magic'; their claims remain infinitely exposed to revision. Historical claims are provisional forever, for good, within an unending series of interventions. In this sense, as based upon no professional *officium*, the historian is not an official. A historian's is the exercise of a general regime of creative *unofficial* learning under conditions that are contingent and, forever, *provisional.*

Legal decision-making, on the other hand, is an *officium*: a right that comes with a duty – a duty of imposing consequences that will have their bearing upon the parties right away; a mastery, but one based upon a ministry.[25] This is why law is not, first of all, a reaction to complexity, or the self-discipline of a legal decision-maker. If law is a decision-producing machine, then the functioning of such a machine relies intrinsically upon time and time-bound self-adaptation; it proceeds by transforming all complexity matters into time matters. After every legal decision, a new time starts to run – this is the meaning of *res iudicata*: to give rise to a sequential order in which earlier own results function as resource of decisions yet to be taken. In Derrida's footprints, Teubner refers to the divide possible/impossible. Luhmann's social systems theory's contributions to modern law relate to (self-)*possibilisation.* Luhmann has famously called his *observer* a scion of the house *devil.*[26] His notion of a *system* has different origins. Social systems, traceable to need and neediness, to the house and the household, to oikonomia, appear after and because of the Fall of the original couple, at a moment when the devil's Fall is already old history. A secularised economic theology and an unending series of variations on the theme of *indispensability*, social systems theory refers to the needs to 'cope' with the system's contingent (untranscendable, unescapable) exposure to the environment. In places like Cockaigne or paradise, no one has ever heard of systems or *oikoi*. They emerge as the reaction of the fragility of the perfect order, whether polis or creation. While the ancient terminology of *oikonomos*, *oikonomia*, *oikeiosis*, etc. covers large swaths of the *meaning*-region of Luhmannian systems terminology (self-reference, most especially, though Luhmann does not seem to have been interested by the connection), the *word* system (Gr. *systema*) had already been used, in antiquity, to refer to entities like bodies, cities, houses, poems, even the cosmos.[27] In its application to household, sustainability, etc. the word appears in the early 20th century, soon supplemented with *environment* as abstraction-increasing codicil.[28] The riddle of the commonality between social-systemic *autopoiesis* and ancient *oikonomia*, house-government (cf. the relevant Aristotelian treatise) remains: both refer to operations that are carried out under conditions of 'being thrown on one's own resources'. Whence their common character of collateral damages, their proximity to the Heideggerian and Blumenbergian theme of *Sorge*/anxious care. A particularly important leg of the journey from paradise to *Sorge* has taken place in the riverbed of *contingency.*

25 Giorgio Agamben, *Opus Dei: An Archaeology of Duty,* see note 4 above.

26 Thus Niklas Luhmann (« Der Beobachter […] stammt aus dem Hause Teufel »). See his yet untranslated *Die Wissenschaft der Gesellschaft*, Frankfurt am Main (Suhrkamp), 1990, 118ff. See Anton Schütz, *Luhmanns unheimliches Argument*, in Albrecht Koschorke, Cornelia Vismann (Hg.), *Widerstände der Systemtheorie: kulturtheoretische Analysen zum Werk von Niklas Luhmann*, Berlin (Akademie-Verlag) 1999, pp. 96–109.

27 Agamben, *Kingdom*, cit., see note 10 above; Marie-Jose Mondzain, *Image, icône, économie.*

28 Gorm Harste, *The Long and (Not So) Winding Road of Systems Theory*, paper presented to the Danish Conference of sociology, 2012; Manfred Riedel, System, Struktur, in Otto Brunner et al., eds., *Geschichtliche Grundbegriffe*, Band 6, Stuttgart (Klett-Cotta) 1989, pp. 285–322.

The decades straddling the year 1300 show evidence of the first official encounter with *things neither necessary nor impossible.*[29] Theologian John Duns Scotus casts the onslaught of admitted contingency in dodgily humorous terms: "People who claim that there is no such thing as contingency need to be subjected to torture—unless and until they are ready to admit that they could as well not be tortured".[30]

The triumphal march of contingency is coupled to that of letting loose the power of God. Yet, the God of Franciscan theology is not only all-powerful (as is Aquinas's as well). He is also all-disciplined, almost like an 19th century Englishman. In one sense, his *potentia absoluta* is a shelter, a hedging intransparency, in the service of his disciplinedness, called by Scotus: *potentia ordinata.* It is this ambitiously complex limitational concept that we need to have a closer look at, considering all that it has in common with a more recent notion from social systems theory, Luhmann's *contingency formula.*[31] Social systems theory was left with the embarrassing question whether the function systems can deliver sufficient stability in the ocean of contingency, in the way, say, in which liberal economy expected just this from the famous 'invisible hand'. As Luhmann's answer was negative, the problem opened was that to which the contingency formula was supposed to provide, not, surely, a solution in the sense of an annihilation or evacuation of the problem encountered, but definitively a *formula* allowing to coexist with it. Schematically, the fact of operating under conditions of functional differentiation exposes each function system to the need of replacing the now absent panoramic master-view by means of distinguishing first- and second-order observer. The multiplicity, in other words, that results from the absence (in Luhmann, as opposed to Scotus) of a *potentia-absoluta*-wielding 'master', gives rise to *contingency formulas* – one for each differentiated function system. The contingency formula thus offers a guideline for coping with the phantom pain that is the fatal legacy of the now unavailable 'mastery-universalism', by narrowing the zone of its legitimate applications – not an easy business, in light of the still widespread conviction that observer-independent universality alone can bestow legitimacy to any claim whatsoever.

V.

Reading Kafka's *Before the law*, Teubner suggests a depersonalising *aggiornamento.* Let the law *itself encounter its law.* In the place of Kafka's man, he puts the legal system. The tale thereby changes levels, from person to function system. A new land surveyor, Teubner measures the distances of knowledge-related rationalities and management-related deontologies.[32] Doing so, he also lays the groundwork of a new understanding of Western legal

29 André De Muralt, *L'unité de la philosophie politique: de Duns Scot et Ockham à Suarez et au libéralisme contemporain*, Paris (Vrin) 2002; Anton Schütz, A Quandary Concerning Immanence, in 22 *Law and Critique*, 189–203 (2011) 197.

30 « [I]sti, qui negant aliquod ens contingens, exponendi sunt tormentis, quousque concedant quod possibile est eos non torqueri » (Duns Scotus, *Quaestiones in lib. primum Sententiarum* [quoted after the edition of Wadding, Lyon 1639, vol. 5/2] dist. 39, quaest. 5). Today, suggesting torture as a learning technique comes as a shock; but behind the claimed innocence of the witticism lurks already the serious modern alliance of contingency and juridification.

31 Niklas Luhmann, *Theory of Society (vol. 2)*, (Stanford University Press) 2012, depicts contingency formulas as *systemspezifische Unbestreitbarkeiten* (« claims that, within the system, cannot be disputed »).

32 Discussing so-called « unbridgeable » conditions, Luhmann, attentive to the negative dialectics of differentiation involved, suggests that the notion of a « total difference » can only refer to such items about whose relation it can be said that their poles relate to each other as « not different, but rather indifferent ».

history, identifying law as communications of lawyers, law-customers, etc. rather than as an artefact of meaning, whether *arché* or *genos*.

Teubner's article *Das Recht vor seinem Gesetz: Zur (Un-)Möglichkeit kollektiver Selbstreflexion in der Rechtsmoderne* contains a steep hurdle for the translator, which is no other than the dialectics between 'Recht' and 'Gesetz', and by the resulting perplexity prevailing in the relationship between the English and most continental European languages in their respective wording of normative matters. 'Recht' embodies the proper name, the normative region's compassing synecdoche; it is a close linguistic relative of 'right' – a *faux ami*, incidentally, in that 'right' applies only to legal subjects, not legal orders. The proper name of the normative sphere in English is 'law' – a word related *not* to *Recht* or *right* but to *loi*, *legge*, *ley*, *lex*, *Gesetz* (and, as vanishing point: legislation).

The translator's nightmare reaches its climax with Kafka's *Vor dem Gesetz*. Often and arguably incorrectly classified as an 'apologue' (an allegorical or moral fable intended to convey a useful lesson), this short prose piece has been translated as *Before the law*. The point here is not about trying alternative translations, but about reminding that English 'law' stands indistinguishably for German 'Gesetz' *and* 'Recht'. Everything looks as if Kafka, not a likely candidate for sloppy use of language, might as well be referring to the normative sphere at large. Suppose that instead of his unsettling prose piece *Vor dem Gesetz*, Kafka had in mind to write, say, an introduction for prospective law students, under the then appropriate title "Vor dem Recht": The difference would not show. Which incidentally might be the reason why discussions of Kafka's *Before the Law* so often read as if they factually were introductions for prospective law students.

If one tries to translate an expression such as Teubner's meta-Kafkian title *Das Recht vor seinem Gesetz*, the resulting aporia offers an insight into the cluttered border-zones between English and German (law *and* language). German *Recht* refers to a process, a problem, even a profession; German *Gesetz* (always with the definite article) designates *that which carries validity* in the eyes of a legislative/law-giving/*gesetzgebend* instance. The fact of accentuating the tension between the two German signifiers by cramming them into one single short phrase underscores the gap. How is one supposed to understand "The law before its law"? Linguistic and non-linguistic uncertainties intertwine. While *Gesetz* is unproblematically to be translated as 'law', *Recht*, the central heavyweight term of German normative language, and thus, the usual suspect wherever the English reader finds the word 'law' in a translation from that language, poses a problem linked to the interference of English 'right'.[33] In Teubner's *prosopopeia*, it is *Recht* that is supposed to take up the man from the country's difficult situation. To understand law as situation-exposed like a person, as Teubner asks his readership to do, corresponds neither to the 'subjective sense' of *Recht* nor to its 'objective sense' (absent from the meaning of English 'right'). Even so, the *experimentum* of substituting *law/Recht* for *the man from the country*, refers to law in the making, to law as a process of reflexive decision-making, as a function system, or a thought process, or as the crossing of both.[34]

Kafka's *Before the law* tells the tale of a human-all-too-human being's ambiguous quest. How can 'the law' take its place? How can the law be confronted to *its* law? The answer is:

33 This is not to question that it is a courageous move of newer translations of Hegel's *Grundlinien der Philosophie des Rechts* to stick to the common etymon of German *Recht* and English *right* and to translate the title with the near-neologism *Philosophy of right*, rather than *of law*. Whoever makes such a radical step is fully aware that it increases, rather than reduces, the difficulty for any non-initiated and non-specialist readership.

34 A core theme of Teubner's work. Cf. Gunther Teubner, *How the Law Thinks: Towards a Constructivist Epistemology of Law*, in 23 *Law and Society Review* (1989), 727–758.

by dint of exposing itself to the impossible possibility of *just* decisions.[35] The issue is turned into one of self-reference; the plot thickens between law and law, between law qua legal system, and law qua the legal system's duty or *officium*. Splitting *law* into two,[36] law judging and law judged, we are effectively given a story about the law, rather than about someone. Derrida sets the stage having *literature* encountering its law (*loi*, *Gesetz*).[37] Kafka's world is full of well-defined agents: land surveyors, country doctors, investigators, new advocates, bank employees, mythological heroes, dogs, mice, etc. Teubner questions that Kafka should be seen as someone whose writing should necessarily specialize on human beings "made of flesh and blood", rather than the selves of the legal institutions (*Rechtsinstitutionen*) of modernity. If the *law itself* has 'legal issues', no wonder that it proceeds by incessant searches *for its own* law, *its own Gesetz*. Why did Kafka, a trained lawyer and an insurance agent, *not* think of explicitly staging "the law's own problems with the law"?[38] The law, in its *first* hypostasis, refers immanently to an *operative* unit, a site of *effectuality*;[39] it refers, in other words, to normative 'business', the Luhmannian sum total of communications that, happening simultaneously, apply recursively-endlessly the guiding distinction of 'lawful/not lawful'.[40] The law, in its *second* hypostasis, refers to a transcendent rule, command, judgement. Law 1 (=Recht), in need of justification, is exposed to the humiliation of being permanently confronted to Law 2 (=Gesetz) and its verdict. In fact, a more traditional bipolar structure, known as "jurisprudential antinomy" between *Recht* and *Gesetz*, is known to any practitioner of legal theory. The problem is, one might distinguish Law-2-*Gesetz* and endow it with no matter which superiority over Law-1-*Recht*; one might subject law understood as the historical account of *its own earlier choices*, to law-as-judgement, or *the impossible law of justice that alone measures the law*: what one will not be able to leave behind, that way, is the loop of reprogramming a finite circular structure of the normative, tautologically defined as a *process that comes up with what it comes up with*.[41] The operation-engendering *business of law* (*Recht*) needs to be understood in relation to the sovereign *imperative of law* (*Gesetz*). But what do we gain from the doubling procedure? The re-conception of justice as *transcendence formula*[42] (by which Teubner innovates with respect to Luhmann's notion of justice as *contingency formula*[43]) modifies the standing of the reference to justice by adding a further leg of proceduralisation/temporalisation – at the price of opening a potential *cascade* of "*Before-the-law*"-thresholds.

35 Gunther Teubner, Das Recht vor seinem Gesetz: Zur (Un-)Möglichkeit kollektiver Selbstreflexion der Rechtsmoderne, in Marc Amstutz/Andreas Fischer-Lescano (Hg.), *Kritische Systemtheorie – Zur Evolution einer normativen Theorie*, Berlin (Suhrkamp), 2016.

36 Ibid., 3.

37 See Jacques Derrida, *Acts of Literature*, ed. by Derek Attridge, New York (Routledge) 1992, 190ff.

38 See Anton Schütz, *Legal Critique: Elements for a Genealogy*, in 16 *Law and Critique* (2005), 71–93.

39 For Giorgio Agamben, *Opus dei: An Archaeology of Duty*; see also Thanos Zartaloudis, On Justice, in 22, *Law and Critique* (2011), 135–153 (147) for the semantics of *operativity* and *actuality*, of *energeia* and *poiesis*, and their respective roles in Agamben and Heidegger, and in Teubner and Luhmann.

40 Niklas Luhmann, *Law as a Social System*, Oxford (Oxford University Press) 2004, 99ff.

41 One needs to nuance this proximity by looking at what distinguishes Teubner's level of locating the site of the *dialogical bias* from Habermas's. But one would also have to allow for a basic objection, shared by both Teubner and Habermas, against what both perceive as instances of *tautological bias*. Both Habermas and, lately, Teubner, take their distances from circular/tautological identity-constructions. They share a common rejection of the hardliners of circularity, such as Scotus, Spinoza, Luhmann, and ironically, Agamben.

42 See Teubner, *Self-Subversive Justice*, 1–23.

43 Luhmann, *Law as a Social System* (engl. tr.), 211 ff. See G. Bryson, Justice as a Kontingenzformel: A 'Hard Case' in Luhmannian Reception History?, in A. Febbrajo-F. Gambino, *Il diritto frammentato*, Milano (Giuffré), 2013.

VI.

By placing either transcendency (Teubner) or bipolarity (Agamben) at the heart of law, both reject the secularisation narrative that epitomises *modo freudiano* the modern legalised present ("Where religion has been, there law shall take over"), by relying upon the modern supersession of the pre-modern religious past. It is in this light that Teubner's (and Luhmann's) efforts of rehabilitating the legal system against its positivist impoverishment deserve to be replaced in the context of the last instalment of *Homo Sacer*, where *use* is centre staged, bringing the politics of *form of life* into yet another undecidable relation to the de-politicising coup d'Etat of *oikonomia*—of 'coping', 'dealing' and 'managing'. The divergence is about the instructions that follow from this. It is tempting to question the wisdom of prescribing more of the same juridifying cures to alleviate damages of earlier such; to ask, for instance, how the "inextinguishable shine" (*unverlöschlicher* [...] *Glanz*, [Kafka, *Before the law*]) relates to what Agamben's theological terminology calls "glory"? Are government *and* glory ingredients of one unique field of tension, one single machinery? Is no step towards governmentality, managementality and juridification, sufficient to dislodge the *glory* element? Is a new oscillation all we can expect?

Yet, self-reference, meaning the increasingly exclusive relevance of earlier own actions in the process of decision-making, appears as the unshakeable foundation of how the modern legal system is likely (and, therefore, also bound) to proceed. The modern legal system is born as a result of often-studied differentiation processes – and has given rise to a long-standing mock-immunological debate about the role of 'justice' in the course of its self-reproduction: If, as Teubner (closer to Derrida than to Kafka) has it, law should encounter justice 'as *its* law', one is tempted to ask: which of the divided legal and philosophical views is closer to law's intrinsic paradox of undecidability? That the function system specialising in decisions is also specialising in undecidability is barely a surprise; at best, it is an example more of the solidarity between the *notion of expenditure* and that of the *cursed part* according to Georges Bataille.

But the issue remains of what, in positivist validity-terms, "impossible justice" might refer to. Two centuries of positivism that start from the Benthamite incubation and are still law's pillar/pillow today, are witness to the historical continuity of the basic teaching. The Austro-Hungarian monarchy—the institutional framework in whose categories Kafka (1883–1924) wrote *Before the Law* in 1914, has been brought up as a lawyer — had omitted to buy itself into the doctrine of progress. "Kakania" was *officially* backwards; the sucking effect from the future that had been unfettered elsewhere had no purchase on it. Nor is it a coincidence, or a paradoxical riddle, that the geographical-historical setting that has given rise to Kafka had also produced, two years earlier, another Prague-born lawyer, Hans Kelsen (1881–1973), whose *Pure Theory of Law* has produced the intellectually most challenging, most unapologetically academic, but theoretically most uncompromising, formulation of the entire legal positivist saga. The gap between the modern-progressive-rationalist content of Kelsen's writing and its authoritarian-speculative form: its internal tension between a social-democratic plus enlightened, science-centred and leftist stance, and the Habsburg-empire inherited middle-European and elitist institutional form and method, has baffled generations of specialized Kelsen-readers throughout the world.

Today, the age-old *fama* of legal positivism's historic mission/*officium* of working towards a global legal revolution, turns out to have been barely more than a 'period-feature'. Those lawyers and law-trained philosophers, who, like Teubner and Agamben, are born in the 1940s, have witnessing the moment at which positivism has been wrapped up in its last twilight. Different from Kelsen, whose formative years coincide with the climax of the modernist trajectory, with the period of the sovereign dignity of knowledge or *epistemic empire* (roughly, the first half of the 20th century), Agamben and Teubner formative years coincide with the slow demise of knowledge and its sovereign pole-position and, in law, the long sequence of post-positivisms. The positivist account of the legal order and the modernist understanding of science had brought the myth of power – the doctrine of an ultimate, unobserved observer, who sees everything as it is – into its final shape. All decisive elements of the doctrine against which Kelsen had fought before his emigration to the United States – excepted only the clerico-fascist control of public life that, in Austria, had preceded the Anschluss – resurface with a vengeance in the 1980s, when the critical legal studies movement, with its notorious thrashing of 'formalist' and 'ossified' positivism, set the pace. But once again, let us not forget that legal positivism has only been a minor foothill of a larger mountainous massive, the end not of history, but of the social leadership of modern science, and the deflation of the unconditional overall trust in it, which had lasted for many centuries.[44] The law, whose autonomy had been shielded, for a century of victorious legal positivism, from the challenges of de-differentiation, is confronted once again with the sirene calls of "opening itself up": Teubner, who, in his Kafka-reading, sentences the *law* to the hardship of encountering *its law*, is a case in point.[45] The unquenchable thirst for what might be called *more-justice-than-possible* goes together with a protean ability of converting into utterly possible arrangements of "enshrining politics" – of "*wrapping up* politics" (cf. artist Cristo) – transforming law, via 'law-plus-supplement', into a theme that is eminently able to be routinized, administered, managed, taken care of. Autopoieticism has no "social function system for transcendence" on offer. In systems-theory, transcendence suggests, if anything, *de-differentiation*. The addictive credit-creation triggered by the financial crisis[46] is a point in case. The question is to what extent the inflationary recourse to critical-legal and neo-constitutionalist transcendence programs needs to be counted as further indicators of addictive de-differentiation.

VII.

Law *struggles* today to supply a self-presentation that convinces as a function system. The late 20th century collapse of the political perspectives and scientifically grounded legal-positivist expectations accompanies an academic programme for law that is eminently expressible and gloriously teachable. Law faculties and schools, often struggling with their fresh students' applications and programs, spread a layer of anagogical 'Good News' about the capacities, chances and inherent powers of the legal profession that often exceed the inflation rates of allowable institutional deficit spending. Indeed, legal education seems to be specifically vulnerable to this anagogical temptation. In 1919, a year before his death,

44 The inversion can be seen at work both within law and without. Cf. the fields of post-colonial and subaltern studies. The question of rehabilitation is, for instance, well presented and re-presented in titles such as Dipesh Chakrabarty *Provincializing Europe* cited after the 2nd edition, Harvard (Harvard University Press) 2007. The title alone brings a fresh breeze, and from the book itself transpires a frank spirit of provocation seasoned with a certain awareness of where the effective stakes are—good news, coming from a region long time inundated with critical Western crocodile tears.

45 Gunther Teubner, A Constitutional Moment? The Logic of Hitting the Bottom, in P.F. Kjaer, G. Teubner. A. Febbrajo, eds., *The Financial Crisis in Constitutional Perspective. The Dark Side of Functional Differentiation*, Oxford (Hart) 2011, pp. 9–52.

46 Teubner, Self-Subversive Justice, 1–23.

Max Weber cast his core judgment on duty in his famous twin papers *Science as a vocation* and *Politics as a vocation*. His critique focussed on the illegitimate surpluses realized by means of fishing in muddled waters. His nemesis was the mutual *contamination* of political militancy and scientific instruction, or, in other words, the consummated disconnection between free-wheeling aspirations and the steel-hard casing of management — the double shipwreck staged by careers in politics and in the Human/Social/Historical Sciences. A century after Weber, the implosion of political agendas based on the tradition of Revolution, Enlightenment and the gigantism of industrialist production, the emerging of the post-industrial university as a factory of self-sufficient discourses smoothly and lucratively self-reproducing on the basis of factually abandoned aspirations to knowledge, give rise to a mounting sea-level of illegitimacy. Luhmann's and Teubner's call for the full recognition of the fact that *finality* (e.g. the claim that law is invested by some law-transcending mission) is now bound to take into account *tautology* (law-does-what-law-does, albeit within the problematic limits of law's contingency formula *justice*), heeded in the moment at which a wholly new 'generation' of more direct means of steering has taken centre stage and functions, often qualified as 'populism', as a new unifying, more exactly short-circuiting, treatment of achieved levels of differentiation and fragmentation. Its appearance very clearly tries to undercut, yet fails to solve, a range of potentially vital problems. The bipolarity at work between *oikonomia*/management and the assertion of the transcendent glory of sovereignty find in the new usurpation of political power a docile, if improbable pupil. Meantime, there is no way of blinding oneself to the fact that slogans like 'impossible justice', and slogans like 'duty-of-self-transcendence', move not in the same but in opposite directions. Clearly, the withdrawal of sovereign politics and the phantom pain it provokes is felt both and equally on the philosophical and on the legal side of the double mirror. The terminologies 'inoperativeness', 'undoing', 'destituent power', 'form [rather than: rule] of life' and 'use', offer striking point-to-point *alternatives to juridification*. The claim to a life capable of living itself out without the help of a legal rule is revealed as the key aspect of the *Homo Sacer* project. Meantime, the *daily growth* of juridification has become part of the routine. The very question of decidability or not seems wrongly posed. The mutual *Mitsein* of *juridification* and *dejuridification* provokes a need of a new institutional vocabulary.

What the controversy shows is that the legal order, operating necessarily under conditions of contingency, stands under a steadily increasing need for compensating supplements. For a long time, it recruited religion; in the past two or three centuries, the soothing glorious supplement had been provided, on the contrary, by the secular preaching of politics. Politics figures as a source of integrity and 'meaning'. During the past twenty years, "the Davos man" (a termed coined at Davos, in 2004, by S. Huntington) has been overtaken by what might be analysed as an *oikonomia*-guided ego-cure in order to heal the *polis* of what appears in its optics as Christian or post-Christian altruism ('populism'). Nearly two generations earlier, Luhmann's theory had launched an attempt to figure out the conditions allowing autopoietic function systems to achieve function-related autonomy.[46] The function system internal contingency formula was destined to overcome the temptation of a reductive, ad-hoc or tit-for-tat conception of coping with any type of upcoming contingency. This is based upon the notion that the system can in no case *learn* from the environment. It can only learn to cope with it. The environment has neither message nor strategy. It has no need to care for reducing un-masterable complexity or contingency; it does not care, it is what it is, that is all. Only the system cares, or learns. All caring and learning takes place in a system. But this poses questions. Some are old: how is social order possible in the absence of an overarching, society-ecumenical order limiting contingency, given that there is no overarching system? How promising are the chances that it emerges spontaneously? Yet, systems without an identity other than the series of their operations do exist and can exist even in the absolute absence of any absolutely compassing instance. Can they be enabled to absorb and manage contingency in a non-fortuitous fashion, by means of an internally forged 'contingency formula'? In order to save the baby while getting rid of the dirty bathwater, Teubner replaces contingency-formula with trancendency-formula, but whether contingency-based in Luhmann, or transcendence-based in Teubner (law-as-business vs law-as-judgment) or bipolarity-based in Agamben (de-juridification vs juridification)—the importance of the 'formula' can barely be overstated, as it is the element that puts a new conception of law in the place of the silently and smoothly running ideal of legal positivism. That Luhmann's term 'contingency formula' comes up in the *contingency-ambitious society* of the German Federal Republic of the late 20th century, is no coincidence. "Transcendence formula" (early 21st century) as well belongs to a strategic campaign, is a witness to its own surrounding circumstances. While the first draws a distinction between the law and its contingent societal environment, the second strives to domesticate the law by getting it under the thumb of the law's duty of transcending itself. But transcending-itself constitutes, applied to the law, a recipe for further juridification.

Part II

On the multidimensional functioning of legal systems

6 Normative force and political intelligence

André-Jean Arnaud

1. From normative force to political intelligence

I have already had occasion to present law in a sociological perspective as a force field where rationalities are found. These days, this field is augmented by the transformations imposed as a consequence of the impact of economic and financial globalisation on the traditional concept of rights. 'Normative force' probably also acquires a fair part of the specificity of its meaning in an intellectual context that cannot avoid referring to the theories of complexity to which too many jurists have remained insensitive to until now.

It is perfectly true that it is high time to start discussing what appeared to be anomalous with regard to the traditional force of the law: the force of directives that have not been transposed, of the number of first articles of certain laws, of the guidelines in the law of competition, of administrative directives, of advisory opinions, of draft projects to reform the law of obligations, of the 'rights to' whose numbers are multiplying, of the tools of corporate social (or societal) responsibility, of trade agreements in labour law and of the recommendations of independent administrative authorities, without counting the many other tools and instruments that are used today, yet are ignored by legal tradition.

Only a recourse to theories deriving from complex legal thinking can enable the diversity both of legal norms and of the multiplicity of contemporary regulations to be accounted for. It is only from this crucible that ideas will come that may enable new generations of jurists to respond to an expectation that is no longer the same as when we were trained, when we were privileged to have as our guides the prestigious authors who forged the concepts that we absorbed and that we counted on transmitting, in our turn, as an intangible, sacred legacy.

Another reason for returning to the theories of complexity resides in the profound mutations that have recently been produced, over and above even the concept of juridicity, in the radical transformation of legal rationality. I refer here, for example, to the 'force' acquired by civil society in the production of a legal decision, an unpredictable interference recently and until now irremediably condemned by those vested with the power to pronounce on the law. We are referred back, necessarily, to the underlying epistemological source of thinking about norms: it is only by getting away from a positivist epistemological approach – the 'one best way' on which the traditional mindset about the law depends – that we can enter the era where, paving the way as we go,[1] it is possible to think differently about the law.[2]

1 "Se hace camino al andar...", Antonio Machado, *Proverbios y cantares*, 29, Campos de Castilla, 1917.

2 On the necessary passage, in law, from positivism to a constructivist project, it is worth referring to André-Jean Arnaud and Maria José Fariñas Dulce, *Une introduction à l'approche sociologique des systèmes juridiques*, Bruxelles, Bruylant, 1998, 167 sq.

As a matter of fact we are navigating in completely interdisciplinary waters here, and this implies a complementary conceptual innovation, by means of transposing concepts from one disciplinary field to another. To speak about the force of law in the sense of its effectiveness, as sociologists of law are accustomed to doing, means to refer to the law and to legal norms in the strict sense. To speak about 'normative force' is to shift the centre of gravity towards the entirety of the social field, i.e. to admit that different normative forces forge bonds with each other and to invite jurists to achieve an interdisciplinary understanding of the law and a complex approach to it.

This is tantamount to saying that it is the entire theory of law that is being questioned. The 'network' outweighs the 'top-down' approach endorsed by our legal traditions. To take 'normative force' into account implies authorising a game that draws its complexity both from the back and forth between the 'creative forces' and the 'receptive forces' of the law and from the practical collisions between legal norms and the ones that emerge in other fields, from ethics to politics via economics and the social field. Our Anglo-Saxon colleagues talk about 'entanglement', a term that is familiar to theorists of complexity. We are here at the antipodal opposites of the linearity and simplicity of the law that modern legal thinking bequeathed to us.

Better, with the 'normative force' thus conceived, it could well be a question of rather more than a concept: we could actually be envisaging a veritable paradigm. Coming from mishandling the traditional paradigm of the law that is identified with that which is obligatory and characterised by static constraint, what we get from a 'pure theory of the law', 'normative force' comes across as something quite different from a simple concept.

If the intensity of the normative force is variable and liable to undergo modulations in its magnitude and with time; if the force of a norm started out in life linked to the conditions both of its issuance and of its reception; if consequences can be drawn about its nature (symbolic or regulatory), or about its quality (original or derived; objective or subjective; intrinsic or extrinsic); if it is capable of being distorted (effectiveness, ineffectiveness, consolidation, obsolescence); and if, moreover, it has any consubstantiality with the law, by means of the *trait d'union* that the normative force establishes between concepts familiar to us, including traditional concepts such as the 'source of law', 'effectiveness', 'creative force', 'normative power', 'normative value' and 'normative scope', to name just a few, then in order to act, this benchmark force that is the normative force certainly does constitute a veritable paradigm, as Kuhn intended it when he defined it, as we remember, as a cluster of universally recognised concepts that are liable, at a given moment and for a certain period of time, to provide a community of researchers with mechanisms for framing problems and finding solutions to both quite well-established and new problems.

Let's say it clearly, without beating about the bush: 'normative force' is a paradigm, a paradigm made up of that cluster of concepts that jurists have received from tradition and of those that they are required to reinvent in the course of the great transformations that are brought about by the recent multiplication of the sources of the law. This proves to be invaluable because a new paradigm is truly called for to understand and integrate the norms that derive from new regulations. These latter have immediately turned out to be numerous, as I have demonstrated elsewhere:[3] norms of regulation that, on the one hand, pertain primarily to the private sphere and, on the other, even when they remain under the authority

3 Cf. *Governar sem Fronteiras – Entre globalização e pós-globalização*, Lumen Juris Edit., Rio de Janeiro, 2007.

of the state, are not always implemented through the law, as is the case of numerous public policies. A new paradigm would also be called for in order to understand and integrate the unusual actors that are civil society or the private sector, the unaccustomed practices that are their methods of implementation and the subversive instrument – or at least one that is considered to be subversive – that is governance.

Building on this vision, what I would like to advance in the paragraphs that follow is a draft of some specific thinking about 'legal intelligence'. I would like to suggest that this paradigm of 'normative force', based on an interdisciplinary approach related to the theories of complexity, could well turn out to be the cornerstone of a 'legal intelligence', as long as we can afford to apply to our field what is represented by the point where geometric lines meet in a work of architecture.

What does 'legal intelligence' mean? First, it is a matter of 'intelligence', in its etymological sense. *Intelligere* means to understand, to discern, to 'read between', so to gather together, to collect and to choose. The ability to collect information, the ability to choose what is most suitable for a given situation, is to be 'intelligent', educated and judicious: a connoisseur. In this sense, there is much talk these days about intelligence in the field of specialisation that borders on the ones touched on principally by this book, notably the economy and strategic research.

The time has come to work on a 'political intelligence' – by which I mean an intelligence of public policies.[4] Reflecting on normative force ultimately responds to a project for establishing such a 'legal intelligence' that still has few parallels in the discourses covering our field of specialisation but which could be translated as "intelligence in the area of elaborating and re-orienting normativity in the legal field".

Is it really necessary, we may ask, to introduce this ostensible innovation? To tell the truth, it does look as though the time is ripe for it. The term has already been used with different meanings and connotations in the social sciences. Goffman, for example, talks about what he calls 'free-floating' intelligence:[5] in this case, we seem to be on the terrain of ethnomethodology, of interactionism and of the theories of knowledge. There is also much talk about artificial intelligence, which is related to an understanding of the underlying mechanisms of thinking and of 'intelligent' behaviour.[6] And this is also related to the approach that we find in the theory of decision-making elaborated by the Nobel Prize for Economics winner Herbert A. Simon, the theory of the complex decision.[7]

4 This is what was undertaken in the framework of the work undertaken by the UNITWIN network of the UNESCO Chair in *Human Rights, Violence: Public Policies and Governance* that I founded at the Universidad Externado de Colombia (Bogota). In addition to that university, the network's other members are the Carlos III in Madrid, the PUC-Rio de Janeiro, the UNISINOS (RS), the Université de Paris Ouest Nanterre-La Défense, the University of Camerino and the UFP, Paraíba. http://www.uexternado.edu.co/esp/catedraunesco/index.html

5 For Goffman, "social life strives constantly and in a thousand ways to grasp and freeze the intelligence that enables us to learn" (*Preface* to Erving Goffman, *Frame Analysis: An Essay on the Organisation of Experience*, Boston, North-Eastern University Press, 1974).

6 On the importance of artificial intelligence in the field of law, see Danièle Bourcier, Patricia Hassett, Christophe Roquilly, *Droit et intelligence artificielle : une révolution de la connaissance juridique*, Ed. Romillat, Orléans, 2000. There are teachings that cover the main domains of artificial intelligence and of aids for decision-making, in particular, adaptive agents and decision-making agents, data mining, learning, optimising and problem-solving, intelligent databases, image and sound processing, multimedia and man-machine interactions. Cf. http://www-master.ufr-info-p6.jussieu.fr/specialite/iad/

7 H. A. Simon, *The science of the artificial*, Cambridge, MA, MIT Press, 1969.

The various meanings attributed to the term 'intelligence' in Anglo-Saxon culture, which is more pragmatic than that of the European continent, include such concepts as self-awareness, communication, planning and problem-solving. It was around these meanings that the Intelligence Service was conceived, for example.[8] Intelligence raises our cognitive capacity: knowing where, when and how to search for information; knowing how to collect it; knowing how to filter and arrange it; knowing what to do to orient future action; knowing with whom to do it; and, in short, knowing the aims not only for a country's security but also in all the areas where decisions have to be made is absolutely vital. For those who have to make decisions, all the difficulty consists in practice in not being overtaken by the quantity and the diversity of information.[9]

These days, it is quite a common occurrence to hear talk of 'intelligence' in a great many specialised fields close to our own specialisation of socio-legal research. This comes across very clearly in the field of economic intelligence or that of strategic intelligence. This latter can be classified under the heading of an approach to processing information that aims to enable decisions to be made in the relevant areas of intelligence, espionage and homeland defence.[10]

With regard to economic intelligence,[11] numerous entrepreneurs have learned and digested the importance of applying it. It is not hard, for example, to find an advertisement for something that calls itself the 'Economist Intelligence Unit' on the Internet, where it is described as a company that provides "a constant stream of analysis and forecasts about more than 200 countries and six key industries", with the capability "to help executives stay informed about decisions concerning their businesses, according to certain intelligence delivered on-line or on paper, in customised searches as well as by means of conferences and exchanges".[12] In addition, we can find a long list of organisation sites related to economic intelligence and an enormous bibliography devoted to the issue.

Economic intelligence uses the latest and most sophisticated information analysis tools so as to avoid missing out on market opportunities because of having failed to obtain and

8 The Secret Intelligence Service (SIS), or MI6 (Military Intelligence, Section 6), is the United Kingdom's external intelligence agency, originally established in 1909. Under the heading of 'Intelligence', item 2, the *Dictionnaire Littré* notes that Chateaubriand used the word 'intelligences' in an English sense that is not foreseen in French: "[The ones that in 1815 were] in the centre of armies and of European diplomacy and, as a consequence, in the centre of all intelligences and all relations", t. XXVI, 194, footnote, éd. POURRAT frères, 1828. Cf. recently Thierry Delpeuch and Jacqueline Ross, *Développer le renseignement en matière de sécurité publique dans les forces de sécurité intérieure - L'intelligence-led policing aux Etats-Unis : enseignements pour la France*, Report to the Delegation on Perspective and Strategy - INTERSECTS project run by the French National Research Agency (INTelligence of Risks affecting SECurity in Sensitive Territories), August 2010.

9 To keep up with today's pace of the volume of information and of digital data produced by billions of people, of devices, of sensors and 'intelligent' equipment of all kinds, systems must capture, transform and analyse all kinds of data in real time… more than 60,000 times per second! Consumers' requirements are such that, just by way of example, during the 2009 French Tennis Open, more than 45,000 points played in the men's singles and women's singles tournaments were registered and processed in real time, enabling tennis fans to understand the key moments in the competition. Cf. ibm.com/think/fr/intelligence_(22 June 2009).

10 http://www.intelligencestrategique.be/site/ase_is-fr/intelligence-strategique/concept-d-intelligence-strategique/

11 Cf. e.g. Mourad Oubrich, "L'intelligence économique, un champ de recherche novateur en management stratégique", in *La Revue des Sciences de Gestion*, Paris, N° 226–227, October 2007, 77 sq.; Maryse SALLES, *Stratégies des PME et intelligence économique. Une méthode d'analyse du besoin*, Paris, Economica, 2nd ed., 2006, and the important bibliography quoted by the author.

12 www.eiu.com/

process the necessary information in good time. New technologies like stream computing,[13] for example, now enable data to be analysed in movement and to correlate them with a view to transforming them into 'intelligence'. In fact, managers now have to react faster than ever before to identify market evolutions and changes in consumer preferences and in forecasts of their best expectation of behaviour: they have to be able to predict the main trends, to cut costs and to keep decision-making and execution times down to a minimum.

Information technology's added value helps managers to know precisely what has happened, what is happening and what might happen. Intelligence can be used as a means for identifying and analysing market evolutions faster than ever before and for optimising even highly complex systems and organisations. These analytical tools enable their users to pass radically from an ordinary decision-making process to a predictive process.

Everyone knows how useful the theoretical development and the subsequent execution of economic intelligence has turned out to be. This discipline (Could we call it a 'science'?) was elaborated to enable business enterprises to respond to a crucial challenge: how to have the right information available at the right time so as to be able to make the right decision. The expression describes an organisation's ability to collect, interpret and exploit the information that makes a decisive difference to the complete success of the decision's consequences. To refer back to the terms coined by Herbert A. Simon, the inventor, as I have pointed out, of a type of decision relevant to the theories of complexity, based on a constitutive – and, more precisely, constructivist – epistemology, one might say: "in order to enable decisions to be reached that are the most satisfactory, as a function of the initial project supported by the organisation that makes the decision".

Now, it appears that this, in practice, is exactly what we are attempting to achieve in numerous contemporary studies investigating the sociology of law and, more precisely still, those studies that can be classified under the heading of a 'political sociology of law'. So why not try to practise 'legal intelligence' by adapting certain principles of economic intelligence to the specificity of the domains covered by public action? All decision-makers would stand to benefit: legislators, judges and administrators.

2. On the necessity of a 'political intelligence'

The implementation of such a 'political intelligence' is thus shown to be inevitable. It is, for example, the great difference between what it once meant to lecture at a university fifty years ago and what it has become today. Half a century ago, the lecturer turned up in his gown, ready to explain the results of his research to his students. He taught them how to gather information that was often far from easy to come by, and he told them how to organise that information in such a way that he would feel that the topic had been tackled, so as to achieve the best effect.

These days, we live in an 'information age', which is said to have succeeded the industrial age. The quantity of information develops at breakneck speed: we talk about 'big data'.[14] Yet, by virtue of the fact that the use of increasingly sophisticated communication tools becomes

13 Cf. *Stream Computing, an* initiative of ATI Technologies Inc., a major company that specialises in producing microprocessors for computer graphics chipsets, notably in partnership with the University of Stanford, PeakStream, Microsoft and Adobe.

14 On Thursday 27 December 2012, the French newspaper *Le Monde* carried an article entitled *Big Data* that specified "The mass of data created by smartphones, computers and tablets on the Internet is exploding with every passing second. Dubbed 'big data' by web experts, this colossal mass is a prodigious market".

easier every day, all students can find just the essential information they need, while all too often deserting the libraries. At the moment, the problem is to know how to teach students to choose, from so much information, what really deserves to be collected and which is the most satisfactory in a given situation. This is one of the new tasks for university professors, a task based on their own experience. And it is an objective that can be achieved. It can in fact be achieved in an excellent manner if we make due use of a tool that is capable of providing us with the elements we need in order to be able to know what has to be collected if we are to make the best decision as quickly as possible, how to bring together, choose and process the information in the best way to achieve this. The tool to which I refer is intelligence.

If economic intelligence was developed to enable groups of businessmen and enterprises to cater for a crucial need – precisely to obtain the 'right' information at the 'right' time, so as to be in a position to make the 'right' decision – can we assert at all that it may not be indispensable for decision-makers in the area of public policies? This is concerned with an organisation's ability to gather, interpret and apply the information that is vital for ensuring the complete success of a decision. In a nutshell, making it possible to achieve solutions for making the decisions that are the most satisfactory in terms of the original project conducted by the organisation that is making the decision. Predicting, anticipating and presenting to decision-makers the elements that will enable them to make a satisfactory decision: this is how to go about working in an intelligent manner; it is to work with intelligence in the field of public policies, to implement political intelligence.

The future will be made up of sharing the specific resources and the skills of each actor who takes part in the decision-making process. This approach of 'participation by sharing' common objectives enables satisfaction to be achieved not only in the results of a decision-making process but also with regard to the knowledge, know-how and methods that have to be submitted to continuous evaluation. This co-operation is fundamental between actors who far too often barely understand each other. The implementation of consistent intelligence strategies in the field of public policies is absolutely essential these days. We no longer live in the days of presumed decision-makers, like the boss described by Charlie Chaplin in *Modern Times*, who knew and had a command of all the information he needed to enable the best decision to be chosen from all the decisions possible. The process of making a complex decision has – or ought to have – categorically replaced the style of decision known as the 'one best way'. We sociologists of law should promote this form of intelligence in the field of law and of public policies.

We should thus insist on the common, essential implication of internal and external competences (let me translate that: the co-operation that is required between scientific research based on civil society and in partnership with it, on the one hand, and on the other, those who hold the reins of government in their hands, or also in certain instances the reins of non-governmental institutions, and, thus, have decision-making power). To be sure, the decision-maker needs the help of specialists, of experts and of consultants. But to what purpose should he choose them solely on the basis of his own views or inclinations? More often than not, he is unaware of the work done by researchers, since he is not close enough to them to take them into consideration.[15] These researchers are, however, some of those who are the best suited both for providing him with information and understanding the basic information, starting from popular sources and in co-operation with civil society, and for presenting him with any

15 It is important to consider the increasing importance of the role played by think tanks: who they are, how they are appointed, how the mandate conferred on them is established and how they function.

potential changes in orientation that may be necessary to improve public policies. They do so in complete freedom, without the slightest personal interest.[16] They are the ones who are best equipped to help the decision-maker achieve an effective balance between observation and interpretation in the light of scientifically evaluated and validated methodologies.

There are already researchers who have been working in the field of sociology of law in this spirit of intelligence in the area of policies, although no general theory has so far been elaborated in this context. Economic intelligence and knowledge management are sometimes taken into account, as is strategic intelligence, but intelligence is only very seldom a matter of discussion in the field of public policies, as a specific, theoretically based tool, overcoming its own methodology and aiming at practicality.

Now, we could rightly wait for researchers who specialise in the field of sociology of law to be invited to present to decision-makers (in both public and private domains) the scientific results they have obtained from research activities focused on collecting and interpreting information about what is expected from enacted law and from public policies, and on how their implementation is thus received. Intelligence in the field of public policies could correspond specifically to what is expected by those who have to make decisions in the areas of law and of public policies, on the part of researchers who work in this field of specialisation, working in a given domain to research public policies whose implementation is short on effectiveness, examining the reasons for this shortcoming and working on governance by analysing the terrain – in partnership with the non-governmental organisations and governmental organisations concerned – and the possibilities for the public policies in question to function well, then proposing projects for redeveloping the public policies to those who are responsible for government.[17]

Like researchers working in the field of economic intelligence, researchers in legal sociology and political sciences should focus on collecting human resources and the technological means used in developing their fields. As in the context of economic intelligence, they need to progress beyond the stage of the pure rationalisation of data collection and of the accumulation of information: they should thus give due consideration to the changes brought about by globalisation and introduce the analysis of complexity into the methodology they use for generating decisions. As in economic intelligence, they should take care to know what is being done outside their own environment.

The ideal thing would be to manage to make conscious use of the specific theoretical bases of intelligence in the field of public policies. But a great deal remains to be done if this is to be achieved: elaborating a real strategy with regard to intelligence in the field of public policies;[18] integrating research tools, raising awareness, monitoring and managing

16 An interesting approach in this respect is that adopted by I. de J. Butler, "Non-governmental Organisation Participation in the EU Law-making Process: The Example of Social Non-governmental Organisations at the Commission, Parliament and Council", in *European Law Journal*, 14/5 (2008), 558–582. The channels of participation mentioned by the author do not take the work of researchers into consideration; what is lacking is in fact a global intelligence about the field of public policies.

17 This is, for example, what UNESCO requested from the researchers who came together in the UNITWIN network of the Chair in *Human Rights, Violence: Public Policies and Governance* mentioned above. These researchers, who come from several continents and different legal and political cultures, worked on questions that are sensitive in their respective countries: displaced populations (Bogotá, Colombia), child labour (Camerino, Italy), street violence (Rio de Janeiro, Brazil), victims of terrorism (Madrid, Spain) etc., but using an identical methodology for what I am presenting here with the name of 'Policy Intelligence'.

18 Cf. e.g. 'Tracking Impact. Case Studies on the Research Policy Nexus', in *International Social Science Journal*, 179/3 (2004).

knowledge in processes that are found to be capable of making information 'useful', i.e. capable of leading in an innovative manner to 'the most satisfactory' decision. This is where the dangers and the limits of intelligence as applied to public policies can be found: economic intelligence and strategic intelligence, which translates as achieving mastery of information, protecting it and using it in what could be called an 'affirmative' manner, but not 'in an offensive way', as is the case of economic intelligence and strategic intelligence.

And there is another danger: that intrinsic to the failure to achieve a situation in which intelligence in the field of public policies is organised in a complete and integrated system of techniques and of human skills. To achieve that situation, all the partners in the project that is the aim of the researchers' activity must acquire an awareness of the benefits that can accrue to them and be prepared to accept the project and participate actively in the process of intelligence in the field of public policies. There is still a great deal to do to convince decision-makers, especially in the public sector, who ought to take an interest in this kind of approach, just as the more alert managers in the private sector have understood that they have a very great interest in profiting from the contributions made by those who apply the approaches used by economic or strategic intelligence.

This procedure, moreover, is not devoid of a third danger. The term 'offensive', for example, which looms large in the approach to the field of economic or political intelligence, is readily perceived as implying a pejorative connotation: the need to engage in such a way as to favour private interests, to the prejudice of others and of the general public interest as it is conceived of in a democratic regime. Intelligence in the field of public policies should be processed using the same methods as economic intelligence or political intelligence, but without necessarily being oriented towards such results. It's a question of ethics in politics.

3. Implementing political intelligence as an asset of normative force

The question we have to ask is this: what should we do to ensure that the 'most satisfactory possible' decision is made, the one that corresponds best to the original project that caused the decision-making process to be embarked on?[19] This can be done if we apply the model of complex decision-making suggested by Herbert A. Simon, which, as I interpret it, implies having recourse to intelligence.

The theory of complex decision-making is actually defined by a certain number of attributes that are associated with the process of intelligence: the existence of a project as an objective to be achieved, the specification of levels specialised in elaborating the decision, thus enabling the project to be executed, and the existence of recurrent exchanges between these levels, for the purpose of improving each step in the decision-making process.

First of all, we can only talk about complex decision-making if there is an original project, i.e. the project that this decision grounded on a complexity-based approach, once made, will enable to be executed. Several questions are generated at this stage. Who constructs the project? Who controls the project's ability to solve the problem that was set at the beginning? Will these tasks be in the hands of the authorities in charge of enacting the law and of framing public policies? If there is no 'participation' in the decision-making

19 Cf. H. A. Simon, *Organizations*, New York, J. Wiley and Sons, 1958; Id., "Theories of Decision-Making in Economics and Behavioral Science", in *American Economic Review*, 49/1, 1959, 253–283; Id., *The science of the artificial*, *op. cit.* The theory behind intelligence and complexity as presented by this winner of the Nobel Prize for Economics was developed by the French economist Jean-Louis Le Moigne.

process – regardless of the type of participation – the decision-making will inevitably remain top-down, which negates the idea of complexity in the decision-making as it is outlined in the theory that bears this name.

Such a complex decision-making process can actually be summarised in three principles. In the first place, the same actors cannot intervene in different phases of the decision-making process, in the knowledge, in the stage of constructing the problem, in that of formulating it as an action plan and in that of implementing it. Second, these three operations must be carried out with the aim of being 'satisfactory' in relation to the project ("satisficing" to cite the language used by Herbert A. Simon). Lastly, relations must be maintained permanently between each of the three levels – constructing the problem, constructing the action plans and making the decisions – that together contribute to providing a public action with a character of continuity, enabling it to avoid the rigid top-down characteristics of decision-making that come in for such frequent criticism in socio-legal studies. When it comes to the law and public policies, participation of this kind in decision-making falls within the remit of intelligence in the field of public policy.

When a French legislator made a decision, in the early 1800s, he knew more or less exactly what he was doing and what it would lead to. This comes across very clearly when reading the writings of Portalis, the cornerstone of the Napoleonic Code. For him, it was not an issue of self-sufficiency, as he wrote about the vanity of all human enterprise; but he never had any hesitation with regard to legislation: he knew exactly what was necessary for the French. That is no longer the case today.

These days – and at whatever level they find themselves – when they embark on the process of elaborating law and public policies, the authorities find themselves having to face up to a global environment of systems subjected to constant change (political, social, economic, religious and other forms of change): these systems are complex in themselves and obey laws of their own. More precisely, as far as the legal system itself is concerned, the authorities ought to give due consideration to the reasoning regarding uncertainty, to contradictory reasoning and to circular causality. The decisions they propose or make in a specific sector are found to have sometimes unexpected repercussions in other areas of social life. The fact is that each result is blocked, is found to be less structural than formal and has to associate the analytical model of decision-making with the way of thinking that led to this conclusion. It is not impossible to break out of this impasse, but the condition is to agree to move away from the principle of the 'one best way' and onto the path of the complex decision.

According to the principle of 'one best way', the traditional process for creating law, calculating what the best possible decision of behaviour will be in each situation, is sufficient for achieving a 'good' decision. Complex decision-making, on the contrary, is based on three hypotheses: first, that problems that require a decision are not given a priori but must be considered as having to be 'constructed'; second, that the fundamental character of the decision is 'teleological', i.e. the decision must be oriented towards a real project; and third, that making a decision is premised on the supposition that the evaluations of each action plan are compared.

Constructing a problem is no simple event, devoid of expression: it is something practical that aims to discover what it is that is not functioning. A series of diagnoses enables the possibilities of implementing the rules put in place by the law and public policies to be evaluated at any moment in everyday life and social practice. In addition, decisions usually exist in terms of the project that will be pursued by them to a good purpose. At this – still conceptual – stage, action plans or possible strategies have to be elaborated that lend themselves to finding solutions to the problems that were formulated at the previous stage. Lastly, there is a comparison between the action plans proposed that aims, after due deliberation, both at selecting a decision from among all the ones that would be possible and, if necessary, at requesting more extensive information, which then implies going back to one of the previous stages: the one where the problem can be reformulated, or the one where other action plans can be sought out. A stage of this kind corresponds to a decision-making process that is no longer related to the idea of optimisation (as in the 'one best way') but to that of searching out solutions that are 'satisfactory' in the light of the criteria collected – in other words, in relation to the complexity that is the characteristic trait of those criteria. In a situation where there is a multiplicity of criteria that are unlikely to be able to be induced to unity, there is no 'optimal' solution, and we have to resign ourselves to dealing in terms of complexity.

A practice of modelling calls attention to the fact that a complex decision does not comprise a simple high-level operation, the choice of the 'optimal' decision, but is the result of the recursive union of three systemic operations. These operations in turn consist respectively in the construction of the problems, in their projection in the form of action plans and in using the action plans to select the most satisfactory solution.[20] What we find ourselves dealing with this way is three sub-systems whose union makes up the complex decision-making system.

The union of the three sub-systems is a sine qua non condition for the production of the complex decision. Another condition is connected to the fact that the process of building the relationship between these systems is recursive. There is a constant back and forth from one subsystem to another: from the one where the selection is made towards the level where the conception of the problems takes place, or towards the one where the action plans are forged, or again from one of these two latter towards the other, to investigate the conditions of the environment and the basic needs, whence the action plans can subsequently be elaborated that will lead to the decision that the decision-maker will make by choosing one of these action plans.

Once this process has been completed satisfactorily, it is possible to choose a decision that is oriented towards a concrete action. Otherwise, the decision-maker can require that more extensive information be made available (which will make it necessary to go back to the stage of construction), or he may demand more reflection (which will make it necessary to go back to the stage of conception). These recurrences are not restricted to a single occurrence and may be reiterated until the decision-maker is in a position to consider the action plan that is ultimately presented to him to be 'satisficing'.

What is most frequently produced in this day and age, both in the political lines and in the legal lines adopted by decision-makers, is that the decisions are officially made in the subsystem of the 'selection' of the decisions, as though it were a question of a single decision-making system, without any subsystems. This makes the decision lose its characteristic of being a complex decision and transforms law and public policies, so products, into a creation of law of the 'one best way' type, related to the 'modern' philosophy (17th–19th centuries) of the state governed by the rule of law.

Intelligence in the field of public policies: to do what, some people may ask? I would answer that the very modelling of a complex action, when associated with intelligence in

20 This is to achieve a decision that respects the quality of 'satisficing', to reiterate the expression coined by Herbert Simon. Cf. Jean-Louis Le Moigne, *La modélisation des systèmes complexes*, Paris, Dunod, 1990, 137.

the field of public policies, can pave the way for a hope that law and public policies may in future cater more responsively to what citizens need. In this way, without abandoning the hope that they may find simple, infallible solutions in a complex society, jurists may make use of this detour through a scientific practice to express the part of the imperatives and of that which remains unexpressed, without falling into the trap either of despondency or of demagogy.

"To know in order to predict, to predict in order to control": I am not rewriting Auguste Comte. Times have changed and complexity has turned our approaches on their heads. These days we would say "to predict, in order to be able to anticipate and make the most satisfactory decision". That is decision-makers' mission. But they must carry it out with good intelligence. That is what legal intelligence is. Thus, does the future consist in the mutualisation of the resources and the skills available from each actor in the decision-making process, for the purpose of achieving common ends and of improving each one's know-how and methods. This co-operation between actors who are thus far blissfully unaware of one another is fundamental. It must be admitted and recognised by everyone. As far as our field of specialisation is concerned, this comes under the heading of what I have called 'legal intelligence'.

There is scope for introducing these issues to universities. Economic intelligence and knowledge management are already frequently discussed there now, strategic intelligence a little less, legal intelligence not at all as yet. This, then, is what could constitute an added value in the teaching dispensed in faculties of law.

7 Balancing legal principles and legal topics

Tércio Sampaio Ferraz Jr.

1. Situating the problem

Jurists have traditionally grown accustomed to handling three core problems of legal theory: identifying the law, interpreting it and applying it. Dogmatic models with concepts, classifications and distinctions seek to build tools to handle these problems. For example, the concepts of validity/effectiveness/abrogation are intended to respond to the issue of identification; the distinction between the intent of the law/the intent of the legislator for the issue of attribution of meaning; the syllogism in which there is a greater premise (valid law), a lesser premise (proven facts) and the conclusion (decision) to justify decisions.

Since the 19th century, continental European (Romanic) legal theory has been producing detailed technology to deal with these issues, mainly with the first two (identification and interpretation), as the problem of application of the law was dealt with in a manner subsidiary to the problems of identifying and interpreting the law, as can be seen in the discussions about the autonomy of procedural law (bearing in mind that until the 1960s, people still spoke of *substantive* law and *adjective* law).

The law was thus interpreted relying on the fiction of codifying the unity of the legislator's intent, which was then ideally conceptualised in the figure of the so-called 'rational legislator'. Legal reasoning, accordingly, meant thinking in terms of a deductive system of law and solving cases by a corresponding systematic classification.

However, the assumption of a rational legislator was never exempt from ideological positioning, based on how relevance is attributed to the main values of the normative system (ideology in evaluating and ranking values). This ideology is implied in legal hermeneutics and may be static or dynamic. It is static when the assumption of a rational legislator favours such values as certainty, security, predictability and the stability of the norms, with primacy of subsumption. It is dynamic when it favours adjustments of the norms and easier operation of the law but casting doubts on the assumed irrefutability and fertility of the legal axioms.

Under such circumstances, interpretation, which is essential for legal thinking, ends up being developed within topics: what ensures the maintenance of a legal system (rational legislator) in light of certain social changes throughout time is precisely a flexible style in which the problems are the starting point, preventing the strengthening of the interpreted laws but not refusing their condition of providing the ground for decisions.

Interpreting the facts themselves (in the sense of 'what will be judged') requires the topical approach, as the facts that the operator of the law deals with knowingly rely on the versions attributed to such facts. The topical version of evidence assumes that nobody can learn the truth inherent to the actual facts by themselves and without additional effort.

The facts must thus be submitted to the technique of successive questions that will be able to make them true, even if they never become fully conclusive. Moreover, the use of colloquial language, with its lack of rigour, its ambiguities and vagueness, would condition jurists to think topically. Therefore, in their rationale, they know that in some respects there is no system that can solve all legal problems on its own, even though it is topically relevant to assume a well-built technical unity.[1]

Although normative 'systems' may for this reason in fact seem more like heteroclite series than the main systemisations of legal science might intend, we must underline the perspective of the assumed system, in which the problems are then selected: those that are incompatible with its structure are rejected and grouped as misplaced problems or false problems.[2] What thus follows is the topical dynamics of the dichotomies of lawful/unlawful, fair/unfair and void/voidable, upholding the requirement that decisions be made according to technical language, while, however, also meeting the need to delimit the distance between the technical procedure and the social relationship under litigation, so that the decision may be made 'in accordance with the law'.

So legal topics are more a style of thought, in practice related to a cultural attitude characterised by a high degree of reliability upon the performance of practical tasks in terms of a theory of viewpoints (*loci*, *topoi*) and a theory of argumentation and reasoning, that is to say considering argumentation both in a strict sense and in a broad sense. In the first meaning, principles are regarded as a presumably organised set of general categories, grouping basic arguments for the decision-making techniques. The set is therefore made up of one or more repertoires (constitutional principles of several types) that ease the task of the *ars inveniendi* of the legal interpreter and applicator. In its broad meaning, argumentation used to be presented as a technique of reasoning that works with a mindset that flexibly ensures the unity of the system (general principles as instruments of completeness of the law).[3]

In the present day, however, the perception of society as an economic society, as an embracing whole concentrated on producing consumer goods, whose consumption is, again, a means for increasing production and so on and so forth, tends to change this scenario by changing the distinctive lines drawn between politics, economics and legal regulation, muddling them. It is not, for example, a question of political exercise by the ones that hold economic power, to the extent that they move from one realm (economic activity) to another (political activity), but of activities with structurally undifferentiated logic so that there is a narrow proximity in the capitalist world between public and private technocracy. Likewise, jurisdictional exercise, which is supposedly politically neutralised by the principle of the division of powers, gains political outlines in which the requirement of prognosis in decision-making turns the verdict into a political anticipation of its political, social and economic effects.

1 Related to these approaches, see Quintilian's division of questions in "indefinite" (*infinitae*) and "definite" (*finitae*) and the problem of their relationship (Quintilian: Institutio oratoria, Harvard University Press, London, 2001, Liber Tertius, 5). See also Theodor Viehweg: *Ideologie und Recht*, in *Ideologie und Rechtsdogmatik*, Klostermann, Frankfurt, 1969.

2 See Viehweg: *Topik und Jurisprudenz*, Beck, München, 1974.

3 See Theodor Viehweg: Some Considerations Concerning Legal Reasoning, in Law, Reason and Justice – Essays in Legal Philosophy, Graham Hughes, New York, London, 1969, p. 266. See also Milagros Otero Parga: Cuestiones de argumentación jurídica, Editorial Porrua, México, 2014, pp. 215, 259. In this sense, Perelman and Tyteca have pointed out the persuasive force of an argumentative reasoning based on a similar formal reasoning: see Traité de l'argumentation, Bruxelles, 1992, § 45.

This does not, however, mean that the jurisdictional power, the judiciary of a sovereign nation, no longer plays a decisive role. Jurisdictional power is not dissolved into the political universal but in fact rethought, appearing in a new guise. Before this, there was an imperial relationship between the judge and those under his jurisdiction, and, as there was not yet any sense of urgency in the economic and social issues, that relationship was external, implying that administering justice (in the sense of making justice come about) was the purpose of jurisdictional activity, which was external to politics. In the current situation, the judiciary cannot be separated from the justice it administers – one is a part of the other. So, it follows that jurisdictional power (one of the powers of the state) becomes a problem of an internal exercise of the acts of management: **judging** as politics, jurisdiction as social and economic policy, all within a technocratic logic: the logic of 'governmentality' (as per Michel Foucault).[4] And a structural triangle establishes itself in its core: empire, judicature and socioeconomic management.

In fact, with the exception of the brutal use of force (seen in the 20th century in Stalinism, Nazism, Fascism and authoritarian regimes in Latin America), the dilemma of a jurisdictional 'management' power has a paralysing function that the contemporary legal system seeks to manage, strategically and even disguisedly, by applying rules of organisation (called the 'politicisation of justice') and by allowing strict risk liability strategies to flourish, sanctioning third-party behaviour, replacing the scheme of lawful/unlawful with the notion of abusive (unlawful due to abuse), which is more compatible with the risk phenomenon (as can be seen, in Roman legal systems, in laws that deal, for example, with anticompetitive practices, in which the rule of reason plays an important role), adopting the direct application of general clauses (such as objective good faith), etc.[5]

In practice, what we see in our current complex technological society is that the activities of control have changed vectors, no longing being aimed mainly at the past but now being concerned essentially with the future. The issue is no longer one of controlling past behaviour but future behaviour. Technological civilisation thus uses its creative capacity in types of government whose most important values are the efficiency of results and a high probability of achieving them. In the legal realm, the courts, traditionally a place where a person is judged and held accountable for his actions, for what he has done, are now called upon to perform a prospective assessment and sit on 'judgement' on 'who' that person is and what he may do. It is within this framework of projection of the sense of law towards the future, towards its reaching out, more than to its preconceived consistence, that the advent of the so-called 'postmodern' state in the legal realm must be assessed.

It was, in fact, the growth of the social state (or, more precisely, of the welfare state) that reversed the basic postulates of the legal concept of the liberal state, beginning with the separation between state and society, which allowed for the corresponding release of legal structures from social structures. In this conception, individual freedom was always construed as a negative freedom, as a non-impediment, and the neutralisation of the judiciary was only a consequential requirement. The social state brought the issue of positive, participative freedom: not a principle to be defended but one to be achieved. Positive freedom changed the right to equality into the right to become equal in the conditions of access to full citizenship. In a mass society, this requirement has the consequence of hypertrophy of the constituted powers. The executive and legislative powers suffer great expansion as they

4 Le Gouvernement de soi et des autres. Cours au Collège de France, 1982–1983, Paris, 2008.

5 See, in the context of *risk*, Rodrigo Octávio Broglia Mendes: *Arbitragem, lex mercatória e direito estatal*, São Paulo, 2010.

are expected to deliver social citizenship and not merely sustain their legal-formal framework. On the other hand, the judiciary increases its discretionary power.

The result is that social rights, a typical product of the welfare state that are not, as it is well known, a type of formal a priori but actually have a potential promotional meaning, are now a requirement of implementation. This changes the performance and function of the judiciary that, in light of such social rights or their violation, they must not only judge, in the sense of establishing right and wrong based on the law (the conditional responsibility of the politically neutralised judge), but also – and above all – examine whether the exercise of the legislative power leads to the achievement of the purported results (the final liability of the judge who, in a certain way, is once again political).

The extensive social standardised mass that transforms society into a consumer society has thus turned the economy into a process of mass production, mass sales and mass consumption, reducing almost all human activities, from arts to leisure, from science to culture, to objects of consumption, i.e. objects that are disposable after use. And it then transforms the previous conception of subjective rights as individual rights by demanding collective protections – collective rights – and even protections that cannot be identified individually or collectively: diffuse rights (environment, free competition, consumer rights, etc.) and the so-called 'homogeneous individual rights' (public health, private health insurance, etc.).

Consequently, litigation now admits and requires even more new categories of rights of action (class actions, for example). Likewise, the position of judges also changes, affecting their political neutrality ('impartiality'), as they are faced with co-responsibility, in which they must correct any deviations from the achievement of the purposes set in the legislative policy. So, this responsibility, which in the classical division of powers belonged solely to the legislative and executive powers, is now also imputed to the judiciary.

In this sense, with today's advent of a technologically standardised mass society (Internet, social networks) and a technologically computerised bureaucratic 'état providence', there seems to be a growing demand for judges to be politically 'de-neutralised' and then called upon to exercise a social and therapeutic function, being released from the tight conditioning of strict legality and the solely retrospective responsibility imposed thereby (to judge facts, as well as to judge the past in the name of the law as given), and invested with a potential responsibility concerned with achieving political purposes (judging in the sense of providing for the future). In this case, judges are no longer exempt, due to the principle of formal legality (*dura lex sed lex*).

This transformation is not merely about correcting the literalness of the law in each case through equity or the obligation to look at the law's social purposes when applying it in court: that already existed. The judge's responsibility now also includes the responsibility for the political success of the purposes imposed on the other powers by the demands of the providence state. In other words, the judiciary becomes responsible for the coherence of its behaviour in accordance with the projects of social changes, just like the legislative and the executive powers, and any unsuccessful decision must be corrected by the judicial process itself.

The new situation actually has a profound impact on two traditional classical legal principles: the principle of the immunity of the state (the king can do no wrong) and the principle of *res judicata*, both of which are founded on jurisdictional activity in the liberal bourgeois state. In the liberal state, both the state, in the quality of a legal entity, and its servants and agents were civilly and administratively liable for violations of citizens' subjective rights, while the judiciary had the final say about unlawful acts. In the liberal rule of law, the basic condition for this now outdated structure of accountability was the judge's immunity with regard to his jurisdictional acts vis-à-vis the parties. This immunity, in turn, was correlated to the principle of *res judicata*. *Res judicata facit jus* was a requirement of the jurisdictional activity itself, arising from the judge's impartiality as a third party in litigation (*tertius super partes*). After all, legal security would be threatened without it, since it would not be possible to comply with the requirement that litigation must have an end, due to the impossibility of revisiting it permanently (*ne lites aeternae fiant*).

By exposing the judiciary to public criticism, primarily by the mass media, today's political 'de-neutralisation' of judges creates a number of tensions between their responsibility and their independence, seen most strikingly in the thesis of external control of the judiciary, which states that, instead of resulting 'logically' from the division of powers, both the immunity of magistrates and the principle of *res judicata* are, in fact, at the service of values, socially relative purposes that the legal system seeks to achieve in several ways. It is as if the fact that appointment of the justices of the higher courts is strictly reliant on the political will of the executive and legislative were suddenly to acquire – suspicious – relevance (as happens in Brazil with the appointment of the justices of the Federal Supreme Court, or the appointment of judges from amongst private lawyers or public attorneys, nominated by their respective class entities).[6]

More to the point, it is clear that binding judges to the law, which is the basis of their neutralisation, ends up generating, for the ordinary citizen, a type of insecurity that did not exist before: insecurity created by the law itself! So compare the security granted by the judiciary against an unlawful act carried out by one citizen against another with the social insecurity of the ordinary citizen when an injunction is granted due to the presence of the legal requirements in light of the risks it may cause for the country's economy, the lawful reorganisation of a financial institution that has rigorously undergone the proper court proceedings as required by a law that is changed due to 'systemic' (financial market) risks to which it may lead, or the (lawful) dismissal of workers being overturned in the name of the social damages it may cause, or holding companies accountable for employees of third-party contractors due to the social function of property, as declared in the Constitution.

And how does the judiciary respond to this loss of its institutional neutrality? How can the 'politicisation' of litigation be tackled in safety? This is where the so-called 'rationalisation matrix', grounded on the works of Max Weber and, more recently, of Habermas and Luhmann, and on a critical discussion, comes into play, focused on replacing the concept of action (and its insertion in the legal realm of freedom) with the concept of communication. This creates conditions for inserting issues of regulation that expose, on the one hand (Habermas), serious legitimisation problems and, on the other (Luhmann), solutions that are supposedly more suitable for understanding the transformations suffered in modern times haunted by the technological society, in which the law loses its characteristics of a hierarchic normative order and becomes a structure with no organising centre, due to the circularity of communicative relations.[7]

This new situation shows how important it is to seek a way to deal with 'common' criteria ('principles'), in which the problem is the perception of legitimising criteria as a type of recognisable code of conduct. Legal interpretation takes on a new role in this scenario.

6 See Mauro Cappelletti, "Who Watches the Watchmen?", in General Report do 11th International Congress of the International Academy of Comparative Law, Caracas, 19 the so-called 'rationalization matrix'.

7 See Orlando Villas Bôas Filho: *Teoria dos sistemas e o direito brasileiro*, São Paulo, 2009.

2. Interpreting the law and its challenges

When applying the law, the judge interprets (what does that norm mean?), i.e. he makes inferences and, thereby, obtains new norms derived logically from valid norms, which are the grounds for his home operative norm (sentence). What is the theoretical status of this operation?

Kelsen's posthumous work[8] adopts a radical position, in an anguished revision of his prior work: since norms are the products of intent (*voluntas*), there is no (logical or moral) regulator in the process of the system's normative expansion. Such radicalism first brought to the debate the need to capture the characteristic normative of law in a manner peculiar to it, i.e. regardless of the normative characteristic of other social practices also grounded on norms. Hence, Hart's criticism of Bentham and Austin and, to that extent, of Kelsen himself.[9]

From the perspective of analytical positivism, however, this debate leads to the assumption that comprehension of the so-called sources of law must be normative, notwithstanding the perplexity produced by its grounds: Kelsen's basic norm and its premise that the system as a whole be considered globally as effective, and Hart's rule of recognition, whose existence is acknowledged as a matter of fact.

Given this factual reality, normative grounds will inevitably be discussed in terms of their legitimisation: recognition, by Kelsen, of an instituting will as legitimate; recognition, by Hart, that certain acts of certain institutions are acts of creation (as mere acknowledgment, from an external point of view; as acceptance of validity, from an internal point of view). Both one way and the other, this identification of the law as a social fact leads us to question the issue of contingency of the norms' content, provided they are valid, considering the relationship between moral values and the law: does the norms' moral merit have nothing to do with their juridical merit, in which case, normative expansion by means of interpretation is a subjective act of valuation, and its normative character arises from will?

The 're-politicisation' of the judiciary – a theory posited in the political realm by those who defend the so-called 'alternative use of the law', and technically called 'neo-constitutionalism', however, presents a problem that is not easily solved. In this sense, it is interesting to see the warning couched in a statement made by Eros Grau, professor of economic law and former justice of the Federal Supreme Court of Brazil:[10]

> Judges, in particular constitutional judges, make intense use of the technique of balancing principles when faced with what the books call a conflict between fundamental rights. As the legal system provides no norm or principle to guide them with regard to which of the principles must be prevail when there is a conflict between them, however, this technique is carried out in the margins of the system, subjectively and in a discretionary and dangerous manner. The option for one principle or the other is determined subjectively, based, however, on the preconceptions of each judge, within the framework of certain ideologies. Either they knowingly adopt a certain legal-theoretical position, or they act at the mercy of those holding the power and the spirit of their times, unaware of the effects of their decisions, in a type of "flying blindly", in the words of Rüthers [2005:233].[11] Both choices

8 Allgemeine Theorie der Normen, Wien, 1979.

9 Juliano Maranhão discusses this matter in his book *"Positivismo jurídico lógico-inclusivo"*, São Paulo, 2012.

10 See: *Ensaio e discurso sobre interpretação/aplicação do direito*, São Paulo, 2009, p. 286.

11 Rüthers: *Geleugneter Richterstaat und vernebelte Richtermacht*, NJW, 2005, p. 2759.

are dangerous. The first because the legal-theoretical position may not be ours; the second because these judges become instruments of those that hold the power. They are always, however, choices submitted to dramatic reflections. I know this because I am no longer privileged by being solely a scholar of the law, by not being bound by the duty to make decisions that will, in any situation, be tragic to those affected by them. Why me? – I've asked myself so many times, when faced with actual legal issues. Who granted me the legitimacy to decide? All legal decisions are dramatic if the judge is not limited to the exercise of merely bureaucratic practices, as a mediocre well-behaved servant.

How does the legal dogmatic rationale react to this?

3. Use of principles and neo-constitutionalism: how to deal with the requirements for application of the constitution and the law

There is now extensive literature (Dworkin, Alexi, Carlos Nino, Zagrebelsky, Atienza, Troper, etc.) that criticises analytical positivism and its exclusion of moral justification from legal argumentation, proposing the contrary, i.e. that legal knowledge and techniques are evidently incapable of cohabiting such a moral exclusion, in particular, in the constitutional realm.

This leads to a type of constitutionalism based on principles and arguments, with a clearly Anglo-Saxon matrix, that not only attacks positivist argumentation (which separates law from morality and rids arguments of their moral burden, giving them one of mere technical efficiency) but also addresses the issue of a conception of legal argumentation called neo-constitutionalism.

Although it is not unanimous, this conception points to the idea that the rights established in the Constitution are not norms but principles in potential conflict and are, therefore, subject to balancing and not to subsumption. What follows from this is a conception of the law as a social practice awarded to judges, a practice of interpretation and argumentation that all operators of the law must be aware of and that posits the issue of distinguishing between 'is' and 'ought', the law as a fact and as a norm.

It is the fact that counts for this conception: it is not validity that rules but actually effectiveness, while fact is treated in a manner appropriate to economic interests and the interests of its operators, which end up repeating and following them due to their persuasive force as an alternative to the crisis of laws and their validity, to the suspicion that social problems may be solved through laws (*legolatry*), etc.

Distinguishing between principle and norm is crucial to this conception. In its most traditional formula (which harks back to Dworkin), it could be summarised as follows:

1 principles do not require specific behaviour but establish either starting points or generic goals; norms, on the contrary, are specific in their issues;
2 principles are not applicable in an 'all-or-nothing' manner, as they enunciate one or more reasons for deciding in a certain sense, without obligation to a certain decision; norms, on the other hand, enunciate dichotomous issues, i.e. they establish conditions that make their application required (with automatic consequences);
3 principles have relative weight or importance, while rules are more strictly imposable; so, principles can be assessed without the replacement of one by another with greater

weight meaning the exclusion of the former; norms, however, while admitting exception, lead to the exclusion of the conflicting provision when contradicted;

4 the concept of validity fits norms well (either they are valid or they are not) but not principles, which, since they are submitted to the assessment of importance, fit more into the concept of legitimacy, although their application is no less immediate than the application of norms.

For some, when seen thus, norms describe the cases to which they apply in a closed manner and are peremptory reasons for action; principles are conceived in an open manner and are non-peremptory reasons for action that may be balanced with other reasons, i.e. with other principles.

This distinction is not clear in itself and deserves consideration. For example, it is not realistic to state that only principles can be balanced, as we also balance rules. For example, between (i) the norm of warranty for defects of sold goods, (ii) the norm of the right to waive such warranty by agreement to the contrary and (iii) the norm of non-waiver thereof, even in light of such an agreement, if the defects were hidden by the salesperson in bad faith. Principles, on the other hand, are not a homogeneous class. Some, for example, are directive (those that govern political, social and economic life: for example, preferential treatment given to small enterprises), and others are merely regulatory (they may be fulfilled but without positive obligation, only negative: the "*principi programatici*" (Crisafulli)[12] of the Brazilian Constitution, for example, include one that states that technological research will be aimed primarily at solving Brazilian problems).[13]

The above notwithstanding, what is seen is that argumentative balancing procedures and the application of constitutional principles, which assume that the operator of the law is authorised to articulate and qualify the public interest presented as a purpose under constitutional provisions, require and imply certain and significant discretion. In this case, the argumentative procedure must assume that the constitutional provisions are subject to a certain fragmentation, with the following assumptions:

Some can be said to be conditionally normative in nature. The state's provisions and its positive participation are *leges imperfectae*, i.e. they cannot be achieved immediately without any action by the interpreter of the law that must, thus, identify the means that enable the purposes to be achieved, be that by social or technical means, so that the norm may become effective. Others are legal-functional in nature. As it is assumed that fixative purposes in the Constitution translate values that do not, however, allow for the perception of binding guidelines, the interpreter of the law must guide the configuration of the desired social order, which will then allow for a 'judicial review of constitutionality' and subsequent constitutional feasibility.

The dogmatic regulators of the balancing of principles are therefore more open and flexible, such as in the case of the rule of proportionality; for example, the articulated and qualified means must be subject to the means available and identifiable, or to the rule of proportionality. So, the state is obliged to achieve its purposes, and the interpreter of the law must consider these from the standpoint of their feasibility.

This is the focus that changes the topical functions of argumentation.

12 *La Costituzione e le sue Disposizioni di Principi*, Milano, 1952, p. 103.

13 See Luigi Ferrajoli: *Constitucionalismo principialista y constitucionalismo garantista*, DOXA, Marcial Pons, num, 34, Madrid, Barcelona, Buenos Aires, São Paulo, 2012, p. 41. See also Ferrajoli: *Il potere giudiziario nel sistema delle garanzie*, in Diritti e poteri, Michelangelo Bovero and Valentina Pazé (eds.), Torino, 2013, pp. 146–166.

4. The use of legal principles and legal topic: from blocking-based argumentation to legitimation-based argumentation

Principle-based argumentation, as a constitutional dogmatic issue, is found in a wide range of possibilities whereby subject-oriented rationality must work in tandem with legislative production (laws, regulations, government policy), whose growing complexity must be directed towards the legitimate implementation of the legal system. This involves constitutional law as a complex phenomenon of communication, not in terms of the extent to which conflicts can be settled with a decision about an act (constitutional/unconstitutional) occurring at a given time in the past but about the future (consistent interpretation, setting binding precedent, resultant fundamental precept, etc.). Here, the purpose of legal topic argumentation becomes to determine the binding sense of legislating in a perspective of innovation, one that can account not just for what happened in the past but also for what may yet happen. Therefore, where in the past acts, omissions, behaviours, limitations, recommendations, government policies and the legal system required the legal action to encompass the legal line of argument in order to acquire a sense of 'ought to be' – whether in terms of that which, according to them, they 'ought to be', or whether in the sense of their 'ought to be' for the recipients, or in the sense of their 'ought to be' for those drafting legislation – now, in a framework that truly considers legal principles, they call for a new manner of dealing with the grounds of the ruling in light of a ruling's future applicability.

In the past tradition of argumentative practice, we used to take constitutional principles topically as a whole incontestable totality, or we established a relevant point of unitary guidance by taking its enforceability, meaning, efficacy or function into account in the constitutional context: the principle as *ground*. Establishing such points implied attributing relevance to them in light of a decision-based objective: controlling constitutionality.

This kind of reasoning is now changing. In general, we can say that balancing principles is linked to topic-argument-based procedures, though less as a procedure based on a constitutional structure that blocks infra-constitutional legislative competence (judicial review) than as a way of thinking about constitutional implementation in light of a political plan determined on a relevant case basis.

In the context of the implementation of the constitutional plan, the interpreter thus presupposes that a constitution expresses the reasons/motives to act in one way rather than another, reasons that lead the interpreter to take a given position in the face of multiple possibilities that are not always congruent when implemented. It thus presupposes that the constitutional interpreter acts for some motive but attributes forward-looking meaning to his/her discourse. This leads to a necessary reference to the hermeneutic premise of not reducing the precept to its text in a new perspective.

Constitutional precepts in the sense of their application are not usually confused with the normative texts that compose the written document. While they hold significant sway, they result from a process that starts from the precept-based text and ends with the drafting of the regulatory precept, i.e. that commences with interpretation and culminates in a ruling. It is precisely this process we call argumentative that takes a topical argumentation in a new sense vis-à-vis its function as a justifier of forward-looking regulation making.

Therefore, when we speak of a topic that balances principles, we no longer conceive them as we did in the past – as a set of legal canons to judge the adequacy of proposed explanations or as criteria to choose legislative circumstances (principle as *ground*) – but as a not-so-rigorously verifiable procedure that allows us to tackle legal questions from a forward-looking frame of mind (principle as *argument*). Given this characteristic of implementing a plan, principles never lose their endeavouring feature, since they neither close nor conclude, but enable much broader decisions to be made than those based on closed norms. They cease to serve as a unitary, though presumed, ground and pave the way for argumentative equivalencies.

Principles thus acquire the condition of *topoi* (viewpoints) as instruments that organise argumentative sets (principles as *loci argumentationis*),[14] whereby the reasonability of rulings seems to be strengthened, despite the enormous contingency generated thereby. Note that, since we are dealing with argumentative sets, the principles thus used do not presuppose or even should not seek a systematised totality. That is to say, they cannot usefully presuppose a principle-based hierarchy endowed with systematic unity. They begin as fragmentary understandings or regionalised precept-based sets understood as alternatives to problems uncommitted to providing holistic solutions. Principles are assumed as significant redundancies that separately guide and orient argumentation capable of justifying a ruling that legitimates possible future consequences – one possible ruling among many but of greater relevance for an identified regional plan.

The topical use of balancing of principles (unlike its use according to legal topic in the realm of subsumption) thus has a less validating function (recourse to the valid rule), but one that is more legitimating of legal decisions, controlling the contingency of the results (future consequences) not by adjusting what happened in the past (the relation between the pre-established norm and the fact) but to what may occur in the future (prognosis of what may be committed to happen).

Principle-based topic or principle as argument therefore develop to be concerned not so much with the burden of proof, the requirement of pertinence and clarity, as far more with the consequence of decisions, enabling arguments to anticipate the legitimacy of what will be and with a persuasive force that relies on a legitimated prognosis and not on past validity.

One example is furnished by the following argument in a case of charges of *slave* labour (labour in similar slave conditions) against a company that sells products purchased from another (wholesale company) that, in its turn, outsources its production, with each one being entirely independent legal entities, without any corporate relationship between them. Slave labour is understood as being work performed in degrading conditions and, thus, invokes the institute of joint and several liabilities of the company that purchases products, together with the company that procures the services and the company that executes the services, based on the concept of strict liability (for the risk, regardless of subjective fault). As this liability is stated in environmental law but not properly in labour law, the argumentative construction in the case in question used constitutional principles, starting with the "principle of human dignity" (Federal Constitution of Brazil, article 1–III), the "social value of work" (article 170, III, VI and VII), of "health" (article 6 and 196) and of "balanced environment" (article 225), then extended this reasoning to the principle of a "safe and healthy working environment" (mentioning article 7, section XXIII, which ensures that workers must be paid a health hazard allowance when they have to work in unhealthy conditions). The arguments used aimed to create a new type of corporate responsibility that requires companies to supervise and

14 "*Locos appello (…) sedes argumentorum, in quibus latent, ex quibus sunt petenda*" – Quintilian, 5, 10, *21* (Harvard University Press, p. 374).

inspect (as a public entity) each stage of the production and sales chain, repairing the undoubtedly morally perverse effects of the economic regime. In other words, principles are invoked no matter if against the legal and even against the express sense of constitutional norms, to legitimise a decision that prospectively corrects the insufficiencies of the law, making a social project feasible.

In this topical use of principles, it is worthwhile to use another example to observe the transition from blocking-based argumentation to legitimation-based argumentation.

One currently familiar issue in Brazil concerns knowing how to tackle the decision to ensure the protection of health in light of, on one hand, a restriction imposed upon freedom of enterprise, in the sense of compulsory planning for private business, and, on the other, the exercise of judging that attributes to the right to the state to intervene in the free market in the name of the right to health. The problem of interpretation lies in how to reconcile conflicts between these rights (freedom of enterprise/health – public welfare).

To assess the matter, two principle-based arguments deserve attention: based on the same constitutional provision of the inviolability of individual dignity, we have on the one hand (i) the introduction of freedom as a moral value (*topos*) to be sought out and achieved by the legal system, with the presence of freedom and the social and free nature of economic activity that, in its turn, sets the standard for state intervention in this realm; and on the other (ii) the right to life as a fundamental valuable principle (principle as a *topos*), from which the social right to health arises and that makes it a duty of the state, hence the need for policies to ensure it is achieved, even if at the cost of free enterprise.

The state's jurisdiction in the field of health requires it to ensure the individual's right to health "through social and economic policies that aim to reduce the risk of diseases and other grievances" (Federal Constitution of Brazil, article 196), in the sense of caring for health and social assistance, over which all federal entities have jurisdiction (article 23, II), including educational policies, through guidelines and publicity campaigns conducted by the public agency itself.

The expression 'social and economic policies' that refers to the state's duty is actually extended topically to a common duty of all agents, whether public or private, to provide health, effected through the aforementioned policies, i.e. by performing health-related services and actions, including preventive ones. Such actions, which include educational action through publicity (sanitary policies of an educational nature), are the state's duty and cannot be transferred to private agents (the blocking-based argument: the constitutional norm sets limits) in the guise of compulsory planning of private enterprise. Yet the topical use of the right to health (human life as 'principle'-*topos*) introduces the possibility to recognise the legitimacy of a normative intervention of the state with the potential to give put the state's duty to execute public policies into proper effect.

What can be seen is that between the formal proclamation of rights (to life – health – freedom – freedom of enterprise) and the actual political status of individuals and groups, with all their differences, there is a vast space occupied by forms of political tension, demanding that the judiciary have a legitimising function and not a properly validating one in the former sense of judicial review. This means that human rights are no longer expressed in terms of *norms* but become *principles*. By extension, we can say that legal procedures based on a line of argument, in contemporary political societies, no longer aim entirely at the adaptive congruency of constitutional norms but actually seek social legitimation through the actual consummation of rights in light of prospective achievement. At first based on the institutionalisation of normative mechanisms (the right to positive provisions), this consummation later receives a status of legitimate transformation based on social prognosis.

5. Conclusion

If, in the past (when fundamental social rights, then called second-generation rights, emerged), the legal argumentation was guided towards postulating an intervention in the manner of a guaranteeing provision (jurisdictional relief: the right of action and court protection), a legitimating argumentation based on principles (not as grounds but as arguments) now begins with the provision of guarantees (the right to social security, to health), and advances to rights to provisions capable not only of protecting the unequal in light of the equal but also of promoting an equality between both, not only aiming at precedents: all are equal before the law, without distinctions of any nature, but aimed at a future dimension; all have the right to equality, i.e. the guarantee that they will become equal. It is in light of this problem of how to achieve social institutionalisation extra-officially (in schools, in hospitals, in factories, in companies) not as a right inherited from the past to be treated equally in spite of inequalities but as one to promote equality where inequalities exist, that legal argumentation exercises a prospective legitimating function (in light of the future) when treating principles as argumentation's viewpoints (*loci*, *topoi*). When they are allowed to be balanced (as ***topical arguments***) and have legitimately equivalent weight – (***pondus***), decisions are committed to the actual consummation of their future consequences.

In sum:

As 'reasons for action', principles begin to be applied directly (and not, as in the past, merely to fill in gaps or in cases of normative obscurity or antinomy). With regard to constitutional dogmatism, the issue is thus no longer the possibility of a correct or objectively valid interpretation but in fact one of determining which one is better or sufficiently justified, given the demands for legitimating future consequences of the cases to be ruled upon.

Luhmann perceived this problem well when he observed:

> (a) "problem arises for the system's redundancies where decisions are based on what will presumably be the case in the future. Since the decision has to be taken now, such justifications move in the medium of the merely probable. This leads initially to an immense increase in the system's variety".

Well, given this increase in variety that results from the consideration of consequences, "it is easy to understand that more recent developments in legal theory have sought support in indefeasible, non-renounceable rights". There is room, however, to doubt whether these rights can nevertheless entirely escape functioning without regard to consequences. "The balancing of interests is, then, a 'programme' for overcoming paradoxes".[15]

This dilemma, to be decided by the interpreter of the law, finally translates into a choice that is not always manifest, within a fundamental conflict between doing what is correct and what is good, which in moral philosophy is expressed, for example, in the division between deontological and teleological theories. Deontological theories correspond to the ideal of human life consisting of acting correctly according to moral norms and principles, in which the ideas of duty and correction (formal justice) are the central themes. Teleological theories correspond to the ideal of human life consisting of the attempt to satisfy certain purposes considered good, underlined by the idea of fairness.

15 *Legal Argumentation: An Analysis of its Form*, in *The Modern Law Review*, volume 58, May 1995, No. 3, p. 294, 295.

As, however, these are choices in which *strict* just/unjust coding fails as a guide, escape routes must be found. And this may be the (successful) role of topical principle-based argumentation, which, by balancing principles and using them as arguments (*topoi* or *loci argumentationis*), does not use them to increase certainty (the generality of common viewpoints – *topoi* – in the former line of argumentation, which was the ground for assumption of the *rational legislator*) but to increase the variety of standpoints that arise from the case at hand, legitimating a balancing of benefits and interests in view of their consequences.

In other – concluding – words, we have an old topic and a new topic of constitutional principles. On the one hand, with the (old) topic use of principle as *ground*, we were (and still are) able to distinguish between erroneous and error-free legal decisions (constitutional/unconstitutional law). On other hand, with the use of principle as *argument* (in the sense of *argument* and *counter-argument*), we can distinguish between good and bad (or less good) legitimated consequences (constitutional/unconstitutional legitimacy).[16]

16 In this sense, we notice a certain systemic confusion between the legal and the political constitution, as distinguished in Febbrajo's analysis: "While for a legal system the constitution is a supreme statute, a sort of basic law, for a political system it is an instrument of politics, in the sense of instrumental politics (which changes states of affairs) or only symbolic politics (which does not). The main point of reference, for this kind of intersystemic connection, is the adequacy of legal norms to the interests and ideals accepted and stabilised within a given society". See Alberto Febbrajo: *Introduction*, in *Law and Intersystemic Communication*, editors Alberto Febbrajo and Gorm Haste, 2013.

8 Questionable neutrality

Personal values in judicial adjudication[1]

Jack Meakin

The perception of objective right takes the color of the subjective mind.

Benjamin Cardozo[2]

1. Introduction

The image presented of neutral or autonomous law is not a formalism that merely provides a deductive method; it refutes the political nature of law by flattening the social conflicts beneath rationalised legal rules.[3] This chapter aims to encourage a socio-legal recognition of personal values in adjudication. The idea of law's neutrality perceives judicial adjudication to be detached and formalistic, and this suppresses fears about legal uncertainty and partiality. Contrary to this orthodoxy, I propose that legal decisions create distance from their author through specialised juridical language and techniques.

Despite judicial attempts to abide by the demands of neutrality, the influence of personal values is unavoidably prescriptive. This chapter will begin by considering the theoretical reliance on a conception of judicial practice that is controlled by the imposition of legalistic filters. To introduce the dominant scholarly treatment of judicial subjectivity, we will consider Ronald Dworkin's conception of judicial practice.

We will move on to discuss the symbolic construction of neutrality as a social fact. This will assess the social demand for neutrality before considering the impossibility of excluding non-legal factors from adjudication. Having insisted upon the inadequacy of traditional conceptions of neutral adjudication in our legal cultures, we will begin to develop a concept of personal values and encourage forthright acceptance of their influence in judicial adjudication.

A concept of personal values, understood as the agent's social normativity, which is engaged in the navigation of socio-legal conflicts, must be embedded within the realist approach to judicial adjudication. I will assess the conceptual tools of habitus, capital and field and argue that the agent cannot be removed in the manner proposed by neutrality; rather, they come to deliberation engaging not just juridical capital but also their categories of perception.

This will enable a preliminary investigation into the influence of subjectivities in judicial reasoning. I will encourage an alternative reading of judgments as law-making through a

1 I wish to thank Adam Czarnota and Scott Veitch for their critical advice and invaluable support, as well as Emilios Christodoulidis for his insightful comments on a previous version.

2 The Nature of the Judicial Process, 1921, p. 110

3 Unger, R. The Critical Legal Studies Movement. *Harvard Law Review*, Vol. 96(3), pp. 561–675. 1983.

discursive analysis of dictum in three right to religious freedom[4] case histories in English and Welsh law. The conclusions of this analysis suggest that our conception of adjudicative practice must comprehend that personal values influence interpretative practice in the following ways: personal values affect the judicial framing of disputes, their interpretation and representation of case facts, and legal authority is invoked as a means to sponsor judiciously constructed argumentation.

2. The absence and presence of personal values

The role of subjective influence in judicial reasoning presents a problem for conceptions of legal practice. This is not, by any means, a new problem and it is a theoretical debate replete with texture and countless interlocutors. I cannot do justice to this debate here. Instead, I will provide a sample of the problem faced by theory and consider the absence and presence of non-legal considerations in Ronald Dworkin's orthodox conception of judicial practice. This provides an introduction to scholarly treatment of our inquiry.

The conflicting accounts of law as an autonomous field or socially reactive was a central concern during the period of 'Free Interpretation of Law' at the beginning of the twentieth century. This movement saw law-making as driven neither by the normativity of individualism or social collectivism, but instead recognised the role of judicial thought as a necessary cog in the common law machine. The important breakthrough here was the move from Mechanical Jurisprudence to Sociological Jurisprudence, and with it, the invitation to a sociologically concerned legal method.

Mechanical Jurisprudence sought universal rules; based on market principles of laissez faire and individualism to generate determinant axioms. Illusions to mechanical application were not value-free – without concern for social impact – but advanced a liberal political ideology of individualism. Therefore, a critique of Mechanical Jurisprudence sought, first, a transparent method with an openness to a decision's ideological aims; and second, for an empirical reorientation of these foundations towards collectivism.[5] Importantly, this was not a period of mere anti-formalism, it was also one replete with fears concerning the subsumption of law by the potential dominance of social factors in a newly opened law-making method. The struggle to accommodate the social normativity of decision-makers in a certain and socially legitimate law can be traced to contemporary theory.

Ronald Dworkin's[6] Law as Integrity recognises judges' complex navigations of competing claims in hard cases. A hard case occurs when there is no suitable existing interpretation of law that can be applied; these cases demand judicial engagement with interpretations of *fit* that are *justified* on the basis of evaluations of justice and fairness. This provides the following understanding of adjudication: that judgments are the result of multiple interpretative considerations, including formal legal principles, precedent, and sociopolitical perceptions, and all are given relative weight according to individual notions of the judicial role.

However, these social and political convictions must 'fit' with "the brute facts of legal history".[7] Meaning previous authority, the nature of that legal culture, combined with general respect for the jurisdiction's doctrine. The question of justification demands a balance of

4 Human Rights Act 1998 Sch.1 Art.9.

5 Garcia-Villegas, M. Comparative Sociology of Law: Legal Fields, Legal Scholarships, and Social Sciences in Europe and United States. *Law and Social Inquiry*, Vol. 31(2) p. 349. 2006.

6 Dworkin, R. *Law's Empire*, Harvard University Press 1986 p. 250.

7 ibid., p. 255.

justice and fairness; this exercise involves the agent's moral and political convictions,[8] but any subjective convictions must align with the jurisdiction's higher order convictions to make law according to community-wide principles. If fit and justification are decided in line with only the judge's conception of justice in that case, then their adjudication ceases to be in good faith.[9] This limits the "role any judge's personal convictions of justice can play in his decisions".[10]

On the one hand, Dworkin cautions against rigid judicial rules of thumb, and frames interpretation as "a moral exercise".[11] but on the other, presents the constraining nature of a community with coherent principles[12] that operate as a necessary check on subjective influences. Law as Integrity recognises non-legal sources and subjective divergences among judges, however, and key to Dworkin's understanding, subjective influence is constrained by legalistic limitations predetermined by the legal culture.

For Dworkin, the subjective is tangible, the judge is aware of the distinct nature of their values, and this ensures their absence in legal interpretations.[13] On this account, judicial value engagement is subject to account and filtered by the requirements of political morality. Political morality in Dworkin consists of the agent's political aspirations, which explains their conception of what the law *should be* and which values *should be* protected by it.[14] While we know Dworkin's theory recognises the role of morality, this is also repressed through the demand for a reference to collective community conceptions of justice and fairness.[15] That judges' political morality is subject to such constraints and filters is central to Dworkin's presentation of 'integrity' as a legitimate political theory of law. These constraints exist as political and associative obligations exerted upon the judge. The former are those specific to the responsibilities of the judicial role and the latter exist where an agent belongs to the social group.[16] In Dworkin's theory, integrity is dependent upon a principled judicial practice.

Karl Llewellyn's *The Common Law Tradition*[17] presents an alternative approach to principled practice grounded in a commitment to legal realism. At the time of writing, there was a prescient fear amongst doctrinal legal scholars about a lack of certainty in 'grand style' decisions, and this had led to a general scepticism regarding judicial practice.[18] Lllewellyn sought to re-establish faith in the judiciary by highlighting the steadying factors on judicial subjectivities. The thesis argued that judicial decision-making emanated from reason, wisdom and situation sense. In addition, 'steadying factors' in adjudication constrained the grand style of reasoning.[19] Although Llewellyn defended the realist perspective that the rule of law is not alone in deciding cases, his characterisation did not accept subjective divergence, but that judges are "guided by something independent of the individual preferences or vagaries".[20]

8 ibid., p. 243; p. 256.
9 ibid.
10 ibid., p. 255.
11 Dworkin, R. *Justice for Hedgehogs*. The Belknap Press of Harvard University Press. p. 409. 2011.
12 Dworkin (1986) p. 243.
13 ibid., pp. 340–341.
14 Dworkin, R. *Justice in Robes*. The Belknap Press of Harvard University Press. p. 13; 21. 2006.
15 ibid., p. 21.
16 Dworkin (1986) pp. 195–196; 216; 183.
17 Llewellyn, K.N. *The Common Law Tradition: Deciding Appeals. Little Brown and Company*. Boston. Toronto. 1960.
18 Twining (2012) pp. 203–206.
19 Twining, W. *Karl Llewellyn and the Realist Movement* (2nd edn). Cambridge University Press. 2012 p. 205; Llewellyn (1960) pp. 60–1; p. 209.
20 Llewellyn in Clark and Trubeck (1961–1962) p. 265.

Against the backdrop of cautious orthodoxies, we must return to a realism prepared to accept that "the socio-political backdrop will no doubt impact on the decision-making process".[21] This, combined with a deconstruction of institutional claims to the contrary, represents the beginning for an embedding of personal values in adjudication theory.

3. The demand of neutrality

Neutrality is a demand to consider the facts, evidence, statutes and precedent without influence from subjective considerations and other non-legal sources.[22] The neutral judge occupies an authoritative position; despite law's social implications and multiplicity of outcomes, this decision-maker has the capacity to cut through the political and take a legal decision for the community as a whole. This has constructed the social image that supports the legitimacy of judicial law-making. This projection leads to societal demands upon judges, despite absent reflection as to whether the imputation of personal values is unavoidable.

Waldron asks us to think what ordinary Americans want from judges;[23] he predicts that decisions should be "according to law" with "objective judgments based on what legal materials require". That his proposal is likely correct presents the problem of sociocultural expectation. It is certainly predictable that the characteristics associated with neutrality are desirable. Fidelity and "deference to enacted rules...[and] a willingness [of judges] to restrain themselves as far as their own political convictions are concerned",[24] appears to immunise law from partiality and provide an exemplary arbiter. Despite ostensible coherence, this lacks greater understanding of the nature of adjudication and the role of non-legal concerns in decision-making.

I propose a deconstruction of this projection, to destabilise the orthodox and encourage concern for the political influence, and social effects, of the judiciary on our law. This requires a reflexive consideration of neutrality and acceptance that formalism is "more rhetoric than analysis, a rhetoric that conceals the actual springs of decision".[25]

Before moving to the next section, we must distinguish neutrality and impartiality. Impartiality is not neutrality; while the latter demands legalistic argument and the objective analysis of materials, the former is defined as honesty, professional integrity and a commitment to considering all forthcoming arguments. For Gunther, impartiality in the application of a norm requires "applicatory meaning"[26] where all available norms are given sufficient consideration to ensure equality before the law.

Friedman defines impartiality as an honesty in decision-making, in coming to what is believed to be the correct decision. However, Friedman does not stick to this simple conception but proposes that "a conscious tilt makes a judge less impartial".[27] Referring here to sufficient judicial concern for social facts in adjudication,[28] the socially ignorant judge is less influenced and more impartial. I encounter two problems here; first, impartiality is

21 Clark and Trubeck (1961–1962), p. 284.
22 Posner (2013) p. 111.
23 Waldron (2014) p. 2.
24 ibid., p. 3.
25 Posner (2013) p. 5.
26 Gunther (1988:257) in Alexy, R. *Justification and Application of Norms.* Ration Juris, Vol. 6(2) pp. 157–70 p. 158. 1993.
27 Friedman, L. Judging the Judges: Some Remarks on the Way Judges Think and the Way Judges Act, in Norms and the Law, Edited by J.N. Droback. p. 156. 2006.
28 ibid., p. 143.

no longer simply honesty but appears more analogous with Waldron's neutrality. Second, to be influenced by understandings of social facts is not a definable accessory. Therefore, I propose a more selective reading of Friedman. Impartiality allows for the unavoidable role of social concerns, yet still demands honest disclosure of political bias and thorough consideration of all arguments.

4. Neutrality as social fact: deconstructing neutrality

In order to question the category of neutrality, it is necessary to confront its existence as a social fact. This section will draw upon Pierre Bourdieu's[29] conception of symbolic capital and the constitutive concepts of the social world – habitus, capital and field. We will explore the role of judicial neutrality as a function of social legitimacy and unpack the promise of a 'neutral' deliberation.

Neutrality and the formalist conception of adjudication are upheld by symbolic capital. Defined by Bourdieu as capital that "is any property (any form of capital whether physical, economic, cultural, or social) when it is perceived by social agents endowed with categories of perception which causes them to recognise it, and importantly, give it value".[30] As structures are accepted, conformed to, and reproduced in the agent's cognitions, we observe the consequence of the state's intentional and "decisive contribution to the production and reproduction of the instruments of construction of social reality".[31] In other words, "symbolic production"[32] produces neutrality as an expectant feature of judicial practice.

If fidelity to legal sources, as formalists propose, at the exclusion of subjectivities is to be achieved, then we must accept an implicit dualism: the juridical habitus operates separate from the habitus as a whole. The juridical habitus is imbued with juridical capital from legal education and subsequent practical experience.

I will argue to the contrary that we must locate the juridical habitus within the agent's wider habitus and recognise the aggregation of influences within the habitus. This means that drawing upon specific knowledge is not an independent operation but mutually constitutive of a person's normative understanding. Therefore, the juridical habitus can be understood as a lens within a lens. It is not possible for an adjudicator to view a case through one lens because the comprehension of legal knowledge is constituted by a variety of social factors. Law functions for a social context and there is no one understanding of this context. There is a necessary blurring of knowledge; we comprehend legal rules against the backdrop of social realities.

Let us first take a step back. Following Bourdieu, habitus is a socially formulated conscious where the agent's conceptions of the social and legal world are formulated; it is here that value is ascribed to particular social understandings. Habitus should be understood as our orientation to the social world, and perception of the conflicts we confront. Consider, for example, the differing recognition of offence and insults depending on varied exposures to diverse social norms during an individual's upbringing.[33]

29 Bourdieu, P. *Practical Reason*, Polity Press 1998 (1994) p. 35.
30 ibid., p. 47.
31 ibid., p. 54.
32 ibid., p. 38.
33 Foblets, M.C. and Renteln, A.D. *Multicultural Jurisprudence: Comparative Perspectives on the Cultural Defense*, Hart Publishing, 2009.

The pervasive nature of perceptions reveals the unavoidable and unknown influence of the agent upon interpretation and decision making. Friedman describes this as a "blindness about ourselves"; the impossibility to exclude those "forces...we are hardly aware of".[34] Any tangible attempts to exclude subjectivities fail to counter the silent conceptions and presuppositions that affect judicial interpretation. Regardless of theoretical or rhetorical attempts at removal, the juridical habitus does not operate alone. When the agent is presented with a value-judgment, their own conceptions about self-evidently defensible values (from the habitus as a whole) are engaged. These conceptions shape the agent as they act "by virtue of a system of preferences proper to him or her".[35] In rejecting the dualism, we recognise that categories of perception are drawn not only from the juridical field but other parts of the social realm.

The habitus is multi-constitutive because it "is the product of the intersection of partly independent causal series".[36] 'Series' refers to the multiple experiences from the various fields to which an agent is exposed. While these 'fields' of specificity contain relative beliefs, norms[37] and by extension, a particular capital. The multiple fields that exert influence upon judges leads to the percolation of non-legal sources in the juridical field, be it as scientific research or judicial perception of a social fact. The juridical field is therefore structured not only by legal rules and precedents but also with specific "social, economic, psychological and linguistic practices"[38] that become recognised practice and affect judicial reason. Importantly, the juridical field unifies juridical capital in one body, and through the process of "differentiation", competences are taken from other bodies and translated into the universalised[39] (seemingly natural and unquestionable) capital of law that we can see in legal argument.

This leads to a necessary concern for juridical tools. They include rhetorical devices that operate not as intrinsic judicial characteristics to solve conflicts in juridical terms but to proclaim neutrality by disguising non-legal factors and the "proportion of arbitrariness"[40] in legal decisions. One way to generate neutrality is through recourse to precedent and principles, "which legitimises the decision by making it seem the result of neutral and objective application of specifically juridical procedures, though it may in fact be motivated by quite different considerations".[41]

For Robert Cover, the use of authorities is an 'employment of force' that commits a 'jurispathic act'. This jurispathic act elevates the interpretation chosen by the judge (who must necessarily kill off other possible conceptions) by appealing to their jurisdiction and the relevant authoritative texts of law.[42] For Cover, this illustrates how the commitment to an objective approach is made by the individual judge, but that it is a metaphor for separation and dedication to the practice of interpretation.[43] In this way, judgments necessarily deploy judicial tools so that they accord with the demands of their practice.

34 Friedman (2006) p. 150.
35 ibid., p. 91.
36 Bourdieu, P. *In Other Words: Essays Towards a Reflexive Sociology*. Polity Press. 1990. p. 91.
37 O'Chase, in Freeman, M.D.A. *Introduction to Jurisprudence*. Sweet and Maxwell (8th edn). 2008. p. 127.
38 Terdiman, R. Translator's Introduction in Bourdieu (1986) p. 807.
39 ibid., p. 46.
40 ibid., p. 826.
41 Bourdieu (1986) p. 832.
42 R.M. Cover *The Supreme Court 1982 Term. Foreword: Nomos and Narrative*. 97 Harvard Law Review 4 1983–4 p. 40; p. 54.
43 Cover (1983–1984) p. 45.

For Bourdieu, juridical language "bears all the marks of a rhetoric of impersonality and of neutrality"[44] as conflicts are "ontologically glorified". Judgments and legal argumentation appear to flow from a universal and predefined set of legal norms without subjective influence.[45] This is a process of neutralisation and universalisation of a social conflict into juridical terms, whereby judges rationalise both social facts and their chosen argumentation into an "objectified and codified"[46] form of juridical capital. This produces a sustained, authoritative and "symbolically effective"[47] judgment detached from subjective influences.

This encourages a reflexive concern for the argumentative practices used in judgments. For instance, we can also draw into question judicial deference to community principles and the wishes of Parliament. This neutralises judicial input to decision-making, disguising the judge's own interpretation of those Parliamentary intentions. And the interpretative practice that reproduces Parliament's intention becomes irrelevant at the moment an interpretation becomes law. In addition, judgments make reference to legal tests or constructs such as the reasonable man, a juridical tool applied by judges to represent a view of the social world. As Broekman explains, such tests are "constructivist and performative".[48] They are not merely descriptive but act as support for the judge's interpretative conclusions about the law.

For Bourdieu, law's autonomy is not an absolute but relative. Law appears an autonomous field, not because it theoretically (or naturally) is, but because it resists external influences and functions by using its own capital to promote its exclusivity and generate the appearance of autonomy as it struggles for social acceptance and legitimacy.[49] This recognises that formalism has produced an ideology of an autonomous law that has become normalised in societal understanding and expectation.

Bourdieu does talk of a neutral space: "inscribed at the deepest level of the habitus"[50] is the judge's ability to assume a neutral distance and ensure disengagement. I do not read this as a proclamation of a formalistic pure neutrality but as a description of the structured social understanding and institutional projection of neutrality, and perhaps even of the attempted isolation of the juridical habitus in juridical practice. Autonomy and neutrality is less an intrinsic characteristic of the judge and more an appearance, an aesthetic of the judiciary.

The formalist rejection of a conceptual effort aimed at locating the non-legal elements in judging would invoke a concern for legal certainty because subjective influence inserts a degree of unpredictability. This chapter does not argue for a more uncertain law but for a textured understanding of the role already played by personal values in judgments. Indeed, a detailed and reflexive understanding of what does, rather than should happen uncovers the degree of certainty we have in practice. In other words, our certain decisions are made with the aid of non-legal subjective influences, and our conceptual and theoretical unfamiliarity calls forth our recognition and exploration of their place in judicial decision making.

44 Bourdieu (1986) p. 819.
45 ibid., p. 820.
46 Bourdieu (1994) p. 47.
47 ibid., p. 52.
48 Broekman, J.M. Legal Discourse and Legal Facts in EYSL European Yearbook in the Sociology of Law 1993. Edited by Febbrajo, A and Nelken, D. Guiffre 1994. p. 187.
49 ibid., Terdiman p. 808.
50 ibid., p. 830.

5. Personal values in adjudication: the concept

Personal values are referred to in this paper as the subjective influence of social understandings to which a judge ascribes value and influence the construction of reasoning. They are 'prescriptive or proscriptive beliefs' that support certain conduct or social realities as preferable to others.[51] This builds upon the rejection of dualism in the habitus set out above, and draws on social psychology and a belief system theory that understands values as central to personality and the primary variable in determinations of social attitudes and behaviour.[52]

Values rationalise certain attitudes (or approaches), and the formation of social understanding constituted by these values 'may produce a self-serving bias'.[53] Cahill-O'Callaghan's recent scholarship recognises the competing values in decisions, meaning judgments are affected not by the unrelenting influence of a single value but, "a more detailed nuanced balancing of competing values which are more diverse than simply a political position".[54]

A candid insight into the place of subjective influence is given by Herman and Jivraj's[55] discursive analysis of judicial representations of non-Christianness in child welfare cases in England and Wales. Herman and Jivraj's concern is for judges' "ways of thinking",[56] and the normativity they espouse. Their conclusions "offer a lens to read English law as resting upon a nominally secular… indivisibilised Christian foundation",[57] where judicial texts can be read as "at times" understood as orientalist, racialized and Christian. This presents judges not as 'simple mouth-pieces' but as an agent that 'make choices about how to present the facts'.[58] Consequently, the legal conflicts are constructed according to conceptions of the social world, and this affects the context and nature of legal decisions.

We have already identified habitus as the site of our "learned yet deep structure of Behaviour",[59] which guides behaviour and constitutes understandings of the social world. Leading to our valuing of an array of often competing values that constitute the agent's concerns for those values that, where they are present in a conflict, become active, and subsequently, shape argumentation. This presents the hypothesis that, the attitude of the agent towards a given concern will likely lead to their preference for such values when confronted by them in deliberation. An understanding of personal values will explore the normativity of judgments and their indivisible effects upon interpretation and the decision-making (law-making) process.

To comprehend this indivisibility of personal values and explore their pervasive influence, I will draw upon the concept of 'doxa' and its construction of a comprehensible social reality. For Bourdieu, doxa is the 'natural world' defined by the established order. An ordered social world is presented through the production of apparently objective structures that are

51 Rokeach in Mayton, D.M. II, Ball-Rokeach, S.J and Loges, W. Human Values and Social Issues: An Introduction. *Journal of Social Issues*, Vol. 50(4) 1994. p. 3.

52 Ball-Rokeach, S.J., Rokeach, M., and Grube, J.W. The Great American Values Test: Influencing Behavior and Belief Through Television. *Social Forces*, Vol. 65(2) (1986) pp. 571–573

53 Kristiansen and Zanna in Mayton, Ball-Rokeach and Loges (1994) p. 4.

54 Cahill O'Callaghan (2013) p. 620.

55 Jivraj, S and Herman, D 'It's difficult for a white judge to understand': Orientalism, Racialisation, and Christianity in English child welfare cases. *Child & Family Law Quarterly*, Vol. 21(3). 2009 pp. 283–308.

56 ibid.

57 ibid., p. 283.

58 Ibid.

59 Terdiman in Freeman (2008) p. 876.

reproduced by and sustained through cognitive structures.[60] In other words, it is the creation of self-evident truths or beliefs. These structures portray the social world as a natural, traditional world and enables citizens to submit to doxic beliefs.[61]

The conceptual tool of personal values recognises this subjective influence of values and their effect upon the construction of the world. Where an agent's subjection to a value is self-evident, it constitutes their common-sense field of 'what goes without saying'.[62] We recall and recognise here the 'misrecognition of arbitrariness';[63] that the agent's comprehensions, and thus, decision-making is unavoidably married to personal belief in a certain social world. Doxic submission explicates the act of reliance upon certain societal facts. To this, we can accept reflexive consideration, but the outcome remains a belief that projects social normativity and is evidently true to the self.

This renders any promise to remove personal values impossible and explainable as an attempt to regain legitimacy, or due to a continued belief in neutrality. There is an assumption that values can be ignored and removed through conscious eradication. The illumination provided by the concept of doxic submission means we cannot merely counteract their influence through conscious self-critique. This fails to recognise the true nature of the agent's relationship with personal values.

Bourdieu suggests that even the most valiant self-reflection would be unable to fully acknowledge the grip of doxa upon our social consciousness. This is explained as our 'intra-conscious';[64] critical analysis of the constructed nature of our beliefs must rely upon certain social truths that we fail to recognise as being uncritically instrumentalised for the purpose of self-reflection. While this circularity specifically applies to doxa, we can transplant the unavoidability of self-evident social reality to the current concern for the non-exclusion of value concerns in decision making.

Personal values are not severable accessories that simply encourage tangible, forthright and extravagant discourse. They play a more concealed role of orientating approaches to value-decisions. They are signposts or anchorage points that wield influence in adjudication. This may accompany active self-reflection upon values, but their intangible place in reasoning means personal values have a presence that defies presumed safeguards on judicial subjectivity.

6. Williamson, Begum and Bashir: considering personal values in adjudication

We have established the hypothesis that the subjective influences of doxic personal values affects a judge's approach to decision making. The following discussion applies the concept of doxic personal values to an analysis of dictum in three cases concerning Article 9 rights to religious freedom.[65] In this analysis, I will suggest a reading of adjudication as influenced by personal values in the following ways:

i The recognition of competing value concerns affects the judicial approach to, and framing of a dispute;

60 Bourdieu (1994) p. 56.
61 ibid., p. 161; 166.
62 Bourdieu, P. *Outline of a Theory in Practice*. Cambridge University Press. 1977. p. 167.
63 Bourdieu (1977) p. 168.
64 Bourdieu and Eagleton (1991) p. 113.
65 Human Rights Act 1998, Sch1. Part 1.

ii Judicial interpretations of case facts are drawn from the evidence presented, and subsequently, represented through judicial understandings of the social world;
iii Judicial interpretations are presented in legal arguments (juridical language) and seek to abide by the doctrine of precedent; these legitimating tools function not only as a requirement of judicial practice but also as validation of legal argumentation, navigated via the subjective influence of the agent's personal values.

The qualitative nature of this analysis has made the stain of the author's own interpretation unavoidable.[66] This is an inescapable truth, but one that does not detract from a candid concern for the relationship between judicial adjudication and the imposition of social normativity in law.

Before continuing, let us consider the type of cases and interpretative practice we are talking about. Some cases involve strict legal rules, therefore limiting the impact of personal values on a decision, meaning there must be sufficient discretion for decisions to be affected. There is however a place for personal values in strict rule decisions; they affect the approach if not the result.

For example, Cowan *et al's* study of District Judges focused upon judicial approaches to decisions in the strict rule area of property possession proceedings.[67] The study presented district judges, who were previously lawyers representing the 'socially disadvantaged', that appeared more inclined to an approach concerned for specific facts despite the case's strict rule nature, compared to an ex-civil barrister inclined towards a patrician approach. Despite a lack of discretion, reasoning was found not to be strictly legal but facilitating subjective influence grounded in past experiences and perceptions. These findings encourage further reflection upon the effects of a judge's conception of the social world on their approach to interpretative practice.

(i) Influence on judicial approach

Judicial approach refers to the judicial formulation of the dispute, their recognition of value in the case before them and the route chosen by their reasoning. The construction of judgments reveals the personal value judgments that aided and shaped the interpretative process.

For instance, in the House of Lords in Williamson[68] head teachers, teachers and parents of children challenged the Education Act's[69] ban on corporal punishment as a breach of

66 Sarat, A. Off to Meet the Wizard: Beyond Validity and Reliability in the Search for a Post Empiricist Sociology of Law, *Law and Social Inquiry*, Vol. 15(1), 1990. pp. 155–170.

67 Cowan et al. (2006) p. 569. Reference is made to the s.5 provision where proof of three months unpaid rent gives rise to the strict rule to order repossession.

68 Regina (Williamson and Others) v Secretary of State for Education and Employment [2002] H.R.L.R. 14; [2002] EWCA 1926; [2005] UKHL 15. In the Administrative Court, Elias J upheld the legislation, finding the claimant's beliefs to fall short of the definition of religious belief in Article 9. The Court of Appeal affirmed the decision on different grounds. Their belief was a religious belief covered by Article 9. It was however only possible for the parents to manifest such beliefs; they were not the teachers' religious beliefs. Therefore, there was no interference with the parents' rights; they could still manifest their beliefs outside of school. The House of Lords, however, found both a religious belief on behalf of the parents and an infringement of Article 9, as the state prevented parents from granting teachers consent to inflict punishment. Focusing on justification under Article 9(2), Lord Nicholls and Lord Walker saw manifestation where an act is 'intimately linked' to religious beliefs, and that a religious practice need not be obligatory (Sandberg 2009). The court, however, dismissed the claimant's appeal as the aims of the legislation justified the infringement, the measures intended to protect children and their welfare were not disproportionate to the resulting infringement upon parent's rights.

69 1998 s.548(1).

their right to religious belief in physical punishment as a duty of education[70] in a Christian context. Lord Nicholls was the first to concentrate on the value of child protection, while fellow justices centred upon minority beliefs and pluralism. It was not predeterminedly necessary to approach the case from Nicholls's perspective, but this was *his* reaction, and the judgment centred upon the value of child protection.

Nicholls references "punishment of children" and then proceeds to account the numerous authorities[71] that proscribe such punishment. Moreover, Nicholls provided his support to the rationale behind the protections offered by such legislation: "That corporal punishment *may* have these harmful effects is self-evident".[72] The semantics used are dismissive of opposition. For Nicholls, it is common sense that "harmful effects" result from corporal punishment.

As a personal value, child protection and its necessity come to the fore and guide behaviour. The judgment's proclamation of self-evidence is reflective of Nicholls's own submission to this axiomatic value. This is presented in the judgment as a self-evidently defensible value position. As such, a defence is mounted for the protection of these values at the expense of counter claims concerning religious belief. Baroness Hale follows this lead, giving central importance to the protection of children.

> If a child has a right to be brought up without institutional violence, as he does, that right should be respected whether or not his parents and teachers believe otherwise.[73]

The onus is again on child protection, emphasising the need to avoid legal (judicial) acceptance of institutional violence. The addition of "as he does" portrays a reflexive answer to the issue, at this moment the agent (Hale) steps out of the juridical discourse to answer the question. It is not however a live debate (even when first aired). There is an unquestioned recognition that children's rights require respect, and the judgment continues in support of their protection. Hale's reasoning remains on this platform despite an expectation for impartial judicial discussion of the parent's claim to an infringement of their rights to religious belief.

The Hale judgment is constructed around a concern about physical punishment's (in) compatibility with human dignity. Baroness Hale states:

> The sort of punishment in which Victoria Climbie's murderers apparently believed is not worthy of any respect at all.... In this case we are concerned with carefully controlled, mild and loving discipline administered in the context of a clear moral code.[74]

Mention of the Climbie murder offers an insight into Hale's deliberation, and the pervasive nature of the habitus, as experiences precipitate Hale's understanding of the line between dignified discipline and undignified punishment – a key issue for the court in deciding whether corporal punishment in schools offended human dignity. The issue could have been broached using legal references; instead a definite source of social concern for child

70 The claim was brought under both Article 9 Human Rights Act 1998, religious belief and Article 2, right to education.

71 [2005] UKHL p. 9.

72 ibid., p. 19.

73 ibid., p. 32.

74 ibid., p. 28.

protection is revealed. While Hale is willing to recognise the "mild and loving" nature of the claimant's intended form of discipline, this does not extend to the construction of a legal argument in their favour. On the contrary, the argument is led by a concern about the protection of children, especially post-Climbie.

That judgments are formulated along lines agreeable to the judge seems an uncontroversial statement, albeit an oft unconsidered one. Value influences may be translated into juridical capital to appear formalistic; however, our analysis suggests that judgments are left with an indelible mark of personal values, recognisable through judicial derision or support for certain values. We can propose, tentatively, that there is an unavoidable relationship with socially formulated subjective influences that dictate which value concerns are evidently (not) in need of legal protection.

(ii) The interpretation of evidence and representation of case facts

(a) Interpretation of evidence

Interpretation by a judge is potentially problematic when they lack expertise of a relevant subject, even more so when, as a substitute, their own somewhat contrasting experiences and perceptions are relied upon.

> The notion that the Shalwar Kameeze school uniform would not accord with essential requirements of Islamic modesty for teenage girls seems to me an extraordinary one.[75]

This is the interpretation of Lord Scott, a white South-African born British judge, and his understanding of a teenage Muslim girl's religious belief in acceptable Islamic dress code. The subject of Scott's deliberation was Shabina Begum who attended Denbigh High School for two years and wore the Shalwar Kameeze, a permitted school uniform for Muslim pupils that do not wear traditional uniform. At the start of her third year, she wore a long jilbab coat not permitted under the uniform policy and, having been sent home to change clothing did not return to school. A claim was brought against the defendant school for both; breaching statutory duty to provide access to suitable and appropriate education under Article 2 HRA 1998 and infringing the claimant's right to manifest religion under Article 9.[76]

The evidence of acceptable dress presented arguments on both sides, but the authoritative manner in which Scott decides against Begum raises the following issue: How did he reach a decisive conclusion on this sensitive issue? It would be irresponsible to speculate as to the exact personal values at play in the decision, but certainly non-legal influences orientate

75 [2006] UKHL 15 p. 27.

76 R (on the Application of Begum) v The Head Teacher and Governors of Denbigh High School. [2004] EWHC 1389 (Admin); EWCA Civ 199 [2005]; [2006] UKHL 15. The Administrative court found the case problematic, construing exclusion from school as resulting from Begum's challenge to school rules as opposed to the school's infringement of religious belief. The judge found there had been no exclusion from the school, reasoning that Begum had made a choice, she was therefore excluded by her own non-compliance with uniform policy. The Court of Appeal allowed the appeal, accepting an interference under Article 9(1) – the appellant's religious belief prevented her from complying with the uniform policy. The court then struggled with Article 9(2), rather than deciding whether interference was justified, Brooke LJ argued the school had incorrectly considered the effects of their rules and imposed the burden that they themselves should have applied a proportionality test: the school had not shown their policy to be 'necessary' and insufficiently considered whether the policy infringed Article 9 rights.

Scott's evaluation of the facts and subsequent approach to the case. The Shalwar Kameeze is but one possibility in the Muslim dress code, more conservative options are available, but it is an 'extraordinary' option for Lord Scott. Is there a threshold for acceptability of religious belief? Can this be legally defined? The freedom of choice is that of the teenage girl, universal doctrine does not state which option is extraordinary; that is a decision left to belief and perception of that belief.

Returning to the Williamson case, judicial uneasiness with corporal punishment as a manifestation of religion extends to the claimant's evidence of belief being recognised as a perverse straining of biblical scripture.

> Plainly not all Christians – I suspect not many – would consider that this and other such texts require corporal punishment to be an integral part of the child's education.[77]

Elias goes on to reject these religious beliefs as being indefensible under the Human Rights Act 1998:

> It may be accurate to say that someone has a religious conviction that everything in the Bible is true, but it would surely be odd to describe, say, a belief in angels as a religious conviction or as itself constituting an article of religious faith.[78]

The claimants' beliefs have gone too far for Elias; according to his understanding of the Christian faith and applied to that of the claimants. The judgment dismisses the validity of these religious beliefs, to the extent that they are presumed analogous to a belief in angels. This jurispathic[79] approach to the facts rejects the alternate construction in support of religious belief.

Moreover, Elias adds the following caveat to the test for defensible beliefs: where beliefs are "unpalatable"[80] they will not be protected by law. This caveat thus provides a judicial dilemma: who decides when a belief becomes unpalatable? Is it the law, or Elias's interpretation of the facts applied to the legal test?

Elias rejects the claim of religious belief because it professes insufficient respect for human dignity as required by Article 9. It would appear that the subjective test of 'unpalatable' is 'ontologically glorified'[81] through its new-found synonymy with the Article 9 requirement of sufficient respect for human dignity. In other words, disrespect for human dignity is unpalatable and the claimants fall under this category. This suggests that the parameters of a legal test for respecting human dignity are understood when we turn to the socially formulated, subjective understandings that inform a judge's treatment of a case's facts and how they are related to legal tests.

(b) Representation of facts

The section above dealt with the interpretation of facts and how they were comprehended by judges. This section is concerned with the (non)use of (ir)relevant facts. Judicial use of

77 [2002] H.R.L.R. 14 p. 3.
78 ibid., p. 10.
79 Cover (1981–1982).
80 [2002] H.R.L.R. 14 P. 12.
81 Bourdieu (1986) p. 846.

case facts is recognized as an act of construction in Herman's history of the word 'Holocaust', and references to the killings of European Jews by the German state in English case law. Where facts are left out, Herman suggests silences are "deliberately chose[n] to deem these facts irrelevant to the legal issue".[82] Judicial reference to the Holocaust and Jews acts as a mnemonic device to remember not the atrocity but to represent presumed idiosyncrasies of Jewishness.[83] Therefore, we become aware of a deeper complexity in tracking the normativity of discourse, as it represents misremembrance, mythology and, therefore, the arbitrary deployment of "phenotypical signifiers or characteristics".[84] Herman thus recognises the agent's creationism in the production of judgments, rejecting the official, formalistic and value-free conceptions of judicial practice; in favour of an approach that unveils formalism as enabling the judge to construct a view of the 'facts'. I suggest alternative portrayals of case facts are thus indicative of the influence of personal value in judgments; where given concerns are, or are not highlighted, we can infer their socio-legal importance.

In Begum, Lord Bingham begins by laying out the agreed facts of the case. A detailed account consuming six paragraphs recounts the actions of the school and their attempts to accommodate Begum. This included: their approval of the uniform policy, the Islamic background of the head teacher, and concerns for social cohesion and tolerance. Only one paragraph[85] considers Begum, noting that she wore the Shalwar Kameeze for two years without complaint and then changed her mind, while her sister had no problem with the uniform policy. The facts that are presented portray a certain image of the case: There is a school that has sought to attain social cohesion, yet now faces a claim of human rights infringement.

Despite an Article 9 case being a question about infringement of a right and justification of the infringement, Bingham's judgment documents Begum's personal choice and her "unwillingness to comply with a rule to which, as I [Lord Bingham] have concluded, the school were entitled to adhere".[86] In dismissing an application of Article 2 (right to education) Bingham notes:

> The respondent's family chose for her a school outside their own catchment area. It was a school which went to unusual lengths to inform parents of its uniform policy... [There is] no evidence to show that there was any real difficulty in her attending one or other of these schools.[87]

Religious belief and the degree of faith is assumed to be a voluntary act. The school's claimed interference is a secondary concern because Begum's right to religious belief is deemed superfluous owing to the opportunity to move school. For Bingham, the facts of Begum's situation were characterised by voluntariness, highlighting that it was not

82 Herman 2008., p. 433.

83 ibid., p. 429; Samantha Knights provides a similarly critical investigation of judicial normativity through a consideration of diversity and Article 9 jurisprudence. Her central argument posits that, "underlying the manipulation of religious identity are serious issues about multiculturalism, diversity politics, and accommodation in the UK". Knights, S. Approaches to Diversity in the Domestic Courts: Article 9 of the European Convention on Human Rights. Ch.15 in Legal Practice and Cultural Diversity, Edited by Ralph Grillo et al Ashgate 2009. p. 283.

84 Herman and Jivraj (2009) p. 286.

85 [2006] UKHL 15 p. 4.

86 ibid., p. 14.

87 ibid., p. 11.

impossible to have practised beliefs elsewhere.[88] Using the doctrine of 'voluntary acceptance' of the circumstance, Bingham ruled that Begum's rights had not been infringed. The case could have been presented via Begum's narrative; we will see from the opposing approaches by judges in the case that judicial reasoning is significantly altered where different case facts are highlighted.

Baroness Hale, Lord Nicholls and Lord Justice Brooke preferred a different interpretation; indeed Bingham, Hoffman and Scott's[89] representations can be juxtaposed with that of Hale, whose minority judgment found an interference with Begum's rights.

> If a woman freely chooses to adopt a way of life for herself, it is not for others, including other women who have chosen differently, to criticise or prevent her.[90]

Hale's chosen approach concentrates upon the rights of Begum as opposed to the extent that the claim is unfortunate for the school. The subjective and legal concerns of Hale are autonomy, individual rights, woman's rights, oppression and liberty.[91] Thus, the case is framed according to the Article 9 test: it is dependent upon whether there was an infringement of Begum's right to wear a religious dress, and only once this is proven can the justifiability of the school's actions be considered.

Bingham rightly notes that Hale and Nicholls are "inclined to a different opinion";[92] and it is exactly the act of "inclination" that concerns our investigation. These disparate judgments show comparatively distinct interpretations, and the varying importance of certain personal values in the elevation of certain facts, leading to different lines of reasoning and conclusions.

(iii) Deployment of precedent in support of personal values

> The fact is that every writer creates his own precursors. His work modifies our conception of the past, as it will modify the future.[93]
>
> *Jorge Luis Borges*

Borges recognised the constructive license employed by those who impose a Kafkaesque reading upon Kafka's precursors. In essence, this project demands reading the contemporary through the historical as though the historical were aware of the contemporary. In law, the idea that precedent predetermined current judicial decision-making rests on the following: we cannot say exactly what the law will become, but once a law is, it was always predetermined to be so. Therefore, if invocation of precedent adapts it to a present that could not have been foreseen, in what way can precedent by itself be instructive?

A judgment employs force upon its precursor (precedent) because law is not static. The intentions of a precedent may be ambiguous and require interpretation and refinement. In addition, our legal community has been developed over time, and to maintain the legitimacy of the rule of law, it is necessary to maintain the relevance of its foundational values

88 ibid., p. 8.
89 ibid., p. 28.
90 ibid., Baroness Hale p. 31.
91 ibid., p. 30.
92 [2006] UKHL 15 p. 11.
93 Borges, J.L. Kafka and His Precursors, in Labyrinths. Penguin Modern Classics. 2000 (1962). p. 236.

and principles. Informed by these reflections, let us explore the use of precedents by the judges in our three cases.

The doctrine of precedent is intrinsic to the English common-law system. The official and prevailing understanding of judicial practice comprehends the deployment of precedent as an act of deference to legal history, rules and a commitment to legal certainty. Through analogy (interpretation and application) legal rules are transposed from a previous case into one where facts are necessarily different but, the same rule applies by abstraction. This demands that judges 'treat like cases alike'[94] with the aim of creating uniformity and certainty in law. Our present inquiry demands a further question: can precedent also work to disguise influence, avert criticism and generate legitimacy?

> Viewed objectively, the act of inflicting corporal punishment is entirely neutral as to the beliefs that inspire it... The infliction of corporal punishment expresses nothing as to the religion of the inflictor.[95]

The above point is the following: the claimants' beliefs cannot have the relation to corporal punishment that they have presented. Lord Justice Buxton sought to apply the Arrowsmith[96] precedent, the key issue in that case was that insufficient mention of pacifism on anti-military leaflets meant the leaflets were not a manifestation of religion. Pacifism had motivated the act, but the act was not a manifestation of that belief. Buxton attempts to deduce the same lack of manifestation from the claimants' testimony by seeing the act of punishment as disconnected ('neutral') in terms of their belief. The court in Arrowsmith analysed a leaflet; Buxton is reliant on the claimant's statements of belief, and necessarily – his interpretation of a theological disconnect between their professed belief and intended action.

While Buxton introduces a conclusive assertion about these beliefs that has been 'viewed objectively', it can be argued that the citation of Arrowsmith also works to legitimise the decision *he* interprets as correct. The non-analogous nature of Arrowsmith's facts with Williamson requires Buxton to make an unavoidable interpretative leap and rely upon his own perceptions and experiences of corporal punishment and religious belief. It is worth noting that Buxton's interpretation of Arrowsmith was rejected by his fellow justices, and the manifestation of belief was declared to be present in the claimants' stated belief in such action.[97]

The role of the judge appears merely facilitatory, with doctrinal application of precedent supporting neutrality's aesthetic. However, by highlighting the deployment of precedent to deny legal recognition of a claimants' religious belief in their actions, we can begin to understand precedent as the 'employment of force'; and, therefore, as a means for legitimating the individual judge's decision-making. Following on from Elias's comprehension of Christian faith above, this is a decision that enters the theological and social arena and attempts to set the socio-legal threshold of religious belief in given actions.

In Williamson, Baroness Hale's choice of authorities follows her attention upon the need to ensure child protection. Hale's distinct approach is supported by authorities not seen in

94 Cownie, F. *English Legal System in Context*, (3rd edn), Lexis Nexis Butterworths, (2003) p. 142.

95 [2002] EWCA 1926 p. 14.

96 Arrowsmith v United Kingdom (1978) 3 EHRR 218.

97 At paragraph 163 Rix LJ, and 286 Arden LJ, [2002] EWCA 1926. Similarly, the House of Lords, [2005] UKHL 15, declared only a limited inquiry into the validity of belief could be conducted by the court, meaning the appropriateness of a belief's manifestation could be assessed according to human dignity but the right to belief is unqualified - The court should not reject as false a claimant's declaration of belief in given actions.

other judgments at any judicial level in the case[98] (a trend that can also be seen in Begum). Support for a blanket ban on corporal punishment to protect the vulnerable is supported by reference to international conventions, reports and a range of "professional educational and child care opinion in support of the ban".[99] The authorities follow a prescriptive belief in the value of child protection – the case materials are chosen by and provide authority for the judgments' concerns about corporal punishment, and not about the protection of religious freedom. Hale's arbitrary submission to her conception of specific issues in the social world demands specific reference to certain authorities in the legal argument.

Undoubtedly, personal values alone cannot construct a judgment; it requires juridical capital, relevant legalistic concerns and support from precedent to ensure a coherent and authoritative argument in law. Precedent is both a requirement of legal argumentation and a legitimating tool in judicial practice. However, the traditional institutional projections can be combined with the reading of precedent as juridical tool. This presents a complicated conception but one that is textured and realistic.

(a) Appealing to a higher authority: the law and reasonableness

Consider Justice Elias's approach to recognising a religious belief under Article 9(1) in Williamson (subsequently overruled):

> There is some attraction in this argument [that religious beliefs respect the integrity of the person], but ultimately I reject it. The law has always shown a respect for the physical integrity of the individual: any intentional assault is unlawful unless there is a defence of justification.[100]

The rejection of religious belief is made by Elias, but in its presentation, this result no longer belongs to Elias. Indeed, the beliefs simply do not fit within the parameters of respect set by *the law*. Judicial use of a legitimate 'other' serves the purpose of authorising Elias's (subjectively influenced) interpretation of a religious belief in corporal punishment. The unavoidability of personal values' influence in judicial practice, meaning the prescription of a particular social normativity onto reasoning, can be recognised through analysis of the juridical tools that project objectivity.

In the same category, a judicial interpretation that declares to act in the manner intended by Parliamentary law-makers is also problematic. Invocation of 'Parliamentary intention' carries with it the invocator's constructive intentions. Unless drawing directly, without deviation upon the higher authority's judgment, the judge cannot directly re-present the intentions of the elected law-making chamber. The declaration of a self-commitment to follow their intentions reproduces the authority and legitimacy of Parliament, the sovereign law-maker in England and Wales, in support of the judicial representation of Parliament's intentions.

Let us turn to another juridical tool that appeals to the law's higher authority – the reasonable man in law. This is the natural person in law, an objective, authoritative structure in appearance. It is also a construct, interpreted and applied by the judge.

98 For example, see para 80 reference to: Hendricks v The Netherlands (1982) 5 EHRR 223; Andersson v Sweden (1992) 14 EHRR 615; Johansen v Norway (1996) 23 EHRR 33.

99 [2005] UKHL 15 p. 31.

100 [2002] H.R.L.R. 14 pp. 9–10.

For example, the approach of the Prison Adjudicator in Bashir[101] was adjudged to be unreasonable. According to Justice Pelling, the reasonable man would have given greater consideration to whether an Article 9 infringement had occurred. This proved that Article 9 rights were not engaged, interfered with or that the adjudicator's actions were justified.[102] In the creation of a legal test that represents social realities, the judge provides a 'doctrinal construction of reality'.[103] Pelling's 'reasonable adjudicator' is a constructed understanding of proper comportment, reliant upon the socio-legal rationale of its constructor. The interpretation in Bashir is presented as *the law's* reasonable adjudicator. This presents a dilemma, to accept either that the higher authority of law is spoken through the judge, or by the judge.

From the disguise of the neutralised and camouflaged reasonable man, we are given an insight into the judge's constitution of the social world (habitus) through their conception of reasonableness, apparently descriptive and representative, but in fact, 'constructivist and performative'[104] in sponsoring a particular legal argument. The interpretations of the judge are therefore formulated behind the objectivity of reasonableness, calling upon the authoritative and legitimating structure of the law's reasonable man, which in turn, creates a new legal test and precedent to be followed in the future. As such, social facts are collapsed and presented as linear as opposed to diverse and questionable. In this realm, the law is not spoken by the one judge but by the legal culture, and disagreement with judge-made law is not reasonable.

7. Conclusion

Jurisprudential literature has been mostly reluctant to accept subjectivities in the interpretation and application of legal arguments, except as a tangible factor constrained by judicial fidelity to legalistic filters. I have sought to unveil this absurdity not from a perspective that rejects correlation between a legal system's judgments but by concentrating on how the institutional image of judicial decision making is presented.

This chapter has encouraged a recognition of personal values and sought to develop our conception of how law is created. This considers the multitude of legal and non-legal considerations that construct a judgment and how normative content enters the law. It was necessary to critically analyse the promise of neutrality and render it an unattainable rhetorical device that evades the pervasive influence of subjectivities.

The concept of personal values illustrates the prescriptive and unavoidable relationship between an agent and their social normativity, and this, in turn, influences their comprehension

101 R (Bashir) v The Independent Adjudicator [2011] EWHC 1108. In Bashir a prisoner was charged with failing to obey a lawful order, to provide a urine sample (under the prison's mandatory drug testing policy) following reasonable suspicion of having taken a controlled substance, contrary to Rule 51(22) of the Prison Rules 1999. Bashir (a devout Muslim) was fasting as part of religious preparation before his Court of Appeal appearance. While the Prison Service Order PSO 3601 allows prisoners to be excused from testing during 'religious festivals which involve total fasting,' the claimant's fast was not seen by the prison adjudicator to fall under the religious festival exception. In a hearing before the Adjudicator the claimant was convicted and imposed a penalty of 14 days' additional detention. The claimant challenged his conviction on the basis it was wrong in law, perverse, and requiring a sample was contrary to Article 9 of the European Convention on Human Rights.

102 [2011] EWHC 1108 (Admin) p. 7.

103 Broekman (1994) p. 187.

104 ibid.

of socio-legal conflicts. While this may not be determinant upon the final decision, submission to personal values impels the defence or promotion of certain argumentation, meaning subsequent judicial representations of a case are underlain by subjective influence. I have encouraged an alternative reading of judgments in an attempt to ameliorate an understanding of the constitutive parts of judicial decision-making. In particular, the non-legal influences that affect interpretative practice and law-making.

The threat to this conception of adjudication is the response that follows recognition of subjective influences. There will be a temptation to devise new judicial practices hoping to eradicate subjectivities; the message from this chapter is of unavoidability and the necessity of acceptance. Otherwise, we regress into a formalistic idea of law detached from social norms. Of course, this cuts against and mitigates the symbolic force of traditional conceptions in favour of an adjudication theory opposed to performative epistemic constructions. Indeed, rather than struggling against realist conceptions of judicial adjudication, the preferable step is renewed concern for the manner that the judicial institution inscribes social normativity into law.

Bibliography

Alexy, R. Justification and Application of Norms. *Ratio Juris*, Vol. 6(2) 1993 pp. 157–70.

Alexy, R. Discourse Theory and Human Rights. *Ratio Juris*, Vol. 9(3) 1996 pp. 209–35.

Ball-Rokeach, S.J., Rokeach, M., and Grube, J.W. The Great American Values Test: Influencing Behavior and Belief Through Television. *Social Forces*, Vol. 65(2) 1986 pp. 571–3.

Borges, J.L. Kafka and His Precursors, in Labyrinths. *Penguin Modern Classics* 2000 (1962).

Bourdieu, P. *Outline of a Theory in Practice*. Cambridge University Press 1977.

Bourdieu, P. The Force of Law: Toward a Sociology of the Juridical Field. *Hastings Law Review*, Vol. 38(5) 1986.

Bourdieu, P. *In Other Words: Essays Towards a Reflexive Sociology*. Polity Press 1990.

Bourdieu, P. *Practical Reason*. Polity Press 1998 (1994).

Bourdieu, P. and Eagleton, T. *In Conversation: Doxa and Common Life. Transcript from Talking Ideas Series Bourdieu and Eagleton*, Institute of Contemporary Arts, London 15 May 1991.

Bourdieu, P. and Wacquant, L. *An Invitation to Reflexive Sociology*. The University of Chicago Press, Chicago 1992.

Bourdieu, P. and Wacquant, L. On the Cunning of Imperialist Reason. *Theory Culture Society*, Vol. 16(41) 1999.

Broekman, J.M. *Legal Discourse and Legal Facts in EYSL European Yearbook in the Sociology of Law 1993*. Edited by Febbrajo, A. and Nelken, D. Guiffre, 1994 pp. 181–200.

Cahill-O'Callaghan, R. The Influence of Personal Values on Legal Judgments. *Journal of Law and Society*, Vol. 40(4) 2013 pp. 596–623.

Cardozo, B. *The Nature of the Judicial Process*. Yale University Press 1921.

Clark, C.E. and Trubeck, D.M. *The Creative Role of the Judge: Restraint and Freedom in the Common Law Tradition*. 71 Yale L.J. 255 1961–1962.

Cover, R. The Supreme Court 1982 Term. Foreword: Nomos and Narrative. 97 *Harvard Law Review*, Vol. 4 1983–1984.

Cowan, D., Blandy, S., Hunter, C., and Nixon J. District Judges and Possession Proceedings. *Journal of Law and Society*, Vol. 33(4) 2006 pp. 547–71.

Cownie, F. *English Legal System in Context*, (3rd edn). Lexis Nexis Butterworths 2003.

Dworkin, R. Hard Cases. *Harvard Law Review*, Vol. 88(6) 1975.

Dworkin, R. Law as Interpretation. *Texas Law Review*, Vol. 60(2) 1982 p. 527.

Dworkin, R. *Law's Empire*. Harvard University Press 1986.

Dworkin, R. *Taking Rights Seriously*. Harvard University Press 1986.

Dworkin, R. *Justice in Robes*. The Belknap Press of Harvard University Press 2006.

Dworkin, R. *Justice for Hedgehogs*. The Belknap Press of Harvard University Press 2011.
Dyzenhaus, D. The Very Idea of a Judge. *University of Toronto Law Journal*, Vol. 60 2010, pp. 61–80.
Dyzenhaus, D. Are Legislatures Good at Morality? Or Better at it than Courts? *International Journal of Constitutional Law*, Vol. 46 2009, pp. 46–52.
Foblets, M.C. and Renteln, A.D. *Multicultural Jurisprudence: Comparative Perspectives on the Cultural Defense*. Hart Publishing 2009.
Freeman, M.D.A. *Introduction to Jurisprudence*, (8th edn). Sweet and Maxwell 2008.
Friedman, L. *Judging the Judges: Some Remarks on the Way Judges Think and the Way Judges Act, in Norms and the Law*, Edited by J.N. Droback. Cambridge University Press 2006.
Garcia-Villegas, M. Comparative Sociology of Law: Legal Fields, Legal Scholarships, and Social Sciences in Europe and United States. *Law and Social Inquiry*, Vol. 31(2) 2006.
Hanretty, C. The Decisions and Ideal Points of British Law Lords. *British Journal of Political Science*, Vol. 43(3) 2013 pp. 703–16.
Herman, D. 'I Do Not Attach Great Significance To It': Taking Account Of 'The Holocaust' In English Case Law. *Social and Legal Studies*, Vol. 17 2008 p. 427.
Jivraj, S. and Herman, D. "It's Difficult for a White Judge to Understand": Orientalism, Racialisation and Christianity in English Child Welfare Cases. *Child and Family Law Quarterly*, Vol. 21(3) 2009 pp. 283–308.
Knights, S. Approaches to Diversity in the Domestic Courts: Article 9 of the European Convention on Human Rights. *Ch.15 in Legal Practice and Cultural Diversity, Edited by Ralph Grillo, Roger Ballard, Alessandro Ferrari, André Hoekema, Marcel Maussen, Prakash Shah*. Ashgate 2009.
Latour, B. *The Making of Law: An Ethnography of the Conseil D'État*. Polity Press 2010.
Latour, B. *An Inquiry into Modes of Existence*. Harvard University Press, Cambridge 2013.
Leiter, B. *Objectivity, Morality and Adjudication in, Objectivity in Law and Morals*. Cambridge University Press 2001.
Llewellyn, K.N. *The Common Law Tradition: Deciding Appeals*. Little Brown and Company, Boston; Toronto 1960.
Mayton, D.M. II, Ball-Rokeach, S.J., and Loges, W. Human Values and Social Issues: An Introduction. *Journal of Social Issues*, Vol. 50(4) 1994, pp. 1–8.
Motha, S. Veiled Women and the Affect of Religion in Democracy. *Journal of Law and Society*, Vol. 34(1) 2007 pp. 139–62.
Posner, R.A. The Decline of Law as an Autonomous Discipline: 1962–1987. *Harvard Law Review*, Vol. 100(4) 1987, pp. 761–80.
Posner, R.A. *Reflexions on Judging*. Harvard University Press 2013.
Sandberg, R. The Changing Position of Religious Minorities in English Law: The Legacy of Begum. *Ch.14 in Legal Practice and Cultural Diversity, Edited by Ralph Grillo, Roger Ballard, Alessandro Ferrari, André Hoekema, Marcel Maussen, and Prakash Shah*. Ashgate 2009.
Sandberg, R. The Adventures of Religious Freedom: Do Judges Understand Religion? Senior Lecturer at Cardiff University – Working Paper presented at Keele University 2012.
Sarat, A. Off to Meet the Wizard: Beyond Validity and Reliability in the Search for a Post Empiricist Sociology of Law. *Law and Social Inquiry*, Vol. 15(1) 1990, pp. 155–70.
Twining, W. *Karl Llewellyn and the Realist Movement* (2nd edn). Cambridge University Press 2012.
Twining, W. Legal R/realism as Legal Theory: Ten Theses, in S. MacAuley and E. Mertz (eds.) *New Legal Realism: Translating Law and Society for Today's Legal Practice*. Cambridge: Cambridge University Press, 2014, pp. 121–46.
Unger, R. The Critical Legal Studies Movement. *Harvard Law Review*, Vol. 96(3) 1983 pp. 561–675.
Waldron, J. *How Judges Should Judge*. The New York Review of Books. August 10, 2006.
Waldron, J. *Unfettered Judge Posner*, The New York Review of Books. March 20, 2014.
Weiler, J. Lautsi: Crucifix in the Classroom Redux. *EJIL Editorial*, Vol. 21(1) 2010. http://www.ejiltalk.org/lautsi-crucifix-in-the-classroom-redux/ last accessed 09/07/2014.
Weiler J. Lautsi: A Reply. *International Journal of Constitutional Law*, Vol. 11(1) 2013 pp. 230–33.

Cases - Empirical Analysis

Regina (Williamson and others) v Secretary of State for Education and Employment [2002] EWCA 1926.
Regina (Williamson and others) v Secretary of State for Education and Employment [2005] UKHL 15.
Regina (SB) v Governors of Denbigh High School [2006] UKHL 15.
R (on the Application of Begum) v The Head Teacher and Governors of Denbigh High School [2004] EWHC 1389 (Admin).
R (SB) v Governors of Denbigh High School EWCA Civ 199 [2005].
R (Bashir) v The Independent Adjudicator [2011] EWHC 1108 (Admin).
Williamson v Secretary of State for Education and Employment [2005] H.R.L.R. 14.

9 The leaking law[1]

Karl Dahlstrand

1. Introduction

This chapter starts with the question of how damages for violation through crime are determined by law. Compensation for criminal injuries is the predominant type of non-pecuniary damages in Swedish tort law. Yet, a fundamental uncertainty exists regarding computation of damages and the legal meaning of 'violation'. The general consensus in the legal profession is that norms for computation of damages for compensation of violation are lacking and that the violation and the financial compensation are incommensurable. The analysis and results of my empirical study show several central dichotomies between formal and informal norms and between the internal and external view of law.

But this is not simply meant as a critique to show a 'gap problem' or a disconnect between 'law in books and law in action'. Rather, I want to illustrate that what can be described as 'leaking law' is a central dimension of a normative system that deals with values, language and the application of general rules through interpretation in a certain context. Accordingly, the question here is *how* the law leaks rather than *whether* it does and, further, if in the eyes of legislators estimating such compensation *should* leak. These aspects raise questions regarding the law's limits or boundaries and inflow to the legal system. My theoretical approach is inspired by analytical jurisprudence and analytical philosophy expressed by questions like 'what is the law?' and 'what is the relationship between law and its context?'. And finally, I will detail later in this chapter with what is meant by 'leaking' and why it is relevant to compensation for violation of personal integrity.

2. Social networking and digital culture

The concept of the Web 2.0 builds on the Internet and the use of modern communication technology being more iterative. Social networking sites like Facebook and Twitter (what we know as *social media*) have brought user-generated content (UGC) into a new social arena for economic, legal, social and political relevance (Byron et al., 2013; Christofides et al., 2012; Freis and Gurung, 2013; Heath, 2012; Hur and Gupta, 2013; Kwan and Skoric, 2013; Mainiero and Jones, 2013; Pedersen, 2013; Visser et al., 2012). From a legal perspective as well, the increase in UGC has become the centre of attention in recent years. This manifests in the increased interest in web-related crimes, including hate speech, defamatory or insulting communication, and communication that incites discrimination (Flowers et al., 2013; Låftman et al., 2013; Mohamed, 2013; Negre and D. V. Go III, 2013;

1 Thanks to Deane Goltermann, John Woodlock and Johan Rosquist for reading and valuable comments.

Perry and Olsson, 2009; Soudijn and Zegers, 2012). I describe here how the Swedish legal system has handled occurrences of cyber hate, and why this branch of law is of interest from the perspective of the sociology of law considering informal norms in relation to formal, or legal, norms (Baier, 2013).[2] The structural coupling between the systems of law and the social and technical environment becomes all the more interesting from a sociology of law perspective when a society becomes more differentiated and complex. But the point here is not the general challenge to structural coupling and internal representations of the environment, rather that the need for empirical knowledge of social norms increases in relation to legal policy for compensation of criminal injuries and compensation for violation of personal integrity (Dahlstrand, 2012).

The Internet is closely associated with the ability to communicate our culture and share knowledge, thereby making it a vital component in an open society and freedom of speech. This complicates the issue of restrictions to the Internet (Collins, 2010). The legal issue deals with the question of the limits and boundaries imposed on individual freedom and responsibility by state-governed law. The issue also has a more practical dimension related to how to provide legal security on the Internet with respect to the economic and legal constraints of individual nation states (Citron, 2009; Citron and Norton, 2011; Guichard, 2009; Karniel, 2009; Lessig, 1999; Schultz et al., 2013). From a historical Swedish perspective, increasing numbers of crime categories have been transferred from private litigation to public prosecution (Lernestedt and Tham, 2011).

In Swedish law, only defamation still falls under private litigation, although the number of situations where the prosecutor may prosecute has increased (Wennberg, 2009). Growing numbers of reported crimes concerning defamation in addition to a greater focus on online hate crime and hate speech has led to renewed interest in criminal and social policy relating to the judicial system's ability to handle these types of crimes.[3] In an attempt to meet the problem of proliferating crime reports, the ability to prosecute for defamation has been increased, as the availability of criminal proceedings for defamation and insult were expanded 1 July 2014. In its bill, the government stated:

> The change means removing the requirement of the Penal Code on special grounds for criminal action for defamation and insult. This means that the public prosecutor and the attorney general will in future be able to assist an individual who has been slandered on the Internet. The effect of this amendment will be that individuals will enjoy a stronger procedural position in defamation cases and an increased protection of personal integrity. The general rule is still, however, that the victim of defamation or insult must make a private claim.
>
> (Government Act 2013/14:47)

In addition, the possibility to receive criminal injuries compensation for crimes of defamation and illegal violation of integrity has recently been introduced in Sweden (Government Act 2016/17:222). Accordingly, new technologies and ways to communicate with each

2 The topic of this text is based on the research project "Kränkningar i en digital kontext" (Violations in a digital context), conducted together with docent Måns Svensson at *The Sociology of Law Department* and *Lund University Internet Institute* (LUii) at Lund University.

3 According to official statistics from The Swedish National Council for Crime Prevention (Brå), seven criminal defamation crimes were reported per 100.000 population in Sweden in 1975, and 133 criminal defamation crimes were reported per 100.000 population in Sweden in 2013 – an increase of 19 times.

other have, in a sense, raised the historically and social-scientifically interesting question of where the boundary lies between public and private in relation to legal measures against defamation. And, is there additionally anything more that raises interest in defamation cases, and the judicial system handling of these types of crimes from a sociology of law perspective? And how is this related to the law as a closed or 'leaking' system?

3. How to compensate the irreplaceable?

The past several decades have seen a growing awareness of such concepts as legal pluralism (though the phenomenon 'pluralism' is, naturally, nothing new in the legal field) and the ways in which various informal dimensions of a formal system, such as law, play an important role. The predominant description of the law during what we call the modern era, especially in a country like Sweden, favours a closed jurisprudence focused on legal provisions. This focus on formal legal rules as the predominant source of law made the court and legal usage less important as a dynamic factor in the legal field. Some refer to a legal pluralist world as "the black hole for modern legal positivism" (Zamboni, 2013). Globalisation and greater social and cultural differentiation, as seen in phenomena such as non-state and multiple identities (Banakar and Travers, 2013), are all closely linked to the use of social media, and will, unavoidably, affect the assessment of specific areas of law.

We can also compare with Lon Fuller and his interactionist social theory in contrast to a view of law as a 'one-way projection of authority', while, on the other hand, an interactional view of law reveals that it is a co-operative enterprise between legislator and citizen, each with reciprocal expectations and each with a role conceived in terms of what the law is (Harris, 1997). Often, such descriptions of the legal system and the legal field are made on a general macro-level, without any reference to a concrete branch of law or rule of law.

For this chapter, I will focus on how compensation for violations that have attracted attention through social media *and* UGC, such as defamation or invasion of privacy, challenges traditional views on how law can be seen as a more or less 'closed' normative system – as it is seen within legal formalism. Given this challenge, sociology of law can contribute with important fresh insights of the social dimensions within which these violations are currently understood (Dahlstrand, 2011). Methods used in traditional legal dogmatism cannot provide the necessary knowledge of the law as a set of social practices or as an aspect or field of social experience (Banakar, 2009; Hydén, 2011). However, of central importance here is that the need for this kind of understanding not only has theoretical interest or is linked to research in sociology of law as a single discipline but is also of practical relevance to the application of law (Dahlstrand, 2012; Dahlstrand, 2013). To understand this practical relevance clearly, a closer description of the current legal area is appropriate.

For instance, the fact that the tort liability provision in the Swedish Tort Liability Act (SkL), Chapter 2, section 3, states that "[A] person who seriously violates another person by committing a crime involving an assault on their person, liberty, peace or honour, shall compensate the damage the violation involves". Liability for damages is thus linked to certain types of criminal acts, and there is a close link between criminal law and tort law, particularly when it comes to defamation. For the compensation to constitute a form of redress to the individual and/or some kind of private law 'punishment', or punishment of the individual who is guilty of the offence, knowledge of the social context where these actions take place is of great interest. So how should compensation for violation through crime be determined, for it to provide a form of redress for the individual's emotions (such as fear, shame and degradation)?

Swedish legislators chose, in these cases, to mandate the person applying tort law to make a discretionary estimate that corresponds to 'prevalent ethical and social values' (Government Act 2000/01:68, p. 51–52, 74). This wording relates back to an understanding that norms connected to how compensation for violations or other types of non-financial damages should be determined are not present (Govt. Act 1972:5, p. 121; SOU 1992:84, p. 133; SOU 1995:33, p. 320; precedent legal case NJA 1991, p. 766; Ekstedt, 1977, p. 91–92). Therefore, the aim is to simultaneously (1) provide complete redress to the victim and (2) ensure that estimation of the compensation amount shall be based on and guided by objective factors (Government Act 1975:12, p. 111; Ekstedt, 1977, p. 90; Government Act 2000/01:68, p. 51).

By tradition, Swedish tort law adopts an ambivalent attitude towards this type of compensation due to the various uncertainty factors that constrain traditional principles and dichotomies in (tort) law. But, as we have seen, this type of compensation plays an important role in the types of violations receiving greater attention due to the widespread use of social media. It is therefore of great interest to study and understand the nature of these damages.

The principal rule of Swedish tort law is that only economic damages can be compensated (Government Act 2000/01:68, p. 17). This perspective has also been reflected in a guiding ruling from the Supreme Court of Sweden, stating: "Swedish law has traditionally adopted a restrictive attitude towards the possibility of imposing entirely non-financial damages based on a violation of somebody's rights or interest" (NJA 2005, p. 462). As a consequence of both the ambivalent attitude towards these types of damages for violation and, the increased attention to this type of compensation, the question of what really constitutes a violation is highly relevant (Dahlstrand, 2013). Is it the illegal or unlawful act, the personal responsibility of the offender, or perhaps the offended person's experience of being violated? It is also vital to consider "what is the ground for damages for violation through crime – *compensation* for a *damage* or a *penalty* for an *offence*"? (Friberg, 2010, p. 927).

Above, I have focused mainly on the widespread use of social media and the increased number of crimes reported concerning defamatory data online. In this light, it is necessary to understand why compensation for violations has reached such importance in legal policy, and to consider the broader picture of higher ambitions to support victims of crimes *and* the legal recognition of discrimination and other violations of human rights and freedoms in society (Diesen et al, 2005; Lernestedt and Tham, 2011).

Still, the difficulties involved in estimating the extent of the violation and awarding redress to the victim through compensation are not isolated phenomena in Swedish law, but involve the general problem known as incommensurability (lacking a common ground from which to make a comparison). Interpretation between different scientific theories or ontological ideas can be impossible, challenging the idea of both the accumulation of scientific knowledge over time and the existence of a neutral language of comparison that can be used to formulate the empirical consequences of competing theories (Feyerabend, 1962; Kuhn, 1962). The problem of incommensurability is also described in legal science, particularly with respect to social and cultural differentiation in relation to evaluation and comparability in law (Sunstein, 1994). M. Jane Radin exemplified the incommensurability problem concretely with respect to compensation, saying: "When someone who has lost an arm in an accident receives $100.000 in compensation through the tort system, what does this transaction mean? Is this that an arm is 'worth' $100.000"? (Radin, 1993–94, p. 56). As described below, the task of evaluating, or estimating, a non-economic damage in money is of great practical and theoretical relevance.

4. An internal view of social rules

The purpose of compensation for violation is to achieve satisfaction for the victim, but there is still the problem of incommensurability between the violation/harm and the task of estimating the reimbursement due for damages. Application of law requires some form of interpretation of social norms (if the determination and the amount are to function as described and not result in a secondary victimisation), as is described within the legislative preparatory work for the act (Government Act 1975:5, p. 121).

The traditional positivist legal view of law requires some kind of 'separation thesis' between law and other normative sources (such as morality) when it comes to legal validity. But in modern legal positivism, a school of thought – Inclusive Legal Positivism – endorses the social thesis in legal positivism and, therefore, would not subscribe to the formulation of the separation thesis. Instead, this school of thought argues that social conventions (or other social sources) can be of relevance when it comes to defining what law is – particularly in the application of law (Coleman, 2001).

Debate has arisen regarding the distinction between hard and soft legal positivism (or inclusive positivism), especially concerning the legal function of providing authoritative and normative guidance about how people should behave and how the law can make a practical difference (the practical difference thesis) (Coleman, 2001; Leiter, 2001). When it comes to the case for compensation for violation, the situation is not that there is any question about validity according to the law, but whether and how this kind of compensation is accepted by the legal profession (that is, the difficulties to evaluate and replace these injuries) – what Hart calls 'the rule of recognition'. H. L. A. Hart (1997, 92) describes law as a system of (social) rules and quotes the rule of recognition "which is in effect a form of judicial customary rule existing only if it is accepted and practised in the law-identifying and law-applying operations of the courts" (Hart, 1997, p. 256).

The question is therefore whether the difficulties arising from this subjective and symbolic form of compensation have the consequence that, even though the victim has the right to compensation according to the law, the practical possibility to obtain satisfaction or redress is limited. A concrete example illustrating this issue is a Swedish Court of Appeal case (Case N° T 107–13) that has attracted much attention. A person who was found guilty of aggravated defamation on the Internet against his ex-girlfriend was ordered by the district court to pay damages of SEK 130.000 but the Court of Appeal reduced this to SEK 25.000.

Explaining this steep reduction, the court stated in their findings that people in contemporary society are in general much more liberal about sexuality and privacy on the Internet, or, as the court put it, "in significant portions of society, it has, over time, become more socially acceptable to be very open and outgoing regarding sexual habits". Both the formulation in the court's findings and the dramatic reduction in damages itself were heavily criticised as they conflicted with the growing attention to the societal and legal problems of cyber bullying and other crimes concerning invasion of privacy on the Internet.

This practical example also shows how compensation challenges traditional concepts, such as the distinction between the internal/external view and its relation to law. It is impossible for those responsible for enforcing this law to maintain its purpose without accounting for relevant social scientific knowledge. On the other hand, the critical and reflective reactions of the general public in relation to the court's action show that people do not 'formally' have a normative internal relation to the stance adopted by the current legal rules about some kind of internal point of view in relation to the law.

To summarise, through a perspective influenced by Hart, the 'open texture' and penumbral area of the uncertainty of legal rules, the view that all rules are 'social', and what MacCormick (1981) has described as a 'hermeneutic' understanding, that legal actions and institutions can be understood only by interpreting the meaning they have for those directly engaged, has the greatest relevance. Understanding the violation, and then the compensation, which is meant to function as satisfaction or redress for the victim, calls for knowledge of an internal perspective of the actual legal field, which can only follow from experience in a social practice where these concepts (constituting the violation) are used and attain their social meaning.

This view is inspired by analytical philosophy and Hart's linguistic empiricism (Cotterrell, 1989). One criticism of the theory Hart presents in *The Concept of Law* (1961) is that there is a 'sociological drift' in Hart's normative legal theory (Cotterrell, 1989), and his combination of the descriptive-explanatory method and addressing the philosophical problem of the normativity of law "is an unsatisfactory hybrid" (Perry, 2001). Therefore, Hart's concepts and description must be interpreted carefully, especially from a sociology of law perspective, and be seen more as a preliminary hypothesis than as empirically verified, or dogmatic concepts bearing the stamp of scientific truth. Still, there is a clear relationship between analytical jurisprudence and sociology of law in the ambition to study legal concepts and the view of language as a means for understanding social reality as practice (Galligan, 2007).

Moreover, perhaps as a consequence of the interdisciplinary potential in his theory, interest in Hart has increased – or, as Wacks puts it in his textbook on legal theory: "Recent years have witnessed an explosion in the development and refinement of many of the ideas originally conceived, in particular, by H. L. A. Hart. With its preoccupation with semantic and conceptual analysis, the source of authority, and objective reality, what was once considered to be rather conservative, dreary, and narrow has become sexy. In modern legal theory circles, it would seem that, in the words of the pop anthem of the nerd, 'it's hip to be square'" (Wacks, 2012, p. 77). Hart, as one of the most well-known modern legal positivists, can therefore function as a 'link' between jurisprudence and social science or other disciplines like psychology, philosophy and semantics. This is especially true in the case of the legal field and legal application, where the social dimension of actual rules has significant relevance, as when a victim has the legal right to compensation and the compensation is symbolic, since it is in these non-pecuniary damages that compensation for the damage caused by the offender is sought (Dahlstrand, 2012; Dahlstrand, 2013). And an understanding of what the rules mean from an 'internal perspective' is of particular importance. This perspective is also an echo from Max Weber. Hart was probably inspired by Weber's views on how understanding social action requires knowledge ('Verstehen') of its meaning, purpose and intention among individuals (Galligan, 2007).[4]

5. The 'leaking law'

That H. L. A. Hart was influenced by the contemporary ordinary language philosophy of Oxford represented by the work of J. L. Austin, Peter Winch, Peter Frederick Strawson,

4 Compare with Weber's famous description of sociology and social action: "...a science which attempts the interpretive understanding of social action in order thereby to arrive at a causal explanation of its course and effects. In 'action' is included all human behaviour when and insofar as the acting individual attaches a subjective meaning to it". Weber, 1947, p. 88

Friedrich Waismann and Ludwig Wittgenstein (Lacey, 2004; Lefebvre, 2011; Stavropoulos, 2001) is clear from formulations such as:

> there is no familiar well-understood general category of which law is a member. The most obvious candidate for use in this way in a definition of law is the general family of *rules of behaviour*; yet the concept of a rule as we have seen is as perplexing as that of law itself, so that definitions of law that start by identifying laws as a species of rules usually advance our understanding of law no further.
>
> (Hart, 1997, p. 15)

Hart wants the reader, with the help of a reference to J. L. Austin, to look not only at the words "but also at the realities we use words to talk about" (Hart, 1997, p. 14). He further urges readers to sharpen their consciousness in "the borderline cases where legal theorists have felt doubts about the application of the expression 'law' or 'legal system'" (Hart, 1997, p. 17). In my opinion, the main theme of *The Concept of Law* (1961) is Hart's description of the internal aspect of rules – what is meant by having an obligation (because it is something different from being forced) – and how obligation is connected to 'the maintenance of social life' and the 'social pressure behind the rules' (Hart, 1997, p. 87). This theme and standpoint can be related to the idea of rule-following behaviour and 'private language argument' as presented by Wittgenstein. The 'private language argument' is a paradox described by Wittgenstein as:

> no course of action could be determined by a rule, because every course of action can be made out to accord with the rule. The answer was: if everything can be made out to accord with the rule, then it can also be made out to conflict with it. And there would be neither accord nor conflict here. (...) So, following a rule is a practice. And, furthermore, since one can think one is following a rule and yet be mistaken, *thinking* one is following a rule is not the same as following it. Therefore, following a rule cannot be a private activity.
>
> (Wittgenstein, 1953 § 201–202)

Thus, following a rule (and for Wittgenstein, language use is a form of rule-following) concerns a social phenomenon as a practice. Interestingly, Hart writes that "[t]he rule of recognition exists only as a complex, but normally concordant, practice of the courts, officials, and private persons in identifying the law by reference to certain criteria. Its existence is a matter of fact" (Hart, 1997, p. 110). Even if primary rules are central to law (as with penal law) governing right and wrong behaviour, secondary rules, such as the rule of recognition, is in a sense 'parasitic' to the primary one, meaning that the rule of recognition raises a question about legal culture and identity that goes beyond the narrow understanding of law in legal positivism.

This raises the question of what the complex operation is whereby the law becomes a part of the existing legal system. Gunther Teubner states:

> The best-known example of legal self-description is Hart's idea of 'secondary rules'. According to Hart, we can speak of law only if the primary rules of conduct are overlaid and regulated by secondary rules of identification and procedure. For Hart, 'the heart of a legal system ... [is] the structure which has resulted from the combination of primary rules of obligation with the secondary rules of recognition, change and adjudication'.
>
> (Teubner, 1993, p. 39)

Teubner describes how legal autonomy develops in three phases, stating that Hart's rule of recognition describes the critical moment when 'partially autonomous law' becomes 'autopoietic law'.[5]

Hart claims that legal formalism is fundamentally mistaken, and theories of law and rules must be understood as social phenomena – rules cannot provide for their own interpretation, "nor can the rule itself step forward to claim its own instances" (Hart, 1997, p. 126). Rudolf von Jhering (1818–1892) claimed early that not even lawyers know the law, (Jhering, 1906) because it is a practical thing that you learn by doing (more art than science, so to speak) (Samuelsson, 2011). Jhering's criticism of his contemporaries' 'Begriffsjurisprudenz' is famous and his teleological legal theory lays the groundwork for the fathers of classical sociology of law, such as Eugen Ehrlich (1862–1922) and Roscoe Pound (1870–1922) (Banakar and Travers, 2013; Modéer, 2009). Hart has even written an article about the link between Jhering, Wittgenstein and Austin, illustrating how they emphasize our attention on reality experienced beyond our conceptions ("Suppose I come across a being that looks like a man, speaks like a man, behaves like a man, and is only one foot tall, shall I say it is a man"?) (Hart, 1983, p. 275).

Wittgenstein's description of the impossibility of private language and rule-following behaviour in his *Philosophical Investigations* (1953) challenges our assumptions about the normativity of rules, because between a rule and its correct application, a gap will always arise. Hence, the rule manifests itself through regular practice (Björkholm, 1997). These ways of thinking break with the traditional view of law as hierarchical, replacing it with an emphasis on horizontal coherence relations of language-games. Aulis Aarnio explains the implications for legal issues as,

> in legal dogmatic reasoning (as a discourse), the notions of world view and form of life have their manifestation in the concept of audience. Through that, the discussions about certainty and the form of life are connected to all that can be said about one correct decision, acceptability and the s.c. majority principle in the theory of legal argumentation.
>
> (Aarnio, 1997, p. 126)

This may seem somewhat indigestible, but Aarnio also commented on this:

> [i]t would be rather naïve to defend the primacy of *Lebenswelt* as the genuine basis of legitimacy. Legal order is a power order and applying law is using this power. This is the reason why the law is – at the same time – 'a citizen of two different worlds'. It is a formal tool to organize social life in a predictable way, but the legitimacy of law (or legal interpretations/decisions) is dependent on linguistic communication and mutual understanding that results in that communication. If for instance the court decisions only follow (blindly) the letter of the law and represent a different value system than the majority of society, people do not trust in decision making any more. (…) [t]he lack of the trust in courts may, by and by, lead to a deep crisis in that society if the courts do not begin to take into account the demands growing up in the *Lebenswelt*.
>
> (Aarnio, 1987, p. 235)

5 See Teubner, 1993, p. 37.

After the above theoretical excursus, I intend to demonstrate in this section the relevance of current theories in analytical philosophy and analytical jurisprudence. Simply put, to fulfil the aim of compensation, the application of the law cannot be of a 'private nature'. That is, the estimation must be intersubjective and reflect the 'form of life' close to the violation and the victim. Civil law is naturally closer to the parties than public law, but in the Swedish legal system, basically all compensation for violations of personal integrity is paid as a part of the criminal injuries compensation by the *Crime Victim Compensation and Support Authority* and decided by the *Criminal Injuries Compensation Board.* The uncertainty related to estimation of violations, and in an effort to attain an effective and predictable reimbursement system, the broad discretion legislated for the authority when applying the law for this compensation may also have exerted influence leading to a more or less 'scant' or restrictive attitude. This, in turn, has resulted in applications of the law that bears the stamp of far-reaching standardisation.

Here, 'leaking law' refers to how compensation for violation through crime should be determined in order for it to provide some redress for the individual's emotions (their fear, shame and degradation). The legislator has chosen to give a mandate to the person applying tort law in these cases to make a discretionary estimate in relation to "prevalent ethical and social values" (Government Act 2000/01:68, p. 51–52, 74). This wording goes back to an understanding of the lack of norms for how compensation for violation and other types of non-financial damages should be determined (Government Act 1972:5: 121). This means that compensation of this kind challenges the law's predictability. The situation can therefore be related to Lon Fuller's principles of legality, and in particular, the failure of congruence between the rules as announced and their actual administration (Fuller, 1964).

6. Not a definition – but a description of law

The attentive reader may now be thinking that if incommensurability exists between the violation and the respective compensation, then surely this incurs that all assessment reflects in some way a 'private' application of the rule. And, if so, then what is the problem? Determining the practical, or actual effect of such assessment, though, is an empirical question related to how individuals assess the violation, or more correctly, how they follow the rule – 'assess violation x so that compensation y gives the offender redress'. Given the incommensurability thesis (Schultz, 2008), response values will show a wide dispersion, or a large non-response for this type of question. To determine how this is, 'really', we conducted two surveys in my PhD project at the Sociology of Law Department at Lund University, which included respondents who had been violated through a crime and received compensation for this violation of personal integrity (N. 300), and a simple random sample of Swedish citizens (N. 1100) (Dahlstrand, 2012). The results show that the respondents surprisingly managed to resolve the task and jointly formed a clear response pattern (Table 9.1):

Table 9.1 Estimation of crime types in legal practice according to two surveys (in SEK)

	Legal precedent	*The public (type value)*	*The public (median)*	*Victims of crime (type value)*	*Victims of crime (median)*
Maltreatment	15.000	50.000	50.000	50.000	50.000
Rape	75.000	100.000	100.000	100.000	100.000
Robbery	10.000	50.000	60.000	50.000	50.000
Sexual harassment	10.000	50.000	50.000	50.000	50.000
Attempted manslaughter	60.000	100.000	120.000	100.000	150.000
Assault	15.000	100.000	75.000	50.000	50.000

The table illustrates that respondents select higher values than what is actually awarded (cf. 'Legal precedent' in the first column reflects amounts actually awarded as reported in the *Review of the Crime Victim Compensation and Support Authority*). Most interesting is the awareness shown by respondents. The two questionnaires were designed as a short vignette where respondents were given a description of an actual case described in the review published by the *Crime Victim Compensation and Support Authority.* They also received minimal background information about the actual criminal injuries and the purpose of compensation for violation of personal integrity.

That the difference between the two respondent groups was relatively small also indicates an interesting aspect about how stable the sense of justice is, in relation to this kind of compensation. Respondents were completely free to choose the amount (in SEK). On an individual level, there were some respondents who chose everything from '0 SEK' to 'SEK 10.000.000'. When the values were calculated as the mean scores, there was also a common feature that the amount increased gradually.

For example, the mean value for 'Rape' was SEK 389.000 in the 'public' respondent group and SEK 209.057 for the same crime in the 'victims of crime' group. For several of the crime types, it is statistically impossible to show any difference between the two groups of respondents (the Mann-Whitney U test gives significance levels as $p = .52$, $p = .55$ and $p = .79$) (Dahlstrand, 2012). This raises the question of when are legal practitioners following a rule in a private way? Is it when they find the answer, as in this case, according to a review from the authority, or when they do it as a private person – and probably act and reason according to social practice and customs as a member of society? (Kripke, 1982)

Even though the consistent survey results were somewhat surprising, a theoretical explanation can be posited as to why the incommensurability thesis can be falsified. Namely, that although a common-sense perspective leads us to believe it must somehow be connected to incommensurability between the compensation and the violation of personal integrity. It is the vagueness relating to the assessment of alternatives that makes it impossible to prove incommensurability. Wlodek Rabinowicz has called this 'the Small-Improvement Argument' in his statement;

> The introduction of x^{-+} does not allow us to definitely rule out the possibility of x and y being equally good, as long as we cannot definitely establish that x^{+-} is not better than y. The following are mutually compatible claims: (i) It is indeterminate whether x is equally as good as y. (ii) It is determinate that x^{+-} is better than x. (iii) It is indeterminate whether x^{+-} is better than y.
>
> (Rabinowicz, 2009, p. 73 f)

The epistemic objection and the vagueness objection make it difficult to argue conclusively, in specific instances, that a case under consideration is indeed an instance of incommensurability, as Rabinowicz describes the situation (Rabinowicz, 2009). Though, compensation for violation of personal integrity will be a contested concept in every case (Radin, 1993) and will be distinguished by vagueness even if this does not mean the same as it did when the incommensurability was taken for granted as a consequence of the vagueness.

As described above, the respondents were not attuned or in agreement on an individual level, even if the table above perhaps gives that impression. And that the respondents often choose regular and round sums such as '50.000 SEK' says more about the social and economic unit of measurement in our society than about a specific violation. However, it is as close as we can get to how people assess a violation compared to the legal application.

Aarnio has described incommensurability and interpretations in relation to Wittgenstein's concept of 'form of life' in a relevant and interesting way:

> The rational argumentation concerning evaluations will not prove to be useless although the ultimate differences in opinion are based on non-rational criteria. On the other hand, the incommensurability of two interpretations does not mean that there are only two or, in each case, a very limited number of interpretations for the common meaning. On the contrary, there is a whole net of such interpretations valid at the same time. An individual may belong to more than one interpretation depending on the life situations. (...) From a slightly different point of view one can say that the concept of form of life and of common meaning consists of an enormous net of fragments and that a certain individual may participate in some but not necessarily in every one of them. In saying this, however, we leave the concept of the form of life itself open.
>
> (Aarnio, 1987, p. 213)

7. Concluding remarks

'The leaking law' as a theoretical concept is a result of the inductive approach and tries to show how the legal field is dependent on its context. Legal rules are built on linguistic statements and these statements, and their sentences, in turn, depend on general language usage. Competency regarding the correct use of language is reproduced socially and its rules are only shown through practical use. For legal positivism, 'the practical difference thesis' means that law (and, specifically, the application of law) must be capable of making a practical difference.

This dimension, or function, has been described in different ways in sociology of law, for example, in Nils Christie's description of how "conflicts as property" (1977) are stolen by the state and its actors, lawyers and judges. The application of law cannot be conducted in total isolation from its context because law is a language-dependent social practice, but if the legal field and the application of the law are conducted in a more self-referential way (cf. Niklas Luhmann's theory of autopoietic social systems), the legal system will likely 'leak' legitimacy. If the law pays more attention to its context, this will probably result in a legal system that 'leaks' legality (Dahlstrand, 2012; Hydén, 2008).

Even if lawyers and the officials in the legal system do not think they are a function – a dependent variable – of this context (socially, economically, politically, etc.), there is recurrent proof that they are (Cardarelli and Hicks, 1993). Thus, the question is rather how deliberately this is done. In some areas of the law, knowledge about the context is of greater interest and relevance as, for example, in the law of tort or penal law, because of their proximity to everyday life – or the 'form of life'. Moreover, Jürgen Habermas has argued that 'law as institution' (as criminal law) can be a powerful and important source of normative integration – particularly in a culture and society lacking common narratives, and that it can function as a bridge between 'lifeworld and system' (Barron, 2002).

Under certain conditions, and in relation to certain social changes, demand increases for knowledge about the situation and where or how the context within the law is situated. The digital society and the increasingly frequent use of the Internet as an important social arena perhaps constitute a situation where the demand for this learning and knowledge exchange is brought up-to-date. This potential conflict between legal concepts and their application, caused by an obsolete 'analogical understanding' in relation to a branch of law dependent upon digital technology, has been studied from a socio-legal perspective in relation to the concept of "path dependence" (Larsson, 2011).

In summary then, one of the strengths of the analytical philosophy described in this chapter relates to how it liberates the internal point of view regarding law and rule-following behaviour and how law runs the risk of being 'a private language' in a society that bears the stamp of a far-reaching differentiation between its sub-systems. Defamation and other violations perpetrated via the Internet raise the question of how to compensate the damage caused by the violation. There is a fundamental uncertainty about the compensation awarded for violation because of the difficulties involved in estimating the violation in monetary units. One way of approaching the issue of compensation is to regard it from a *user perspective* and, thereby, attain an understanding of the concept through the way it is used, as well as through the individual skills of a person putting the concept into practical use meaningfully in social and cultural practice.

References

Aarnio, A., *The rational as reasonable. A treatise on legal justification.* (Dordrecht: D. Reidel Publishing Company, 1987).

Aarnio, A., *Reason and authority. A treatise on the dynamic paradigm of legal dogmatics.* (Aldershot: Ashgate, 1997).

Baier, M., *Social and legal norms towards a socio-legal understanding of normativity.* (Farnham: Ashgate, 2013).

Banakar, R., "Law through sociology's looking glass: conflict and competition in sociological studies of law", in *The new ISA handbook in contemporary international sociology: conflict, competition, and cooperation*, (ed.) D. Kalekin-Fishman, A. Denis, (London: Sage, 2009).

Banakar, R., Travers, M., *Law and social theory.* (Oxford: Hart Publishing, 2013).

Barron, A., "(Legal) reason and its 'others': recent developments in legal theory", in *Jurisprudence and legal theory: commentary and materials*, (ed.) J.E. Penner, D. Schiff, R. Nobles, (London: Butterworths, 2002).

Björkholm, T., "To reach bedrock – Wittgenstein on rules and rule-following behaviour", in *Elsa Eschelsson*, (ed.) N. Jareborg, (Uppsala: Iustus Förlag, 1997).

Byron, P., Albury, K., Evers, C., "It would be weird to have that on Facebook. Young people's use of social media and the risk of sharing sexual health information", *Reprod. Health Matters* 21, (2013), 35–44.

Cardarelli, A.P., Hicks, S.C., "Radicalism in law and criminology: a retrospective view of critical legal studies and radical criminology", *J. Crim. L. & Criminology* 84, (1993), 502–553.

Christie, N., "Conflicts as property", *The British Journal of Criminology* 17, (1977), 1–15.

Christofides, E., Muise, A., Desmarais, S., "Risky disclosures on Facebook: the effect of having a bad experience on online behavior", *J. Adolesc. Res.* 27, (2012), 714–731.

Citron, D.K., "Cyber civil rights", *Boston Univ. Law Rev.* 89, (2009), 61–125.

Citron, D.K., Norton, H., "Intermediaries and hate speech: fostering digital citizenship for our information age", *Boston Univ. Law Rev.* 91, (2011), 1435–1484.

Coleman, J., "Incorporationism, conventionality, and the practial difference thesis", in *Hart's Postscript*, (ed.) J. Coleman, (Oxford: Oxford University Press, 2001).

Collins, M., *The law of defamation and the Internet.* (Oxford; New York: Oxford University Press, 2010).

Cotterrell, R., *The politics of jurisprudence: a critical introduction to legal philosophy.* (Pennsylvania: University of Pennsylvania Press, 1989).

Dahlstrand, K., "How to compensate the irreplaceable? A socio-legal research project within victimology about the relation between formal and informal norms", in *Norms between law and society*, (ed.) H. Hydén, (Lund: Lund Studies in Sociology of Law, 2011).

Dahlstrand, K., *Kränkning och upprättelse: En rättssociologisk studie av kränkningsersättning till brottsoffer.* (Lund: Lund Studies in Sociology of Law, 2012).

Dahlstrand, K., "Norms about norms: a Hartian perspective", in *Social and legal norms. Towards a socio-legal understanding of normativity*, (ed.) M. Baier, (Farnham: Ashgate, 2013).

Diesen, C., *Likhet inför lagen*. (Stockholm: Natur och kultur, 2005).

Ekstedt, O., *Ideellt skadestånd för personskada*. (Lund: Juridiska föreningen i Lund, 1977).

Feyerabend, P.K., "Explanation, reduction and empiricism", in *Scientific explanation, space, and time*, (ed.) H. Feigl and G. Maxwell (Minneapolis: Minnesota Studies in the Philosophy of Science, Volume III, 1962.

Flowers, A., Zeadally, S., Murray, A., "Cybersecurity and US legislative efforts to address cybercrime", *J. Homel. Secur. Emerg. Manag.* 10, (2013), 1–27.

Friberg, S., *Kränkningsersättning: Skadestånd för kränkning genom brott*. (Uppsala: Iustus, 2010).

Freis, S.D., Gurung, R.A.R., "A Facebook analysis of helping behavior in online bullying", *Psychol. Pop. Media Cult.* 2, (2013), 11–19.

Fuller, L., *The morality of law*. (New Haven: Yale University Press, 1964).

Galligan, D.J., *Law in modern society*. (Oxford: Oxford University Press, 2007).

Government Act, 1975:12.

Government Act, 2000/01:68.

Government Act, 2013/14:47.

Government Act, 2016/17:222.

Guichard, A., "Hate crime in cyberspace: the challenges of substantive criminal law", *Inf. Commun. Technol. Law* 18, (2009), 201–234.

Harris, J.W., *Legal philosophies*. (London: Butterworths, 1997).

Hart, H.L.A., *Essays in jurisprudence and philosophy*. (Oxford: Clarendon Press, 1983).

Hart, H.L.A., *The concept of law*. (Oxford: Oxford University Press, 1997).

Heath, S., "A jungian alice in social media land: some reflections on solastalgia, kinship libido, and tribes formed on Facebook", *Jung J. Cult. Psyche.* 6, (2012), 110–127.

Hur, J.L., Gupta, M., "Growing up in the web of social networking: adolescent development and social media", *Adolesc. Psychiatry* 3, (2013), 233–244.

Hydén, H., "Using law as a model. Different approaches to the understanding of normative decision making," in *Contributions in sociology of law*, (ed.) H. Hydén, P. Wickenberg, (Lund: Lund Studies in Sociology of Law, 2008).

Hydén, H., "Understanding law in society. Developments in socio-legal studies", in *Understanding law in society: Developments in socio-legal studies*, (ed.) K. Papendorf, S. Machura, K. Andenæs, (Münster: LIT Verlag, 2011).

von Jhering, R., *Geist des römischen Rechts*, (Leipzig: Breitkopf & Härtel 1906).

Karniel, Y., "Defamation on the Internet – a new approach to libel in cyberspace", *J. Int. Entertain. Media Law* 2, (2009), 215–239.

Kripke, S., *Wittgenstein on rules and private language*. (Cambridge: Harvard University Press, 1982).

Kuhn, T.S., *The structure of scientific revolutions*. (Chicago: University of Chicago Press, 1962).

Kwan, G. c. e., Skoric, M. m., "Facebook bullying: an extension of battles in school", *Comput. Hum. Behav.* 29, (2013), 16–25.

Lacey, N., *A life of H. L. A. Hart. The nightmare and the noble dream*. (Oxford: Oxford University Press, 2004).

Larsson, S., *Metaphors and norms: understanding copyright law in a digital society*. (Lund: Lund Studies in Sociology of Law, 2011).

Lefebvre, A., "Law and the ordinary: Hart, Wittgenstein, jurisprudence", *Telos: A Quarterly Journal of Critical Thoughts* 154, (2011), 99–118.

Leiter, B., "Legal realism, hard positivism, and the limits of conceptual analysis", in *Hart's postscript. Essays on the postscript to the concept of law*, (ed.) J. Coleman. (New York: Oxford University Press, 2001).

Lernestedt, C., Tham, H., *Brottsoffret och kriminalpolitiken*. (Stockholm: Norstedts Juridik, 2011).

Lessig, L., "The limits in open code: regulatory standards and the future of the Net", *Berkeley Technol. Law J.* 14, (1999), 759.

Låftman, S.B., Modin, B., Östberg, V., "Cyberbullying and subjective health: a large-scale study of students in Stockholm", *Sweden. Child. Youth Serv. Rev.* 35, (2013), 112–119.

MacCormick, N., *H.L.A. Hart.* (Stanford: Stanford Law Books, 1981).

Mainiero, L.A., Jones, K.J., "Workplace romance 2.0: developing a communication ethics model to address potential sexual harassment from inappropriate social media contacts between coworkers", *J. Bus. Ethics* 114, (2013), 367–379.

Modéer, K.Å., *Juristernas nära förflutna.* (Stockholm: Santérus förlag, 2009).

Mohamed, D., "Combating the threats of cybercrimes in Malaysia: The efforts, the cyberlaws and the traditional laws", *Comput. Law Secur. Rev.* 29, (2013), 66–76.

Negre, F.M., Go III, D.V.G., "Curbing domain name registration abuse: a legal framework in the implementation of the anti-cybersquatting provision of the cybercrime prevention act of 2012", *Ateneo Law J.* 57, (2013), 949–1000.

NJA 1991, p. 766.

NJA 2005, p. 462.

Pedersen, S., "UK young adults' safety awareness online—Is it a 'girl thing'"? *J. Youth Stud.* 16, (2013), 404–419.

Perry, B., Olsson, P., "Cyberhate: the globalization of hate", 18, (2009), 185–199.

Perry, S.R., "Hart's methodological positivism", in *Hart's postscript: essays on the postscript to the concept of law*, (ed.) J. Coleman, (Oxford: Oxford University Press, 2001).

Rabinowicz, W., "Incommensurability and vagueness", *Aristotelian Soc. Supplementary*, 83(1), (2009), 71–94.

Radin, M.J., "Compensation and commensurability", *Duke Law J.* 43, (1993), 56–86.

Samuelsson, J., *Tolkningslärans gåta: En studie i avtalsrätt.* (Uppsala: Iustus förlag, 2011).

Schultz, M., *Kränkning: Studier i skadeståndsrättslig argumentation.* (Stockholm: Jure, 2008).

Schultz, M., Wiklander, G., Bardon, J., *Näthat: rättigheter och möjligheter.* (Stockholm: Karnov Group, 2013).

SOU, 1992:84., *Ersättning för kränkning genom brott.* (Stockholm: Allmänna förlaget, 1992).

SOU, 1995:33., *Ersättning för ideell skada vid personskada.* (Stockholm: Allmänna förlaget, 1995).

Soudijn, M., Zegers, B., "Cybercrime and virtual offender convergence settings", *Trends Organ. Crime* 15, (2012), 111–129.

Stavropoulos, N., "Hart's semantics", in *Hart's postscript. Essays on the postscript to the concept of law*, (ed.) J. Coleman, (red.), (Oxford: Oxford University Press, 2001).

Sunstein, C.R., "Incommensurability and valuation in law", *Michigan Law Rev.* 79, (1994), 779–861.

Teubner, G., *Law as an autopoietic system.* (Oxford: Blackwell, 1993).

Wacks, R., *Understanding jurisprudence. An introduction to legal theory.* (Oxford: Oxford University Press, 2012).

Weber, M., *The theory of social and economic organization.* (New York: Free Press, 1947).

Wennberg, S., *Introduktion till straffrätten.* (Stockholm: Norstedts juridik, 2009).

Visser, B.J., Huiskes, F., Korevaar, D.A., "A social media self-evaluation checklist for medical practitioners", *Indian J. Med. Ethics* 9, (2012), 245–248.

Wittgenstein, L., *Philosophical investigations.* (Oxford: Wiley-Blackwell, 1953).

Zamboni, M., "A legal pluralist world'… or the black hole for modern legal positivism", (Available online at http://papers.ssrn.com/sol3/papers.cfm?abstract_id=2251017, accessed 2014-08-26).

10 The postmodern administrative law

Karl-Heinz Ladeur

1. The autopoiesis of law and the emergence of global administrative law

In systems theory, the focus of the observation of the legal system shifts from norms to decision-making, i.e. the legal system is regarded as being composed of decisions, not of persons and not of norms as the object of application to specific cases. At least, this is constitutive of the difference between centre (decisions) and periphery (legislation) of the legal system. This may sound counter-intuitive to traditional approaches to law, and it may not do sufficient justice to the practice of contracting[1] and other transactions, which do not take on the form of a binding decision.[2] However, this discussion will not be taken up here. The autopoietic construction of the legal system as processing from decision to decision is opposed to a more traditional conception of decision-making as deriving (specific) decisions for cases from a (general) norm that is integrated in a whole system of legal rules and – super-imposed at this level of norms – a set of principles that integrate the law in a system. The focus of the following analysis is more on the inevitable autonomy of not only judicial but also administrative decision-making, which allows for a recognition of the creative normative function of the processing of administrative decision-making.[3] Modern administrative law cannot, of course, deny a creative element that is termed 'discretion', although this leeway for administrative autonomy is hidden within the idea of a legislative delegation of power.[4]

a) No administrative law beyond delegation of power? The self-generative function of administrative law

'Delegation' includes the assumption that the domain of options within which the 'delegated' power of administrative decision-makers can develop is defined by the legislator. However, global administrative law is confronted with the design of forms, instruments and

1 See in a theoretical perspective Karl-Heinz Ladeur, *Das subjektive Recht als Medium der Selbstransformation des Rechts and Gerechtigkeit als deren Parasit*, 109, 114 *et seq.*, in *Zur (Un-) Möglichkeit einer Gesellschaftstheorie der Gerechtigkeit* (Gunther Teubner, ed., 2008).

2 Jerry L. Mashaw, *Reluctant Nationalists: Federal Administration and Administrative Law in the Republican Era 1801–1829*, in 116 *Yale Law Review*, 1636 (2007).

3 See only the overview in Francesca Bignami, *The Administrative State in a Separation of Powers Constitution: Lessons for European Community Rule-Making from the United States*, Jean Monnet Center for International and Regional Economic Law and Justice, New York University, 1999; for a critique see Jerry L. Mashaw, *Federal Administration and Administrative Law of the Gilded Age*, om 119 *Yale Law Journal*, 1362, 1377 et seq. (2010).

4 See Eberhard Schmidt-Aßmann, *Das allgemeine Verwaltungsrecht als Ordnungsidee* (2nd ed., 2004).

procedures beyond the established rules of general administrative law and its inherent structuring function.[5] As will be shown in more detail below, the fundamental forms and components of general administrative law have not been developed by the legislator nor by the judiciary (which has made some of its implicit rules explicit), but by an experimental search process of the administration itself.[6] The ensuing 'reverse' process of norm-generation – from administrative experimental rule generation to explicit stabilisation through courts, and finally, through legislation – appears to be incompatible with the traditional understanding of the separation of powers.

This unavoidable self-generative element of the legal system is due to the fact that we have to distinguish – from explicit rule-making – an evolutionary process of self-transformation of (not only administrative) law, which is due to the dynamic of society at large, including its knowledge basis and the social norms and expectations that try to cope with the societal complexity. The legal system is linked permanently to the 'collective knowledge' of society[7] and the basic forms of attribution of responsibility: in modernity, we can first observe the emergence of the 'society of individuals',[8] which provokes the rise of a new administrative law based upon individual decisions. The next stage of the evolution of administrative law is characterised by the new paradigms derived from the requirements of the 'society of organisations' and its consequences (such as planning law, the forms of the welfare state, *etc.*) The forms and procedures of this new stage of administrative law had to be found in an experimental process first and could afterwards be integrated in new types of laws and legal procedures of decision-making. We are now confronted with a new change of paradigm, the rise of the 'network society', which, again, demands new administrative forms and procedures for decision-making in conditions of increasing complexity. With Jerry L. Mashaw, one might describe the evolution of administrative law as underlying a "cyclical oscillation between categorical and contextual norms".[9] Administrative law is deeply characterised by paradigmatic transformations that are initiated by administrative decision-makers in experimental processes, and finally, stabilised by court practice and the legislator.

The hypothesis that underlies the following reflections is based upon the assumption that the globalisation process does not invade a stable domestic administrative (or private)

5 The role of courts in the development of general administrative law is overstated when the latter is reduced to *judge*-made law, see Benedict Kingsbury, *The Concept of 'Law' in Global Administrative Law*, in 20 *European Journal of International Law*, 23 (2009): from the absence of a legislative delegation of power to administrative deciders does not follow a supplementary norm generating role of courts alone, administration itself has to be regarded as the creator of the instruments and forms of administrative law; the role of the judges consisted rather in the doctrinal stabilisation of the institutions of general administrative law, for the role of doctrine in general administrative law see Eberhard Schmidt-Aßmann, *Allgemeines Verwaltungsrecht als Ordnungsidee* (2nd ed., 2006) 3 et seq. and Jens Kersten & Sophie-Charlotte Lenski, *Die Entwicklungsfunktion des Allgemeinen Verwaltungsrechts*, in 42 *Die Verwaltung*, 503 (2009); Oliver Lepsius, *Themen der Rechtswissenschaftstheorie*, 1, 27, in *Rechtswissenschaftstheorie* (Matthias Jestaedt & id., eds., 2008). For a critique of simplistic "functionalist" conception of legislation as the (generative) democratic will see Martin Loughlin, *Public Law and Political Theory*, 60 (2003); Id., *What Is Public Law?*, 151 et seq. (2003).

6 One can even speak about the "fact" in legal contexts as not being a "truth" but the product of a legal procedure, Barbara J. Shapiro, *A Culture of Fact. England*, 1550–1720, 11 (2000).

7 Norbert Elias, *The Society of Individuals* (1939 in German, 1991).

8 Jerry L. Mashaw, *Accountability and Intellectual Design: Some Thoughts on the Grammar of Governance*, 115, 154 et seq., in *Public Accountability: Designs, Dilemmas, Experiences* (Michael Dowdle, ed., 2006).

9 This is why the question posed by Carolyn J. Hill & Laurence E. Lynn, *Is Hierarchical Governance in Decline? Evidence from Empirical Research*, in 15 *Journal of Public Administration. Research and Theory* (2005) 173, 189, is legitimate though the authors' quantitative focus on the permanence of hierarchical structures of decision making is only of limited analytical value.

legal system from outside but that it is also a consequence of an evolutionary process that disrupts the legal system from within. It goes without saying that this evolutionary model does not assume that the new paradigms replace the older ones completely,[10] but that we have to conceive of the legal system of postmodernity as being multi-layered because the new paradigms are based upon a secondary respectively tertiary remodelling of the preceding one. This hypothesis can explain the unavoidable and legitimate creative role of administrative agencies in the new transnational realm of decision-making and allows for a more systematic self-reflection of the dynamic process of change in administrative and private law.

b) A side look at private law: Is Lex Mercatoria *law?*

Some legal theorists have put forward the claim that global law, the *Lex Mercatoria* as a self-organised practice of privat,e law, in particular, has to be regarded as 'less closed' and less autonomous.[11]

However, this would be a misunderstanding: as will be shown later, global law differs considerably from state-based law; this notwithstanding, the law should not be regarded as losing its autonomy under conditions of globalisation. Instead, the network paradigm can contribute to a better understanding of the new types of transnational legal practices: *Lex Mercatoria* lacks the coherence and methodological foundation of traditional private law,[12] but this is not a problem, because the common frame of interests of (mainly) big transnational firms can compensate for the lack of guidance of the arbitration practices. Its openness is further attenuated by the practice of referring to clusters of arbitration decisions and the UNI-DROIT-principles.[13]

The disruptions and fragmentations emerging from the evolution of the "global law beyond a state"[14] or, rather, from a heterarchical "network of networks" of law with varying combinations of characteristics according to actors, transactions, knowledge bases do

10 Assuming only a "relative autonomy" and reducing the law finally to what the judge say what the law is: Michel van de Kerchove und Francois Ost, *Le droit ou les paradoxes du jeu* (1992); for an alternative position see G. Teubner, *Breaking Frames: The Global Interplay of Legal and Social Systems*, in 45 *The American Journal of Comparative Law*, 149 (1997); Id. & Peter Korth, *Zwei Arten des Rechtspluralismus: Normkollisionen in der doppelten Fragmentierung der Weltgesellschaft*, 137 in *Normative Pluralität ordnen* (Mattias Kötter & Gunnar Folke Schuppert, eds., 2009); from a political science perspective Alec Stone Sweet, *The New Lex Mercatoria and Transnational Governance*, in 13 *Journal of European Public Policy*, 627 (2006).

11 Wolfgang Peter, Jean-Quentin de Kuyper & Benedict de Candolle, *Arbitration and Renegotiation of International Investment Agreements*, 152 (1995); Paul Lagarde, *Approche critique de la Lex Mercatoria*, in *Etudes offertes à Berthold Goldmann*, 125, 133 (1983); Andreas Abegg, *From the Social Contract to a Social Contract Law. Forms an Functions of Administrative Contracts in a Fragmented Society: A Continental View*, Center for the Study of Law and Society Faculty Working Paper, February 2008.

12 Axel Metzger, *Extra legem, intra ius. Allgemeine Rechtsgrundsätze im Europäischen privatrecht*, 533 (2009); Ursula Stein, *Lex Mercatoria*, 242 (1995); for the evolution of its self-reflexive momentum see also Gunther Teubner, *"Global Bukowina". Legal Pluralism in the World Society*, in *Global Law Without a State*, 12 (1997); Andreas Fischer-Lescano & id., *Regime Collision the Vain Search for Legal Unity in the Fragmentation of Global Law*, in 25 *Michigan Journal of International Law*, 999 (2004); Peer Zumbansen, *Piercing the Legal Veil: Commercial Arbitration and Transnational Law*, in 8 *European Law Journal*, 400 (2002); Gralf Peter Calliess & M. Renner, *From Soft Law to Hard Code: The Juridification of Global Governance*, SSRN-WP 2007; Andreas Fischer-Lescano, *Transnationales Verwaltungsrecht*, in 63 *Juristenzeitung*, 373 (2008); see also the contributions in: *Internationales Verwaltungsrecht* (Christoph Möllers, Andreas Voßkuhle & Christian Walter, eds., 2007).

13 See Gunther Teubner, Breaking Frames, *Economic Globalization and the Emergence of Lex Mercatoria*, in 5 *European Journal of Social Theory*, 199 (2002).

14 Kingsbury, *supra*, note 9; David Dyzenhaus, *The Concept of (Global) Administrative Law*', IILJ Working Paper 2008/7, www.iilj.org; for lex mercatoria Teubner, *supra, note* 17; id. & Korth, *supra*, note 14.

not – according to systems theory – call into question the autonomy of law as a self-constructing system that operates with its own tool box and observes itself within its own horizon, which cannot *but* draw a distinction between itself and its environment (the other systems in particular) and is not just driven by external forces (like the political or the economic system).[15]

However, it is not without consequence that it is not just from the point of view of systems theory that the question "is global law 'law'"? has to be raised.[16] The doubt that the question may be answered in the negative is one of the uncertainties that irritate the professional observers of the practices that are termed 'global law' as opposed to international law.[17] This is probably one of the reasons why N. Luhmann took the view that the 'world society'[18] – beyond the legally-structured nation state and the international public law as centred on the nation state as well – is increasingly governed by 'cognitive' rules,[19] and not in any traditional normative mode.

c) Global law – Is it law?

In the present discussion on global law, the question 'Is it law?' has been raised in particular by G. Teubner,[20] and, recently, by B. Kingsbury.[21] The recognition of a possible 'generation of norms as a spontaneous process' between equal private actors seems to be quite acceptable for traditional approaches to law.[22] However, this is different with reference to

15 Kingsbury, *supra*, note 9; see also Alec Stone Sweet & Florian Grisel, *L'arbitrage international: Du contrat dyadique au système normatif*, in 52 *Archives de Philosophie de Droit*, 75 (2009) who focus on the judge-like stabilisation of a "dyadic" normative practice by a third party; this view underestimates the autonomous creative potential of a transsubjective practice.

16 See Eberhard Schmidt-Aßmann, *Die Herausforderung der Verwaltungs-rechtswissenschaft durch die Internationalisierung der Verwaltungsbeziehungen*, in 45 *Der Staat*, 315 (2006); Franz C. Mayer, *Die Internationalisierung des Verwaltungsrechts* (2006); Auby, *supra, note* 1; Stefano Battini, *Amministrazioni senza stato. Profili di diritto amministrativo internazionale* (2003); Sabino Cassese, *Lo spazio giuridico globale* (2003); id., *The Globalisation of Law*, in 37 *New York University Journal of International Law and Politics*, 976 (2006); Richard B. Stewart, *The Global Regulatory Challenge to U.S. Administrative Law*, 695.

17 For the concept of the "world society" see Niklas Luhmann, *Die Weltgesellschaft*, 51, in *Soziologische Aufklärung*, 2, (id., 1975).

18 David Kennedy, *The Mystery of Global Governance*, 37, 58, in *Ruling the World? Constitutionalism, International Law, and Global Governance* (Jeffrey L. Dunoff & Joel P. Trachtman, eds., 2009).

19 Gunther Teubner, *Self-Constitutionalization of Transnational Corporations? On the Linkage of "Private" and "Public" Corporate Codes of Conduct*, in 17 *Indiana Journal of Global Legal Studies*, 617 (2010); id., *Constitutionalising Polycontexturality*, in 19 *Social and Legal Studies*, 17 (2010); id., *The Corporate Codes of Multinationals: Company Constitutions Beyond Corporate Governance and Co-Determination*, 203, in *Conflict of Laws and Laws of Conflict in Europe and Beyond* (Rainer Nickel, ed., 2010); see also id., *supra*, note 10, 3; see also Jean-Marie Guè Henno, *The End of the Nation State* (1995), 100.

20 Kingsbury, *supra*, note 9; for a critique see Ming-Sung Kuo, *Inter-Public Legality or Post-Public-Legitimacy?, A Response to Professor Kingsbury's Conception of Global Administrative Law*, in 20 *EJIL*, 997 (2009); see also Ralf Michaels & Nils Jansen, *Private Law Beyond the State? Europeanization, Globalization, Privatization*, in 55 *American Journal of Comparative Law*, 843 (2007), who give an overview of the discussion and demonstrate the primarily semantic character of the controversy; Gralf-Peter Calliess & Peer Zumbansen, *Rough Consensus and Running Code. A Theory of Transnational Law*, 79, 113 (2010), take the view that elements of domestic law that are transplanted to the transnational sphere of law undergo a "transmutation"—one may think that this is but another version of the semantic controversy.

21 See Christoph Möllers, *Transnational Constitutionalism Without a Public Law?* 329, in *Transnational Governance and Constitutionalism* (Christian Joerges, Inger-Johanne Sand & Gunther Teubner, eds., 2004).

22 See with reference to (domestic) standards Veeck v. Southern Building Code Congress International, 293 F3d 791, 799 (5th Cir. 2002); Harm Schepel, *Constituting Private Governance Regimes*, 161, 162: in Joerges et al., (eds.), *ibid.*

public law, which seems to be based upon the will of an institutionalised legislator or a delegation of law-making power.[23] Some authors even go so far as to deny any evolutionary dimension of public law that is said to be 'intentionally steered'.[24] Traditional public law still draws on the forms that have emerged in the realm of the nation state, and tends to deny the legal character of the new phenomena of global law when it seems to transcend the borders of international law.[25] The uncertainties of the new legal order that no longer fit in the forms of law, which have been moulded by, and with reference to, the state are expressed by the use of the term 'soft law'.[26] Jerry L. Mashaw has convincingly argued that the doubts of the 'lawness' of global administrative law stem from the same origin as the conventional ignorance of the generative power of administration that manifests itself in the emergence of the 'internal administrative law' in the 19th century.[27] In the following, it will be shown that the basic transformations domestic administrative law has undergone in the last decades can only be explained if such an evolutionary dimension of public law, which opens a new perspective also on the emergence of global administrative law, is recognised.

In international private law, the question of whether Lex Mercatoria is law is controversial.[28] In global administrative law, the question can, apparently, be left open according to many authors, because domestic administrative practice has also acknowledged a number of forms of preparations, of internal rule-making, procedures that have a strong impact on the legal processes without being (unanimously) regarded as being legal acts or legal norms in the stricter sense.[29] G. Teubner – as a private lawyer – is focused on private legal norms and takes the view that it is "global civil society" to which the new forms of societal legal norms can, and, indeed, have to, be attributed as an authoritative "source" of law beyond the state. This approach presupposes a new "societal constitutionalism"[30] that stipulates a

23 Möllers, *supra*, note 25, 330, 338.

24 For the sources of international law that are relevant in global administrative law See Benedict Kingsbury, Nico Krisch & Richard B. Stewart, *The Emergence of Global Administrative Law*, in 68 *Law and Contemporary Problems*, 15, 29 (2005); for the necessity to go beyond these norms in the traditional sense see Christian Tietje, *Recht ohne Rechtsquellen?*, in 24 *Zeitschrift für Rechtssoziologie*, 27, 40 (2003).

25 Pierre-Marie Dupuy, *Soft Law and International the Law of the Environment*, in 12 *Michigan Journal of International Law*, 420 (1991); Kenneth W. Abbott & Duncan Snidal, *Strengthening International Regulation through Transnational New Governance: Overcoming the Orchestration Deficit*, in 42 *Vanderbilt of Transnational Law*, 501 (2009); for the far spread conceptual vagueness see also Anne Peters & Lucy Koechlin, *Towards Non State-Actors as Effective, Legitimate, and Accountable Standard Setters*, 492, 495, in *Non-State Actors as Standard Setters* (ead, ead., Till Förster, and Gretta Fenner Zinkernagel, eds., 2009).

26 Mashaw, *supra*, note 6, 1470, 1476.

27 See Ralf Michaels, *The True Lex Mercatoria: Law Beyond the State*, in 14 *Indiana Journal of Global Legal Studies*, 447 (2007) (that lex mercatoria can neither be reduced to "anational" law nor to a derivative of state law but hat attained a new quality of a law beyond the state that combines diverse elements); see the documentation of the controversy in Klaus-Peter Berger, *Formalisierte Oder "Schleichende Kodifiizierung" des Internationalen Wirtschaftsrechts* (1996) (containing a differentiated discussion of all major pros and cons with reference to the question "is it law"?; see also (skeptically) Jan Kropkoller, *Internationales Einheitsrecht*, 123 (1996); more positively: Ursula Stein, Lex mercatoria 211 et seq. (1996); Hans-Joachim Mertens, *Das Lex Mercatoria Problem*, in *Festschrift Odersky*, 857, 860 (Reinhard Böttcher et al., 1996).

28 Joel Reidenberg, *Lex Informatica: The Formulation of Information Policy Rules through Technology*, in 76 *Texas Law Review*, 553 (1998) (describing the normative effects of technology on the legal structure of transactions via information technology).

29 David Sciulli, *Theory of Societal Constitutionalism: Foundations of a Non-Marxist Critical Theory* (1992).

30 Gunther Teubner, *Verfassungen ohne Staat? Zur Konstitutionalisierung transnationaler Regimes*, 49 in *Recht ohne Staat* (Klaus Günther & Stefan Kadelbach, eds., 2011).

law-making potential beyond the traditional forms of the state.[31] The spontaneously generated norms of transnational operations (not only commercial in the narrower sense but also including the "Lex Digitalis" of the global communication order or Lex Sportiva[32] as the law of the transnational sports organisations and their rule-making requirements) are not generally recognised as law [33] by state-based tribunals, whereas, in fact, as long as this 'law' can make use of its own institutions (the international mediation procedures), it is, at least, a functional equivalent to law in the stricter sense. G. Teubner takes a more principled approach and, as a consequence of the acknowledgment of the norm-giving power of the 'global civil society', attributes legal character in the stricter sense to Lex Mercatoria – following the terminology of H.L.A. Hart – because it has generated its own "secondary rules", i.e. procedures of reflection, distinction and control, as opposed to non-institutionalised norms of morality, etc.[34] This reference risks to be reductionist because it sets aside the paradox of the self-generation of the law as a social practice, as a 'language' with its eigenvalue, and to end up in a circular argumentation that shifts the criterion for the recognition of 'lawness' just to a meta-norm.[35] Such an approach tends to neglect the emergent character of legal institutions that are only stabilised by secondary norms 'after the fact'. The following analysis tries to shed some light on the historical transformations within domestic administrative law that generate new institutions in emergent processes for a better understanding of the specificity of a global administrative law perhaps not 'without the state' but with 'entangled hierarchies' that do not (yet?) allow for a clear distinction of 'primary' and 'secondary norms'.

2. The historical evolution of general administrative law

In a deeper sense, a law that – as one might rephrase the above-mentioned quotation from the recent book of Joyce Appleby – rests on the assumption that 'nobody is in charge of the collective order', is 'positive'.[36] As a consequence, it is 'non-instrumental', in the sense that it refers to a 'relationship in terms of rules'.[37] Clearly, the individual is not – in a meaningful sense – to be presupposed as the creator of his or her own self. Individuality is – itself – a social form that underlies permanent change.[38] The non-instrumentality of the 'positive' law and its corresponding conception of individual freedom do not invoke the 'voluntary

31 Reidenberg, *supra*, note 32; Birgit Rost, *Die Herausbildung Transnationalen Wirtschaftsrechts auf Dem Gebiet der Internationalen Finanz- und Kapitalärkte*, 251 (2007); Christopher M. Bruner, *States, Markets, and Gatekeepers: Public-Private Regulatory Regimes in an Era of Economic Globalization*, in 30 *Michigan Journal of International Law*, 125, 165 (2008); Franck Latty, *La Lex Sportiva. Recherche sur le Droit Transnational* (2007).

32 See for this argument with reference to the Lex Mercatoria Berger, *supra*, note 31, 75; for a theoretical reconstruction of an autonomous law beyond the state ee Gunther Teubner, *Breaking Frames: Globalisation and the Emergence of Lex Mercatoria*, in 5 *European Journal of Social Theory*, 199 (2002).

33 See Teubner & Korth, *supra*, note 14.

34 Cf. Jean D'Aspremont, *Hart et le positivisme postmoderne en droit international*, in 113 *Revue Generale de Droit International*, 635 (2009); also Niklas Luhmann, *Law as a Social System*, 123, 125 et seq. (2004).

35 Joyce Appleby, *The Relentless Revolution: A History of Capitalism*, 248 (2010).

36 Michael Oakeshott, *On Human Conduct*, 140 (1975); Terry Nardin, *The Philosophy of Michael OakeshotT*, 202 (2001); see also, Edward F. Mcclennen, *Rationality and Rules*, 13, in: Peter A. Danielson (ed.), *Modeling Rationality, Morality and Evolution*, 13 (1998).

37 See, generally, Markus Schroer, *Das Individuum der Gesellschaft* (2003); Jean-Claude Kaufmann, *L'invention de soi: Une Théorie de l'identité* (2004); Kenneth J. Gergen, *The Saturated Self: Dilemmas of Identity in Contemporary Life* (1992); Joanne Finkelstein, *The Art of Self-Invention* (2007).

38 Wolfgang Streeck, *Re-Forming Capitalism. Institutional Change in the German Political Economy*, 156 (2010).

disposition of self-interested economic actors'.[39] They presuppose an acentric society the collective order of which resides in the permanent emergence of innovations that establish a 'play of ideas',[40] a pool of variety that contains an excess of possibilities over reality generated from the practices of cooperation, competition, imitation and experimentation in society. Clearly, this process generates not only spontaneously but also in a reflexive form of second order observation of the very rules and patterns its own infrastructure, meta-rules and stabilising institutions. However, it is most important to underline that the individual as a merely 'self-interested economic actor' is primarily not a myth of liberal society, but one of its critics. This can be demonstrated by referring to the present discussion of the protection of the 'commons' of culture against private appropriation in the digital world and its equivalent in the genetic engineering. The relationship between privately-owned knowledge and the 'intellectual commons' is a permanent problem of liberal society, but one should not overlook the collective, albeit distributed, character of the core of the 'common knowledge' of society,[41] which was characterised by open access and restricted by patent law only to a limited extent. In the economic order of the liberal society, a 'culture of improvement'[42] is enshrined, which was always open to knowledge transfer that was, to a large extent, not only accepted as being unavoidable but also as being productive for the permanent generation of technological innovation and competition. This process does not exclude 'public intervention' – on the contrary, apparently, the public knowledge infrastructure in countries such as Germany in the 19th century had a positive impact on the culture of innovation.[43]

a) The 'acte administratif' as the main form of administrative action in the 'society of the individuals'

The legal norms basically do not 'steer' society in modernity, but protect the self-organisational potential inherent in the unrest that it introduces in the 'society of the individuals'.[44] This self-organisational potential comes to the fore when the legal system is challenged by the dynamic knowledge base that generates 'experience' as a distributed type of knowledge that no longer accepts a central privileged point of observation of society that is either 'given' by tradition or claimed to be possessed by the political sovereign power in the European absolutist states.[45] In Germany, this 'sovereign' knowledge, which combines normative and empirical aspects inasmuch as it claims that the administrative state holds this privileged position that allows us to know what the requirements of the public order are, is termed '*Polizeiwissenschaft*' ('police science').[46]

39 Appleby, *supra*, note 39, 156.

40 See for this concept Herbert Gintis, *Rationality and Common Knowledge*, in 22 *Rationality and Society*, 259 (2010).

41 Robert Friedel, *A Culture of Improvement: Technology and the Western Millennium* (2007).

42 See generally Rainer Wolf, *Der Stand der Technik* (1986); Miloš Vec, *Recht und Normierung in der industriellen Revolution*, 272, 367 (2006).

43 See only Appleby, *supra*, note 39, 248.

44 See on the emergence of the public knowledge that is needed for the government of the absolutist state Michel Senellart, *Les arts de gouverner. Du regimen medieval au concept de gouvernement*, 236 et seq. (1995).

45 Matthias Bohlender, *Metamorphosen des Gemeinwohls - von der Herrschaft guter polizey zur Regierung durch Freiheit und Eigentum*, 247, in: *Gemeinwohl und Gemeinsinn -Historische Semantiken politischer Leitbegriffe* (Herfried Münkler & Harald Bluhm, eds,. 2001).

46 See for the development in Germany Michael Stolleis, *Geschichte des öffentlichen Rechts in Deutschland*, 2 (1800–1914), 410 et seq. (1992): the concept had found its contours only at the end of the 19th century; the same goes for France, cf. Philippe Belaval, *Foreword*, in: Cédric Milhat, *L'acte administratif: Entre processus et procedures*, 7 (2007).

The new administrative law of the second half of the 19th century[47] undergoes a fundamental change when it accepts that the concept of order mainly refers to a factual normality and its description by societal experience, and is no longer based upon the traditional knowledge of the sovereign state.[48] This is why it would be superficial to take the "*acte administratif*" ("*Verwaltungsakt*"), the sovereign unilateral administrative decision that has binding force ***even if*** it is not in conformity with the law, at face value.[49] It is meant to deliver 'fixed points' in the 'floating mass of administrative activities'.[50] Both legislation and legal doctrine were more interested in very broad issues of the general legal order, whereas the operation with the increasing complexity of technical knowledge and industrial innovation were left to the discretion of administrators.[51] The '*acte administratif*' corresponds to the distributed logic of the 'private law society' (*Privatrechtsgesellschaft*)[52] that processes innovation, experiment and social experience.[53] The authoritarian character[54] of the "*acte administratif*" (*Verwaltungsakt*) should ***not*** be taken at face value; it is an extremely modern instrument that has demonstrated its flexibility even under postmodern conditions of complexity.[55] It is a form of a flexible public intervention that corresponds to the character of the positivist law 'without a goal' of its own.

The '*acte administratif*' has both an external function (in the limitation of subjective rights) and an internal function that allows administration to process rational decision-making on a case-by-case mode[56] from which a structure emerges that can be deciphered both by the administrative practitioners themselves ***and*** by private actors. In this way, the '*acte administratif*' is 're-coded' as an infringement in personal rights while, at the same

47 In a theoretical perspective see Pierre Macherey, *Petits riens. Ornie`res et derives du quotidien*, 21 (2009); id., *De Canguilhem à Foucault. La force des normes*, 77 (2009).

48 The focus of German (and French) administrative law on the Verwaltungsakt ("acte administratif") is said to have focused on state intervention and to have neglected the role of the administration in the development of benefits administration and infrastructure in particular, Kersten & Lenski, *supra*, note 9, at 504; but this is far from convincing because the American evolution follows the same track without being focused on the "administrative act", Mashaw, *supra*, note 7.

49 Otto Mayer, *Deutsches Verwaltungsrecht*, I, 95 (1914).

50 Vec, *supra*, note 46, 281; Erkco-Volkmar Heyen, *Deutschland*, in: *Geschichte der Verwaltungsrechtswissenschaft in Europa*, 29, 32 (id., ed., 1982); H. Berthélémy, *Traité de droit administratif élémentaire* (8th ed., 354) et seq. (1916) for the regulation of "installations classées".

51 It is not a coincidence that one of the founders of modern public law in Germany, Carl Friedrich von Gerber, *Grundzüge Eines Systems des Deutschen Staatsrechts* (2nd ed., 1869) was first a private lawyer; his focus on the "will power" ("Willensmacht") of the state and its putative "blindness" to political goal finds its reverse side in the openness toward the observation of the social dynamic of a liberal society; see also Carsten Kremer, *Die Willensmacht des Staates. Die gemeindeutsche Staatsrechtslehre des Carl Friedrich von Gerber*, 296 (2008) (for the relationship between goals and "willpower").

52 The work by Reimund Schmidt-De Caluwe, *Der Verwaltungsakt in der Lehre Otto Mayers* 63 et seq. (1999) and Michael Stolleis, *Geschichte des Öffentlichen Rechts in Deutschland*, II, 332 et seq. (1992) overstate the political connotation of the emerging German administrative law in the 19th century and neglect its internal rationality; more differentiated Thomas von Danwitz, *Verwaltungsrechtliches System und Europäische Integration* 31 et seq. (1996); Roger Müller, *Verwaltungsrecht als Wissenschaft*, Fritz Fleiner 1867–1937, 100 (2006).

53 The focus on willpower fits in the general trend towards a social-darwinian "vitalism" as a far spread everyday philosophy in Germany that is neither liberal in a political sense nor democratic but not antimodern; see Jürgen Große, *Lebensphilosophie*, 89, 101 (2010), where the momentary expression of willpower in response to a situation is highlighted.

54 Karl-Heinz Ladeur, *Die Zukunft des Verwaltungsakts*, in 86 *Verwaltungsarchiv*, 511 (1995).

55 Marcel Gauchet, *L'Etat au miroir de la raison d'Etat: La France et la chrétienté*, in: *Raison et Deraison d'Etat*, 193, 237 (Yves-Charles Zarka, ed., 1994).

56 Douglass C. North, John J. Wallis & Barry R. Weingast, *Violence and Social Orders: A Conceptual Framework for Interpreting Recorded Social History*, 261 (2009).

time, it is processed in the administrative decision-making procedures that contribute to the stabilisation of the impersonal interrelationships[57] that allow for the self-organisation of society. This evolution corresponds to the rise of 'realism', a social ideology that challenges the holistic conceptions of German idealism and opens a perspective on the dynamic of 'will power as the point of departure for a new construction of society – as distinct from tradition.[58]

It is not by coincidence that Philippe Belaval, a member of the French Conseil d'Etat, in his preface to a book on the modern use of the '*acte administratif*' refers to the 'plurality of the architects' of the concept[59] – a view that presupposes that the elements of architectural design are predetermined and given.[60] From a postmodern perspective that takes into consideration the approaches of comparative research in literature that try to describe the text as a paradoxical effect of an anonymous intertextuality, the co-presence of other texts that interfere with the production of meaning beyond the will of the author,[61] one might get an idea of how basic concepts of public law such as the '*acte administratif*' (*Verwaltungsakt*) in continental European law can only be regarded as the result of a process that writes itself within an 'environment of possibilities' ('*environnement des possibles*').[62] It is the emergent product of a discontinuous process of variation of cases, the stabilisation of 'local equilibria', and of transcending them in crises and of the search for new 'local equilibria'.[63] Certain possibilities are given up, others are retained and interwoven in a multitude of inclusive options and exclusive constraints.[64] Without a 'discursive memory' that links – in retrospect – the distributed intertextuality of the implicit[65] construction of a basic legal institution to a prospective generative dimension within a domain of options that is only – to a limited extent – the object of explicit design, a productive role of the legislation is inconceivable.[66]

57 See the wonderful book by Jacques le Rider, *L'Allemagne au Temps du Réalisme. De l'Espoir au Désenchantement 1848–1890*, 33, 46, 52 (2008).

58 Belaval, *supra*, note 50, 7.

59 See from a perspective of the humanities Michel Charles, *Introduction à l'étude des textes*, 221 (1995).

60 Gérard Genette, *Palimpsestes. La literature au second degré*, 8 (1982).

61 Charles, *supra*, note 63, 102.

62 Charles, *supra*, note 63, 102.

63 This reference to the acentric intertextuality of the selftransformation of law may in fact be more adequate to legal theory than the focus on "evolution" which can only be used in a more or less metaphorical way because there is no functional equivalent to genes in the legal system; see for the observation of oscillatory processes at the "borders" of the legal system Fabian Steinhauer, *Gerechtigkeit als Zufall. Zur rhetorischen Evolution des Rechts*, 94 (2007); Marc Amstutz, *Evolutorisches Wirtschaftsrecht*, 271 et seq. (2001); Gunther Teubner, *Autopoietic Law: A New Approach to Law and Society*, 221et seq., 226 (1988) (the focus on "pattern prediction" still remains vague and is ignorant of selftransformation processes that the system cannot control), Niklas LUHMANNN, *Die Gesellschaft der Gesellschaft* 1, 549 (1997) takes the view that the "evolution of ideas" is context dependent and does not underlie the control by argumentation—what this means for the evolution of system remains unclear; critically Robert W. Gordon, *Critical Legal Histories*, in 36 *Stanford Law Review*, 57, 81 (1984); also Lawrence Rosen, *Law as Culture*, 56 et seq. (2006).

64 Michael Polanyi, *Personal Knowledge. Towards a Post-Critical Philosophy* (1998).

65 This does not mean that no radical reform is possible because the model that could only be briefly sketched cannot exclude that search processes end in a lock-in that blocks any productive experimentation; see the paper by Daron Acemoglu, Davide Cantoni, Simon Johnson & James A. Robinson, *The Consequences of Radical Reform: The French Revolution*, Discussion Paper 2010, http://econ-www.mit.edu/files/5644 (arguing plausibly that the Napoleonic reforms introduced in several German territories at the beginning of the 19th century had lasting positive effects on the economic development.

66 See Ralph Michaels, *Umdenken für die Unidroit Prinzipien: Vom Rechtswahlstatut zum Allgemeinen Teil des transnationalen Vertragsrechts*, in 73 *Rabels Zeitschrift für Ausländisches und Internationales Privatrecht*, 866 (2009).

This is why the requirement of a democratic legitimation for both private *and* public law can only be acknowledged to a very limited extent.[67] The administrative law of the 'society of individuals' is closely linked to the logic of private law and its reference to the self-organisation of differentiated societal systems (the economy in particular). It introduces a similar logic into public law because its cognitive frame of reference is now the society and its practical knowledge basis and not 'police *science*' as in the past.[68] Police power, which is the core of administrative decision-making, refers to a societal dynamic conception of the 'normality'[69] – not to factual tradition and not to a privileged knowledge possessed by the state.[70] However, the close link between the normative and cognitive elements of the definition and the protection of 'public order' is preserved,[71] even though it has to be observed and reflected in a much more sophisticated mode than in the past.[72] This is all the more the case because knowledge takes on a dynamic character itself[73] – in the same vein as the law. The state makes itself 'understandable' by laying open the knowledge base that it wants to establish for administration[74] and the world has to be made calculable.[75] 'Experience' is based upon self-transformation of society as is the legal system.[76] This new perspective changes the status or the rule in general: it is generated 'bottom-up' from individual behaviour, and not from a totalising point of view,[77] which would be incompatible with the experimental order established by private law. This new dynamism comes to the fore both

67 Bohlender, *supra*, note 49; the mostly smaller German states in the late 17th and early 18th century had tried to epitomise an administrative rationality as the legitimation basis of public power, Yves-Charles Zarka, *Philosophie et Politique à l'Âge Classique*, 158 (1998); Michel Senellart, *Les Arts de Gouverner. du Regime Medieval au Concept de Gouvernement*, 282 (1995); id., *"Juris peritus, id est politicus"? Bodin et les thèoritiens allemands de la prudence civile politique au XVIIe sie`cle*, 201, 216 et seq., in: *Jean Bodin. Nature, histoire, droit et politique* (Yves-Charles Zarka, ed., 1996) this allowed for the development of a compromise between an approached which remained focused on the state and an approach which described the state as a function of society. Because of the rise of a fragmented "special knowledge" as a basis for public decision making it seems doubtful that the concept of "police science" can be revitalized under conditions of postmodernity, See however the contributions in: *The New Police Science. The Police Power in Domestic and International Governance* (Markus D. Dubber & Mariana Valverde, eds., 2006).

68 See the famous "Kreuzberg"-judgment of the Prussian Higher Administrative Court (Oberverwaltungsgericht) of June 14th, 1882, Reports (OVGE)) Vol. 9, 353; See Volkmar Götz, *Allgemeines Polizei- und Ordnungsrecht* (13th ed.), 18 (2001); for the historical development in France, in particular the flexibility of the emerging police law see Paolo Napoli, *Naissance de la police moderne: Pouvoirs, normes, société*, 15 (2003).

69 Bohlender, *supra*, note 49; for the US see T.R. Powell, *Administrative Exercise of the Police Power*, in 24 *Harvard Law Review*, 268 (1911); for France Senellart, *supra*, note 48.

70 Paolo Napoli, *Misura di polizia. Un approccio storicoconcettuale in età moderna*, in 44 *Quaderni Storic*, I, 523 (2009).

71 For the broad conception of "police" in the ancien regime See Pasquale Pasquino, *Theories of the State in Early-Modern Europe*, 42, 61, in: Dubber & Valverde (eds.), *supra*, note 71.

72 One element of the new coordination between state and society in the 19th century is the rise of statistics and its use by both public and private actors: Theodore M. Porter, *Lawless Society: Social Science and the Reinterpretation of Statistics in Germany, 1850–1880*, 351, in: *The Probabilistic Revolution*, Vol. 1 (Lorenz Krüger, Lorraine J. Daston & Michael Heidelberger, eds., 1987).

73 Marcel Gauchet, *L'Etat au miroir de la raison d'Etat: La France et la chrètientè*, 193, 237 in: *Raison et Deraison d'Etat* (Yves-Charles Zarka, ed., 1994).

74 Alain Desrosières, *The Politics of Large Numbers. A History of Statistical Reasoning* (1998); Francois Ewald, *L'Etat Providence* (1986); Theodore J. Porter, *The Rise of Statistical Thinking* (1986).

75 Alexandre Lefebvre, *The Image of Law. Deleuze*, Bergson, Spinoza 15 (2008).

76 Claude Gauthier, *L'invention de la Société Civile*, 233 (1993).

77 The police power as a "governmental practice" of the state preserves its forms but it exchanges the cognitive schemes it draws on; see Paolo Napoli, *"Police". La conceptualisation d'un modèle juridico-politique sous l'Ancien Règime*, in 20 *Droits* 183 (1994) and 21 *Droits* 151 (1995).

in police law, which observes the new economic and technical dynamism referring to the distinction of 'danger'/normality (in conformity with experience), and models its 'control project' on the patterns of the societal self-understanding of technology (control of steam engines, gas containers, safety of buildings, *etc.*).[78] The 'normal' is not dangerous.[79]

The state even intervenes in the activities to distribute experience in society when its knowledge remains restricted to local or regional communities. It presses for the establishment of private self-organised organisations which are meant to evaluate and promote experience that can be regarded as reliable (Technischer Überwachungsverein, TÜV, Verein Deutscher Ingenieure, VDI, *etc.*).[80] And both private law and public law have to refer to this 'normal' knowledge when it comes to the question of whether damage (caused by the explosion of a gas container, for example) was to be attributed to 'negligence' (*ex post*) or whether it had to be regarded as 'dangerous' by police (*ex ante*). This does not mean that the economic system or technology impose certain rules on the legal system and call its self-construction into question – not at all. Legal rules cannot be processed without a reference to societal rules and the self-generated 'internal law' of administration[81] – this constitutive link between recurring patterns of behaviour in society and the normative patterns that have to be constructed, observed and tested in the legal system, is essential to the legal rationality.[82]

Administrative law is driven by two contradictory forces: on the one hand, the administrative agents behave as a 'community of experimentalists',[83] which operates with a kind of implicit horizontal linking from case-to-case, whereas courts, on the other hand, have a tendency towards a type of explicit conceptual re-coding, which tries to limit the processes of self-organisation that are necessarily inherent in the administrative practice. There is a permanent interplay between these two types of internal and external stabilisation of the administrative legal process. However, it would be superficial to regard the judicial practice as the creator of the institutions of administrative law.[84] Its stabilisation is the outcome of a cooperative process that is only moulded in statute law much later. This process can be regarded as a distributed evolutionary process[85] that draws upon the different functions of administration and judiciary.[86] The autonomy of the 'relational rationality' of administrative decision-making should not be derived from 'expertise'[87] in a stricter analytical sense, but is due to the evolutionary character of the dynamic self-transformation of society: this evolutionary process that subsumes administrative law to a permanent unrest from which new patterns and instruments of decision-making are generated can be described as drawing on

78 Karl-Heinz Ladeur, *Coping With Uncertainty: Ecological Risks and the Proceduralisation of Environmental Law*, 299, in: *Environmental Law and Ecological Responsibility: The Concept and Practice of Ecological Self-Organization* (Gunther Teubner, Lindsay Farmer & Declan Murphy, eds., 1994).

79 Wolf, *supra*, note 46.

80 Mashaw, *supra, note* 7, 1413, 1461; the concept goes back to Bruce Wyman, *The Principles of Administrative Law Governing the Relations of Public Officers* (1903).

81 Lefebvre, *supra*, note 79, 59.

82 See generally Peter Ochs, *Peirce, Pragmatism and the Logic of Scripture*, 107 (1998).

83 Mashaw, *supra* note 7, 1378.

84 See Müller, *supra*, note 56, 86 in particular; generally Wolfgang Meyer-Hesemann, *Methodenwandel im Verwaltungsrecht* (1981).

85 See for a critique of the Chevron-approach Elizabeth V. Foote, *Statutory Interpretation or Public Administration: How Chevron Misconceives the Function of Agencies and Why It Matters*, in 59 *Administrative Law Review*, 673, 677 (2007).

86 See for this argument Long Island Care at Home Ltd. v. Coke, S. Ct. 127 2339, 2346–47 (2007).

87 Christiane Chauviré, *Peirce et la signification. Introduction à la logique du vague*, 201 (1995).

an 'abductive' approach (following the terminology of Charles S. Peirce),[88] which is a reasoning that creates a new meaning from the observation of 'cases' and conflicting rationales, and leads to a broadening perspective on the societal pool of variety beyond the possibility of inferring a new stable rule that can be 'applied'.[89] It is more a kind of a 'move' within a game with incomplete rules that emerge from the game itself. This is a logic of incompleteness that is not accessible from a control-project that epitomises conformity to rules.

But to describe administrative law and its institutions in the 19th century as judge-made law misses the point: it is mainly an autonomous product of administration itself both in Europe and the United States:

> The structures and processes of administrative adjudication were de- signed and built almost entirely by the administrative agencies them- selves.[90]

This is true also for the United States: Jerry L. Mashaw has epitomised the generation of 'trans-substantive' internal rules of decision-making by administrative decision-makers in the 19th century.[91] For the United States, it is quite characteristic that the existence of much of this earlier administrative law was even denied at all,[92] mainly because it did not fit in the model of accountability and legitimacy of law. The US administrative law is not based upon a focal construction like the French and German '*acte administratif*' ('*Verwaltungsakt*'); however, it is also centred on the search for the adequate forms of intervention into individual rights and the processes of self-organisation that their use unleashes.[93]

b) On the embeddedness of the legal system in the 'epistemic knowledge base' of society

Historians of social and economic institutions, such as Joel Mokyr, have underlined – with good reasons – the hypothesis that one should not overestimate the role of formal institutions in the evolution of modern western societies.[94] Cultural beliefs and self-enforcing practices of trust-building and reputation were at least as important as formal institutions.[95] The complex legal system is rooted in a broader 'epistemic knowledge base'. We will see later that the one-sided perspective on the legal system in the stricter sense leads to futile questions on what the legal nature of 'global administrative law' really is.[96] This approach either leads to the fixation of a traditional static concept of law or the problematical assumption that a global civil

88 See in defense of the rationality of administrative decision making Jerry L. Mashaw, *Norms, Practices, and the Paradox of Deference: A Preliminary Inquiry into Statutory Interpretation*, in 57 *Administrative Law Review*, 501 (2005).

89 Mashaw, *supra*, note 7.

90 Mashaw, *supra*, note 7, 1377, 1466.

91 Mashaw, *supra*, note 7, 1378.

92 Frank J. Goodnow, *Comparative Administrative Law*, 6 et seq., 371 et seq. (1905).

93 Joel Mokyr, *Institutional Origins of the Industrial Revolution*, 4, 22 (2008).

94 Avner Greif, *Institutions and the Path to Modernity: Lessons from Medieval Trade* (2006); Douglass C. North, *Understanding the Process of Economic Change* (2010).

95 See only Kingsbury, *supra*, note 9; for the relationships between global administrative law and traditional international law Sabino Cassese, B. Carotti, L. Casini, M. Macchia, E. Macdonald & M. Savino, *Global Administrative Law. Cases, Materials*, Issues (2nd ed.), XXV, www.iilj.org

96 For a critique see also Möllers, *supra*, note 25, 329; Christian Tietje, *Transnationales Wirtschaftsrecht aus öffentlich-rechtlicher Perspektive*, in 101 *Zeitschrift für Vergleichende Rechtswissenschaft*, 404, 418 (2002); Rost, *supra*, note 35, 87.

society can be regarded as generating and 'constitutionalising' its own legal system beyond the state.[97] The focus should, instead, be on the permanent unrest inherent in the experimental acentric order of (post-) modern society that introduces an evolutionary 'drift'[98] into the cultural memory of society, which is also a challenge for the legal system, because there is a close interrelationship between the cognitive and the normative rationality of society.

The knowledge order of society was (and is) constituted in a way that not only differentiates between general knowledge ('in the books' and in practical experience) and privately appropriated information (legally-protected by patents or practical processes of keeping know-how secret in firms) but also left open a broad range of operations of freely sharing information (which seems to be regarded by many protagonists of the Internet world as something completely new, which is definitely not the case). Robert C. Allen calls this phenomenon "collective invention",[99] which includes, for example, the spread of the steam engine as a basic innovation of the 19th century. Especially in the UK and later also in Germany and other countries, social conventions and 'self-enforcing modes of behaviour'[100] were much more important for the stabilisation of the legal system than the formal adjudication by independent judges of individual cases of conflict. It is quite characteristic that the goals of policing in Germany included the preservation of 'public order' (as opposed to 'public security'[101] in the narrower sense) i.e. the observation of the 'appropriate' behaviour in public and the respect for social conventions (below the level of formal law) such as disciplined and controlled self-presentation in public, including basic norms of politeness, clothing, cleaning, sexuality[102] etc.

These remarks should have made it clear that, in the 'society of individuals'[103] of the 19th century, both public and private law were based upon complex layers of social knowledge, conventions and professional practices, all of which were enshrined in the public order at large or in social and technical experience. The 'administrative act' was, as seen in the perspective opened here, not a relic of the absolutist state, but a modern instrument of rationalising administrative practices and of co-ordination between the society of the individuals and the preservation of 'public order'.[104] It turns it into the new experimental order that can no longer draw on a fixed set of rules and traditions. Its new form is a product of the evolutionary 'drift' of the development of administrative law, which can only *ex post* be stabilised by 'judge made law' or later by the legislator.

3. The remodelling of the traditional administrative law

The exchange process between the law and the structured practical networks that generate and distribute societal experience is in constant flux.[105] A distinction has to be made

97 Francisco J. Varela, Evan Thompson & Eleanor Rosch, *The Embodied Mind: Science and Human Experience*, 200 (1993).
98 Robert C. Allen, *Collective Invention*, in 4 *Journal of Economic Behavior*, 1 (1983); Mokyr, *supra*, note 97, at 22.
99 Mokyr, *ibid.*, 12.
100 For Germany see Volkmar Götz, *Allgemeines Polizei- und Ordnungs-recht* (13th ed.), 43 (2001).
101 See for the policing of prostitution Jacques Berlière, *La police des moeurs sous la IIIe République* (1992).
102 Nobert Elias, *supra*, note 11.
103 Gauchet, *supra*, note 77.
104 For an overview of the function of the "Verwaltungsakt" in present day German administrative law see Christian Bumke, *Verwaltungsakte*, 1031, in: *Grundlagen des Verwaltungsrechts*, Vol. 2 (Wolfgang Hoffmann-Riem, Eberhard Schmidt-Aßmann & Andreas Voßkuhle, eds., 2008).
105 For the different bridging concepts that are used for the transfer of knowledge into the legal system see Ladeur, *supra*, note 83.

between the continuous flow of information that emerges from the permanent variation within societal knowledge basis, and the momentary suspension of normality by the rise of new factual paradigms that induce a kind of 'break of symmetry' in the interrelationship between technical normal knowledge and the feedback loops that have to be designed within the legal network of networks. This was, for example, the case when the knowledge process became more dynamic and, as a consequence, the concept of normality had to be reframed: increasingly, this dynamic is reflected in the legal system when the question is raised as to whether bigger firms have a duty to take an active part in the creation of knowledge and are no longer allowed just to adapt to the current 'state of the art'[106] or when (in administrative law) the orientation on experience and 'danger' (in the end: damage) is at stake.

The hitherto central unilateral administrative decision is in decline – not only in global administrative law. Things get more complicated to judge if one bears in mind that this is also true for domestic law. At the global level in particular, not only informal measures and procedures take the lead over the "*acte administratif*" as expression of the internal sovereignty of the state but also the norms that are referred to in global law are mainly not legal norms that are part of international public law, but factual standards or, if one may put it this way, self-organised 'norms in being', procedural rules in particular.

The same goes for the concept of 'person' as a cornerstone of the liberal positive legal order: this concept draws on the stability of roles and the attribution of future-oriented expectations to legal actors abstracted from the stability of tradition.[107] Once the person is supplemented by the organisation and – recently – by networks of relationship, one may assume that the fundamental relevance of the person has changed as well. The role of the person is mediated by its position in organisations and networks.[108] Expectations can be multi-faceted under both conditions of complexity[109] and the dynamic of self-transcendence of liberal society. This dynamic allows for a new type of reflexivity of the legal order, which can operate with an open linkage between norms in the stricter sense and a whole range of different types of 'social norms',[110] which, in the past, remained more or less hidden in the administrative practices.[111]

The new reflexivity gives sufficient space for a 'management of rules' that remodels the distinction between legal and factual norms: the spontaneous character is replaced more and more by explicit 'standards' that demonstrate a new fragmentation and heterogeneity within the social knowledge base: experience-based knowledge has to distinguished from the 'best available knowledge',[112] in particular. Knowledge is further dynamised. This development includes the necessity to find procedural meta-norms for the observation of the new versions of the 'loops' between both types of rules because there are, of course, problems that raise the question of how a norm has to be characterised: this is the case when the

106 Irène Théry, *La Distinction de Sexe: Une Nouvelle Approche de l'Egalite*, 384 et seq. (2010).

107 The reverse side is to be seen in the fact that the natural person as opposed to the "legal person" in the stricter sense has also been transformed: Increasingly norms are integrated into the legal system that refer to the individual "personality" as the object of care and assistance.

108 Théry, *ibid.*, 140.

109 It is not a coincidence that at the beginning of the 20th century neither doctrine nor legislation had taken much account of the relationship between legal and social norms, Vec, *supra*, note 46, 281.

110 Calliess & Zumbansen, *supra*, note 24, 250 et seq.

111 For the meaning of this and other bridging concepts in environmental law see Ladeur, *supra*, note 83.

112 For the concept see James S. Coleman, *Social Structure and a Theory of Action*, in: Peter M. Blau (ed.), *Approaches to the Study of Social Structures* (Peter M. Blau, ed., 1975), 76; Charles S. Perrow, *Complex Organizations. A Critical Essay* (3rd ed., 1986).

rights of persons who did not participate in the creation of the norm are infringed. However, this is not often to be assumed, because, in the society of organisations,[113] persons are, in many constellations, legally represented by organisations or are subsumed under new general patterns of expectations beyond the classical 'no harm' principle (for example, protection by public insurance, transformation of liability, including strict liability, the creation of group rights, such as the rights of workers and consumers). Often, no external effect of norms can be observed because it is only the general framework of decision-making that is touched by an organisational process. Many social norms are more a kind of functional equivalent to the process of self-construction of experience as a collective, distributed knowledge base.

The more complex type of administrative decision-making that comes to the fore in the domains of planning, high technology (nuclear power, genetic engineering) and risk, in particular, demonstrate that the construction of a balancing decision in these fields is not equivalent to the classical type of a judgment based upon a 'statutory interpretation'.[114] The interplay between administrative decision-making and the law is historically changing: the external legislative norm or the judicial decision-making processes can exercise their stabilising role once a certain 'internal' administrative practice has settled in a rule-like manner, while, in times of transformation, administrative horizontal-heterarchical approaches of processing from case-to-case in a creative way tend to experiment with new forms of administrative operation that do not follow rule-like patterns. This is creative function that one may call the 'modernising mission,' which David A. Strauss attributes – with good reason – to the judiciary, but which includes – in a differentiated way – the administration, as well.

113 See for Germany Rainer Wahl, *Herausforderungen und Antworten: Das Öffentliche Recht der letzten fünf Jahrzehnte*, 43, 51 (2006).

114 See David A. Strauss, *The Modernizing Mission of Judiciary Review*, 76 Chicago Law Review 859, 894 (2009).

Part III

A conceptual discussion

11 The sociological observation of the theory and practice of law

Niklas Luhmann

When sociology set out on its historical path, it found that most fields of human activity were occupied by interpretations and theories. There were innumerable religious interpretations, including elaborate systems of dogmatics. There were moral conceptions and ethical theories. The meaning of economic activity had been explained, partly within the context of private rationality, partly in the meta-context of a national and international economic order that developed under its own impetus. There were theories of the state, constitutional conceptions of order, theories of education and, not least, a multitude of terms of conflict that emerged in the wake of the French Revolution and industrialization.

In this world, it was not easy to define the meaning and the purpose of the new discipline that called itself sociology. Historical and ideal, political relativism alone could scarcely provide a justification for adding a further variant. The unity of the new discipline demanded that the subject of this discipline should itself be regarded as a unity, regardless of all other disciplines dealing with human thought and action. As a result, a new concept of society emerged, at least in outline; one that was neither a continuation of the old European tradition of a *societas civilis* nor of the economic concept of society of the 19th century. Taken to its logical conclusion, this would have meant that all knowledge, from scholasticism to the theory of relativity, from interpretations of the Trinity to Mendelian genetics and including sociology itself as a product of society, would be delivered into the hands of sociology.

However, neither a theory nor an empirical methodology for coping with this task were available. Besides, if sociology were to press its claims, it would have had to take a preeminent place in the system of scientific disciplines. Yet, this system of disciplines had only just replaced the hierarchical order that still predominated in the 18th century, newly consolidating itself in a strictly horizontal juxtaposition – a structure that, because it had established itself in society, sociology would have had to accept and to explain.

No wonder that in such a situation a huge gap was bound to emerge between the claim and the realisation. A study of authors who are today regarded as classics in the subject shows that this situation in fact proved stimulative and led to the development of great theoretical outlines. But it did not make possible a theoretical consolidation – a deficit from which the subject still suffers even today. Only one attempt at theoretical consolidation was undertaken: Talcott Parsons's theory of the general system of action. However, this theory, significantly, at first omits the problem that is under discussion here – namely, the problem that those who act always know why they act, thus, how they act and that they can base this knowledge on an elaborate semantics that orientate it. Parsons's theory avoids this problem by starting out with an analysis of the components of the idea of action; it then discovers this and incorporates it by building it into the theory again as 'culture'. Undoubtedly a brilliant construction, but one which is achieved at the price of reduction to a merely analytical conceptual apparatus and, ultimately, of the levelling of the problem to one of the components of action.

Whatever one may think of this attempt – sociology must always know more than those who act themselves know – either by relativizing their own knowledge as culture, as one factor among others determining action, or by introducing a general motive of suspicion and refusing to accept the meaning that the person who acts regards as persuasive but instead describing this meaning as a rationalisation, an effect of socialisation, of deprivations or of compensatory necessities.[1] Structuralism, with its 'deconstruction' of the individual, has also followed this path (on its significance for legal theory cf. C. Heller, 1984). The empirical technique of the analysis of latent structures or network constellations is another possibility. However, none of these theoretical approaches has yet succeeded in explaining the practical mode of functioning of *highly developed cultural forms* that have arisen in a kind of feedback relation from the problems of interpretation and which, in literary or professional terms, take care of action. These points of departure have certainly formed the basis of research in the sociology of law, but they have not yet produced a satisfactory *sociology of the theory of law*; and without this, there can be no satisfactory sociology of the legal system that is reflected in such a theory.

II

I will attempt to show that new developments in the direction of a theory of *self-referential systems* open up new perspectives for this problem. I refer above all here to the theory of 'autopoietic' systems, i.e. systems that reproduce themselves by their own means, to 'second order cybernetics', which is concerned with the connection between self-reference and observation, and to studies that either include the well-known paradoxes of self-reference in their logical calculation (see Varela, 1975: 5–24) or else treat them as a datum of empirical systems (see for example Barel, 1979; Hofstadter, 1979). These theoretical adventures occur in areas of interdisciplinary discussion. They have as yet scarcely even been noticed by sociology itself. (An attempt to outline at theory of social systems is found in Luhmann, 1984). The following reflections are therefore not based on any form of established consensus either in the world of sociologists or in that of jurists.

Both the legal system and the system of the sciences, including the discipline of sociology, will here be regarded as self-referential systems. Every one of these systems itself constitutes that which functions as the unity for the system. This applies not only to the unity of the system, to structures and processes, but also to the elements of which the system consists (autopoiesis). Within this continual production and reproduction of unity, distinctions are necessary in order to describe what is and what is not used as a unit. (We base this thesis of a basal function of distinction and indication on Spencer-Brown, 1972). As soon as this distinction is itself described, i.e. itself becomes the object of the same distinguishing operation, a paradox arises.[2] The unit, which can only be described by means of a distinction, cannot distinguish itself against the distinction. This would mean questioning the right (or wrong) of distinguishing between right and wrong. And yet it is precisely this paradox on which all self-referential systems are based – because they do *not* make it the

1 Philippe van Parijs (1981) contains the thought-provoking assertion that there exists a kind of «authoritative self-knowledge» of the person who acts (129).

2 The logic of Spencer Brown therefore excludes this case or treats it as a cancellation of the distinction. But see also Varela (1975) who includes it as the third value of self-indications in his calculation.

object of their own operations. 'Summum ius, summa iniuria' – these words may be uttered as a despairing exclamation, but also 'uttered' in the sense that this principle cannot be introduced into the system as a directive, although it is precisely the principle on which the system is based. A paradox is not a contradiction, and therefore, the 'dialectic's' promise of synthesis does not help. The paradox does not maintain that right *equals* wrong, it argues right *because* wrong. This problem cannot be resolved by logic. But it can be *deparadoxified* by the *coding* of the system.

By accepting a binary code (right/wrong) the system compels itself to bifurcation, and it recognizes operations as belonging to the system only if they bow to this law. As in 'The Garden of the Paths which Bifurcate', it is still conceivable that one could walk both paths at the same time; but the meaning of time that would be necessary for such an act is not statable in the system; it must, in turn, be deciphered (Borges, 1972). But this significant silence of the paradox can be solved by other means, can as it were be better solved technically, by coding. When systems are based on a coded difference (true/untrue, right/wrong, having/not having), then all self-reference occurs within these codes. Self-reference within these codes is operationalised as a relation of negation in which third possibilities and contradictions are excluded, and precisely this procedure, which establishes the code, can then no longer be applied to the unity of the code itself.

Unless, that is, by an observer.

III

Whereas the theory of law and juristic dogmatics are involved in the reproduction of the legal system and, therefore, have to undergo this deparadoxification and coding, sociology can observe and describe the paradox that founds the system. This leads it neither to suspicion of motive nor to superior knowledge. On the contrary, from this mode of observation, sociology learns that, if it were itself the theory of law, it would also have to enter into a deparadoxification of the system. The observation of the paradox only brings sociology back to the question of how it can deparadoxify its own paradox as a science – the paradox that there are propositions that are false because they are true. A system cannot be self-referentially structured without coming up against such problems. This is precisely the advantage of observation from outside: it makes it possible to describe a different system as self-referential-closed.

The sociological analysis of the workings of the law has produced useful insights on a number of points. The so-called 'labelling approach', for example, describes the distinguishing and descriptive procedures of the policy by means of distinctions (based on theories of profession, organisation and social strata) that transcend the distinction between right and wrong, whereas the police simply work on the assumption that thieves are thieves and murderers are murderers. In the following section, we will adopt a more systematic approach that takes up theories of labelling, of class justice, of unequal access to law, etc. In the process, a number of subjects that have a tradition both in the theory of law and in sociology will have to be reformulated.

First, the old problem of the facticity of normative validity. In this context, it is certainly correct, though scarcely very productive, to repeat Kelsen's dictum that jurisprudence is concerned with the validity of norms, whereas sociology is concerned with facts (Kelsen, 1922). The next question is how this difference is dealt with in sociology. An answer that predated Kelsen and that has scarcely been developed since is that provided by George Jellinek and Max Weber, who argued that sociology dealt with the factual conviction of the (legitimate) validity of norms (Jellinek, 1959: 333 f.). Here, the relation is defined or psychologised in circular terms (a fact to which Kelsen rightly objected). One can move beyond this state of theory, which has led to the stagnation of the entire discussion of 'legitimacy', if (as a sociologist) one sees the normative quality of a communication in the *facticity of a contra-factual expectation* (Luhmann, 1983a: 40 ff.). According to this definition, an expectation makes a normative claim if its communication promises that the expectation will be retained even in the event of disappointment. This is at first merely a statement of subjective intention. Law then comes into being when normative claims of this kind are selected and generalised. They are valid if they are adopted by others, if they are given permanence, i.e. can be repeated in other cases, and if, for this purpose, they can be put into a general, relatively context-free form. The semantics of the verb 'should' symbolises the result of such a process of generalisation.

Once this definition of norm is accepted, it can be incorporated into a theory of the autopoiesis of the legal system. Autopoiesis means that a system reproduces the elements of which it consists from the elements of which it consists in a recursive-closed order. This happens or does not happen from moment to moment; there are no half-measures and no third possibilities. Thus, the autopoietic communication of law, in everyday life as well as in the organised, decision-making practice, transfers normative quality from communication to communication and, thereby, reproduces itself. According to the code of law, this can occur both through the communication symbol 'law' and through the communication symbol 'injustice' (but not, for example, through the communication symbol 'useful'). Contrary bivalence guarantees the universality of the code. It can be applied to all human behaviour and to all circumstances relevant to it, for all this is either lawful or it is unlawful (but not, to some extent, lawful).

The strict recursive closure of the system, which in sociological terms, corresponds to the social differentiation of a function system for law, means that there can be neither normative input nor normative output. Law cannot import legal norms from its social environment (there is no 'natural law') nor can it transmit to it (legal norms cannot be valid as law outside law). Normativity is the internal modality of operation of law, and its social function lies precisely in the fact that it fulfils the task of the provision and modification of law for society. Every contact of the legal system with the environment must therefore use a different form of expectation. Every orientation of law towards the environment uses the form of cognition. In other words, it is based on expectations that are changed if they are disappointed. In diametrical contrast with the normative attitude, the cognitive attitude is willing to learn. It must presuppose a mode of learning that sufficiently clearly outlines what alternative expectations are available if an expectation is disappointed. In so far as such modes of learning can be developed, law can also learn and adapt to its environment.[3]

This theoretical concept enables us to reformulate the constitutive paradox of law: the legal system operates under normative and cognitive premises; at the same time, it is unwilling or willing to learn according to its own structure that, in each case, differentiates. It is a closed and an open system; closed because open, and open because closed (Morin, 1977). Closure and openness do not contradict each other, because they are not defined in terms of a relation of mutual exclusion; their antithesis, however, subjects the system to the specific demands of deparadoxification. The question therefore is: how can the system

3 It should be noted here that learning as a process is a purely system-internal process, an element of the autopoiesis of the system, because the system obviously cannot learn outside itself. (Cf. Maturana, 1983).

combine not-learning and learning in the sense of a relation of mutual intensification, and thereby, fit itself into social evolution?

IV

For the continual recombination of closed reproduction and open orientation towards the environment, i.e. of normative and cognitive patterns of expectation, the legal system has at its disposal two interrelated modes of communication: *decisions* and *arguments*. Legally binding decisions come into being because the legal system lays claim to the political system's capacity to force through collectively binding decisions even in the teeth of resistance. The inclusion of a capacity to learn is here mediated by decision-making programmes whose application is geared to the circumstances of the individual situation. If this is not sufficient, provision is made for the changeability even of decision-making programmes, and this ultimately leads to the principle of the *positivity of law*. Law is then valid *by virtue* of decisions that make it valid. The legal system itself is obliged to believe in this ground of its validity. Sociology, on the other hand, is in a position to trace this ground of validity back to a paradox and to draw its conclusions from this: positive law is valid *because it could be changed by a decision*, although at the moment no one intends to do so or has the possibility of setting a process of change in motion. Validity is accordingly based on the possibility of its negation. To use a figure of speech familiar from system theory, one can say: law produces the possibility of its nullification, as a rule it inhibits this possibility but it disinhibits this inhibition under certain special circumstances (which, from the viewpoint of currently valid law, may also include 'accidents').

The argumentation with which scope for decision-making (on whatever level) is restricted and decision-making burdens without decisions are reduced raises different system problems. But, here too, a difference can be ascertained between the system-internal attitude and its sociological observation. Within the legal system, one is obliged to believe in the possibility of substantiation, of producing reasons, though not obliged to believe in specific reasons themselves. As the generic term for all valid grounds, reason is virtually indispensable (sociologists in particular will acknowledge this fact). In the past two decades, the juristic style of reasoning has been both violently and superficially criticised, the two main charges being those of class justice and the insensitivity of the juristic technique.[4] Sociological observation using system theory adopts a quite different approach.

Its starting point is the question of how it is possible for arguments, instead of being merely isolated and juxtaposed, to relate to one another to a greater or lesser extent and positively or negatively. Using a term from information theory, this interrelation can be described as redundancy. This means that the information value (surprise effect) of an argument is reduced by the fact that other arguments are already known.[5] The ordering of the arguments – to the extent that arguments are marshalled in 'concentrated' form – makes the search for information unnecessary (redundant), and thus, leads to a decision.

4 Interest in practical philosophy and rational argumentation has revived as a counter-movement to the critique based primarily on Marx. Cf. for example: Dreier (1981) In this discussion Habermas perhaps comes closest to the paradox by inclining towards both sides.

5 This concept of redundancy presupposes *difference* of arguments and is based on relations between them. A different application of the concept of redundancy describes the *equality* of elements. Redundancy is then based on the elements of the system itself and is equivalent to entropy. For the concept of redundancy used here see also Atlan (1979).

Sufficiently concentrated redundancy is a prerequisite for the possibility of replacing one argument by another with regard to the consequences: for the same reason, it is a prerequisite for recognising the dispute value of an argument and for being able to continue the dispute as a dispute about arguments. Only redundancy makes it possible, on the basis of argumentation, to determine what a decision is being made about. Only thus can the decision produce a result that is comprehensible in the same way by all involved, and if redundancy is too slight then not even this can be guaranteed, however great the will to produce a decision and the power to enforce it. To this extent, it is perfectly justifiable to play argumentation off against 'decisionism'. Nonetheless, redundancy has qualities that are both familiar and unfamiliar for the operation of law. Redundancy is symmetrically structured. If one argument reduces the information value of another, the converse is also true. If one substantiates with reasons, this is only because reasons substantiate. Furthermore, redundancy increases in disputes and, as every family therapist knows, in pathological cases. One word leads to another – and for the observer, this has scarcely any information value. The interest of the legal system in cases coming to litigation cannot therefore simply be interpreted as an interest in the increase of redundancy. The professional lawyer must be able both to use and to reduce redundancy. He must be able both to reduce and to increase, and thus, to direct, the uncertainty that results from dependence on further information. On a trivial level, he may do this simply by leaving the parties involved in the dark about his own position (Luhmann, 1983). A more powerfully objectified form is the asymmetrisation of redundancy, the stylisation of argumentation as a search for impartial reasons.

Theories of juristic argumentation that from the outset define argumentation as an attempt at substantiation[6] thereby deprive themselves of possibilities of observing the legal system. The sociologist, as an observer, will wish to leave the question of attribution open, i.e. the question of whether the reasons are chosen because of the substantiation or the substantiation because of the reasons. And he will wish to investigate how the lawyer sets about the task of increasing and reducing redundancy at the same time (Lautmann, 1972). He will wish to observe the manner of dealing with the paradox of the system.

V

Older forms of juristic argumentation assumed law to be a totality consisting of laws, precedents, concepts and 'commonplaces', and attempted to derive a decision from this. The argumentation was required to explain the concrete in terms of the general, and the arsenal of reasons was treated as already established. This mode of argumentation, known as 'conceptual jurisprudence' or 'analytical jurisprudence' has now been universally rejected. It has, at least in theory, been replaced by a more pragmatic, utilitarian, sociotechnical, consequence-oriented perspective. Decisions are expected to be justified by their results and the argumentation has to be formulated accordingly. Yet results are not simply facts but differences. The crucial point here is how much difference the decision (or the justification or the rule on which it is based) generates in comparison to what would be generated without it. Since 'interest jurisprudence' has become generally accepted, it has come to be considered good juristic style to use as arguments and to evaluate the results and the consequences of decisions. This mode of argumentation and decision-making is not uncontroversial, but

6 See Alexy (1978) which takes up Habermas' ideas and conforms to prevalent legal-theoretical and legal-methodological opinion.

it seems to be indispensable because it is impossible to get anywhere without it. Sociology was at first pleased to note that with interest jurisprudence and consequence orientation, the demand for empirically and sociologically founded knowledge also increased. But with greater distance (also to itself) it soon realizes that the demand cannot be satisfied in this way. Who can say with the necessary certainty whether the 'consequences' that are not directly produced by the decision will actually follow? Who can rule out the possibility that unforeseen consequences will result that would subsequently change our assessment of the decision? Indeed, who can guarantee that the assessment itself will be upheld consistently? These questions are part of the standard repertoire of decision theory and of sociology and cannot simply be ignored. If the legal system nonetheless does practise consequence orientation, it does so without taking these reservations into account. In many cases, this may be both harmless and correct. However, the theoretical principle that justification can ultimately be sought only in consequences leads back to the paradox that the impossible is postulated as necessary.[7]

Secondly, it is necessary to point out that the principle of consequence orientation cannot be generalised. It must remain the preserve of the professional practice of lawyers and the organised legislative or judicial business of decision-making. If everyone oriented himself freely according to consequences, this would be equivalent to one of the 'strange loops' with which paradox draws attention to itself.[8] For the normal consumer of law, consequences depend primarily on whether or not he is caught, whether the opposing party goes to court or not; in other words, whether the legal system is brought into play or not. This can also be formulated as a 'free rider' problem. The function of law would then be to prevent 'free riding', i.e. benefitting from order without complying with it. It would be paradoxical then to introduce precisely this as a legally justified paradox into the legal system.

Paradox here does not mean impossibility in the real world or the cessation of the autopoietic reproduction of the system. On the contrary, it is precisely the processing of the paradox, precisely the self-deparadoxification of the system that is of interest here. When, from this perspective, sociology examines the consequences of an increasing consequence orientation in the legal system, two hypotheses suggest themselves: the differentiation of the system into an organisational-professional business and its 'public' will be intensified, and at the same time, juristic practice, which must after all maintain this differentiation, will be empirically overtaxed and made insecure. It seems that the older, hierarchical-authoritative forms of the establishment and administration of law from above are being replaced by a new differentiation that assumes that the people abide by the rules while lawyers can modify them with regard to their consequences.

VI

For the legal system itself, the paradox of its self-reference leads to blurrings of its self-observation, such as one often finds in the paradoxical drawings of Maurits Escher. Most things function, but there are also elements of meaning that cannot be unequivocally fixed. Two significant traditions of legal thinking have dealt with this problem, and I would suggest that sociology could start a third tradition.

7 It should be noted that the necessity of the impossible implies a logical reversal of the definition of contingency. Contingency is something that is neither necessary nor impossible, and precisely, this ultimately defines the possibility of decision.

8 As in Hofstadter (1979): «something in the system acts on the system as if it were outside» (691).

The problem of the *derogation* of law arose within the conceptual framework of natural law. There were cases, such as theft out of sheer necessity (Montes, 1925: 260–274, 352–361) or the higher public good of maintaining order or reason of state in which a violation of the normally valid law had to be accepted (Mattei, 1953: 49–60). Interpretations differed as to whether such cases should be regarded as violations for understandable reasons of natural law or whether they could be justified within the framework of natural law, for example, as restrictions of property or as a privilege of state power (*ius eminens*). In addition, the classical tradition, using terms such as epiekeia, aequitas, justness, provided the possibility – in anticipation of logical types – of assuming a kind of 'fallback' law behind law. In any event, jurists were confronted with the logical imperfection of the legal order and, at least in individual cases, had to come to terms with the experience that law was obviously putting itself in the wrong/making itself unlawful.

With the greater differentiation of law and a greater systematisation of its autonomy, this range of possible solutions seems to have lost its plausibility. It was replaced – as if Gödel had already been heard of – by the assumption that the logical closure of the system could not be brought about internally but only ab extra. This 'ab extra' was at first the will and the special providence of God.[9] With increasing secularisation, this was replaced by the concept of political force (which, in turn, gradually shifted from 'potestas' to 'potentia' and 'vis'). After the collapse of the natural law of interpretation of the contract, which could justify itself only by circular arguments and could not solve the problem of the right to resist, the only possibility that remained was to attribute the origin of law to pure force[10] (10). Kant systematised this idea.[11] Since then the idea – an idea that is familiar but controversial – has developed that force, although it is not in its origin legally qualifiable, nonetheless leads over to law – or, to quote a recent formulation, "*in ogni violenza vi è un carattere di creazione giuridica*" (Resta, 1984: 10). However, the origin in force is not here meant as a historical thesis that no longer concerns us today. If one interpreted the thesis of the origin of law in force historically, this would merely lead back to self-reference, namely, to the view that as law moves away from its origin, it must posit itself as origin.

But force is a permanent, though external, concomitant phenomenon of law. From the perspective of law, which wishes to lay claim to force lawfully, not unlawfully, this is an externalisation of the internal logical imperfections of law, a form in which the establishing

9 In the 16th and 17th century, this was conveyed in the idea of the immediate legitimation of political power. In Pedro Barbosa Homen, politics is «esta especial providencia divina». Discursos de la juridica y verdadera razon de estado (1629). Quoted from Pierre Mesnard, Barbosa Homen et la conception baroque de la Raison d'Etat, in Castelli (ed.), *op. cit.*, p. 109–116 (113).

10 A meticulous justification (every other assumption would have to seek the origin of law in law itself and therefore be circular) is to be foundin Linguet: (1767; esp. vol. 1, p. 284 ff.). Here we also find one of the earliest sociological analyses of law: «c'est la société qui a produit les loix, et non les lois qui ont produit la société». (230). And also the following argument against the circular justification of law: «Toute règle commune suppose des rapports, et la découverte de ces rapports, des connaissances; mais celles-ci, d'où naissent-elles?» (234).

11 In a section, which is aptly entitled «Vom zweideutigen Recht» (Of Ambiguous Law), Kant adopts the traditional modes of posing the problem. Justness is defined as «a law without compulsion», the law of necessity as «compulsion without law» and the problematic is attributed to the imperfection of the legal order, «for this ambiguity is due to the fact that there are cases of questioned law which no judge can be called upon to decide». Quotations from the appendix to the introduction to the Rechtslehre, Metaphysik der Sitten 1. Quoted by the edition of von Kirchmann, (1870: 35 f.) Kant systematically traces this «ambiguity» back to a confusion of the objective and the subjective grounds of the practice of law. This, in turn, is based on the questionable assumption that there is a subject capable of judging whether it is objectively or subjectively determined, by compulsion or by freedom, in his actions.

paradox is admitted. It implies in this form that the legal system can cope with any blurring, with structural contradictions, with 'gaps in the law', etc., because ultimately whatever is decided is covered by political force. The external reference of force is reintroduced into the system as ambiguity, and both then conceal the paradox. The ambiguity is textualised, and it can then be shown from the texts that, in the individual case, something has to be clarified. The 'deep structure' that generates the rules and the arguments is ultimately legally conditioned force. However, as this can no more be changed than the paradox, the only possibility that remains is to cultivate the legal culture and to cover force with a filigree of carefully thought out figures, so that in normal circumstances, decisions that qualify and disqualify themselves as force occur only in isolated cases. Force then camouflages itself as permissible discretion, as a vague concept of law, as a methodologically not checkable choice of method of interpretation and one need only ensure that not too many ambiguities of this kind are admitted (cfr. Ladeur, 1984). Ultimately, the jurist can decide on all legal matters, though not always in a specifically juristic manner.

All this is correct, but is the theory satisfactory? The concentration on an external perspective allows one to adopt a position for or against law. If one is against it, one calls the external perspective force. If one is for it, one calls it peace. In this way, the dispute can rage on infinitely. The internal reproblematisation of force is also aptly described as the art of dealing with ambiguity. Such insights remain indispensable, yet one is still entitled to ask whether a richer theory, which says more than just this, is possible.

The problem of paradoxical self-reference has many facets, which become visible depending on the theory used to construct self-reference, or more generally, depending on how one observes them. The two theories that we have discussed, the derogation theory and the force theory, interpreted the paradox as a contradiction or a blurring and attempted to dispel it. Sociology tends in its theoretical structures, most of which are superficial, to hold up paradoxicality, for example, the equivocation of force as society's bad character.[12] With a theory that regards self-reference as a constitutive structure of systems and, therefore, considers paradoxes as a real phenomenon, one arrives at completely different points of departure. The rich and potentially highly developable repertoire of system-theoretical analysis can then be directly related to the paradoxical unity of the legal system. The theory of law can then be built into a more general theoretical framework that enriches it with possibilities of comparison. Observation from the viewpoint of how a system orders its self-reference, deparadoxifies its paradoxicality, asymmetrises its recursive symmetry causes *every* solution of this problem to appear contingent. However, as a functional analysis, it restricts the perspective to other, functionally equivalent possibilities. The question is then: in what specific conditions can closure and openness of the system both be realised in conditions of increasing complexity? Or how can the transformation of (symmetrical) redundancy into (asymmetrical) justifications safeguard itself against recursiveness? Or how is it possible to cause the unity of the difference of law and injustice or of law-establishing and law-maintaining force (Benjamin) to appear as a relative blurring in the system and, thus, to bring it into operations of the system? Or then: what consequences can be expected if this fails? Or to take a concrete example: what are the prospects of terrorists who bank on Benjamin's speculation that the people 'secretly admire' the violent actions of the 'big criminal' (see Benjamin, 1977: 179–203).

12 It should not go unmentioned that most sociologists are dissatisfied with *this* sociology, so that they usually pursue their research without a universal theoretical framework.

We cannot go into these questions at this point. In conclusion, it need only be pointed out that they are of little significance for the legal system, a fact which also follows from the theoretical approach outlined here. The problem does not lie in the supposedly huge gap between (abstract) theory and (concrete) practice. It arises directly from the theory of autopoietic systems. Science reproduces itself as science and not as law. Law reproduces itself as law and not as science. Reproduction occurs on the level of factual elemental events, on the level of communication from moment to moment. This necessitates a minimum of structural effort but not, or only very seldom, of reflection. As its complexity increases, law may develop techniques of grouping similar cases together, of pinpointing preliminary decisions of a similar kind, of storing conclusive experiences topically or in concepts; it may, particularly in connection with the training of legal practitioners, develop formulas for learning and more systematised dogmatics that will increasingly embrace different cases from the perspective of one principle. Finally, it may differentiate efforts to establish a philosophy or a theory of law, in which the unity of the system, despite internally necessary distinctions, is reflected.

All this is of little significance in the everyday rebirth of law. In certain cases, the theory may provide assistance in justifying decisions. But one does the theory greater justice if one realises that it itself chooses cases in order to reproduce itself as practice of its own kind. The theory of law has itself come to the conclusion that "what is necessary for the reproduction of theoretical practice is not control of the full run of legal outcomes, but rather continuing domination over paradigmatic or semiotically central events" (Heller, 1984: 189). Theory itself determines what cases come into question for this purpose, for ultimately, it is the theory that may have to change itself on the basis of case results.

If this applies to the immanent relation of theory to practice within the legal system, then it applies all the more forcefully to theories that sociology produces as part of its own autopoiesis and uses for the observation of the legal system. Here it is a matter, in the first instance, of studies to enable further studies, of truths which are capable of being passed on in such a way that on further treatment they can become truths or untruths. The institutional coupling of training and theory reproduction at universities has here led to false assessments that require urgent correction. And precisely sociology, which ought to retain a sense of the real circumstances, ought to realise this before all others.

Assuming that this occurs, it seems reasonable to forecast good prospects for closer co-operation between the sociology of law and the theory of law. Both sides have a substantial amount of ground to make up in terms of theory and of the general state of interdisciplinary discussion. The theory of self-referential systems contains an offer to open up discussions. Not an offer of a merger! Theses such as paradoxical constitution and contingent deparadoxification, openness by virtue of closure, the introduction of the distinction between system and environment into systems, access to reality of 'second order cybernetics' on the basis of observation, and other such theses are all based on differentiation. They begin and end the analysis not with unity but with difference. Ultimately, they are all based on an assumption that every logic of reflection must presuppose: that every evolution and every build-up of rich complexity draws borderlines and that it is only in this way that the world will be capable of observing itself.

References

Alexy, Robert (1978), *Theorie der juristischen Argumentation*, Frankfurt.

Atlan, Henri (1979), *Entre le cristal et la fumée: Essai sur l'organisation duvivant*, Paris.

Barel, Yves (1979), *Le paradoxe et le systeme: Essai sur le fantastique social*, Grenoble.

Benjamin, Walter (1977), Zur Kritik der Gewalt, in *Gesammelte Schriften* (vol. II), Frankfurt.

Borges, Jorge Luis (1972), El Jardin de senderos que se bifurcan, in *Ficciones*, Madrid.

Dreier, Ralf (1981), *Recht – Moral Ideologiez Studien Zur Rechtstheorie*, Frankfurt.

Dworkin, Ronald (1978), *Taking Rights Seriously*, Cambridge, MA.

Heller, Thomas C. (1984), Structuralism and Critique, *Stanford Law Review*, 36.

Hofstadter, Douglas R. (1979), *Gödel, Escher, Bach: An Eternal Golden Braid*, Hassocks, Sussex.

Jellinek, George (1959), *Allgemeine Staatslehre* (3rd Edition, 6th reprint), Darmstadt.

Kelsen (1922), *Der soziologische and der juristische Staatsbegriff*, Tubingen.

Ladeur, Karl-Heinz (1984), *Abwägung – ein neues Paradigma des Verwaltungsrechts: Von der Einheit der Rechtsordnung zum Rechtspluralismus*, Frankfurt.

Lautmann, Rüdiger (1972), *Justiz – die stille Gewalt: Teilnehmende Beobachtung and entscheidungs-soziologische Analyse*, Frankfurt.

Linguet, Simon-Nicolas-Henri (1767), *Theorie des lois civiles, ou Principes fondamentaux de la société*, London.

Luhmann, Niklas (1974), *Rechtssystem and Rechtsdogmatik*, Stuttgart.

——— (1983a), *Legitimation durch Verfahren*, Frankfurt.

——— (1983b), *Rechtsoziologie* (2nd Edition), Opladen.

——— (1983c), Die Einheit des Rechtssystems, *Rechtstheorie*, 14.

——— (1984), *Soziale Systeme: Grundiss einer allgemeinen Theorie*, Frankfurt.

Mattei, (de) Rodolfo (1953), Il problema della Deroga e la Ragion di Stato, in E. Castelli (ed.), *Cristianesimo e Ragion di Stato*, Roma-Milano.

Maturana, Humberto R. (1983), Reflexionen: Lernen oder ontogenetischen Drift, *Delfin* 1, II.

Maturana, Humberto R. and Varela, Francisco (1980), *Autopoiesis and Cognition: The Realization of the Living*, Dordrecht.

Mesnard, Pierre (1953), Barbosa Homen et le conception baroque de la Raison d'Etat, in E. Castelli (ed.), *Cristianesimo e Ragion di Stato*, Roma-Milano.

Montes, P. (1925), Precedentes doctrinales del «estado de necessidad» en las ombras de nuestros antiguos teologos y jurisconsultos, 142 *La Ciudad de Dios.*

Morin, Edgar (1977), *La Méthode*, Paris.

Parijs, (Van) Philippe (1981), *Evolutionary Explanation in the Social Sciences: An Emerging Paradigm*, London.

Resta, Eligio (1984), *L'ambiguo diritto*, Milano.

Rottleuthner, Hubert (1981), Zur Methode einer folgenorientierten Rechtsanwendung, in *Wissenschaften and philosophic als Basis der Jurisprudenz*, Supplement 13 of the Archiv für Rechts- und Sozialphilosophie, Wiesbaden.

Spencer-Brown, George (1972), *Laws of Form* (2nd Edition), New York.

Varela, Francisco (1975), Substantive and Reflexive Elements in Modern Law, *Law & Society Review*, 17, 259.

12 Some problems with 'reflexive law'

Niklas Luhmann

I

'Reflexivity' means that law, as an autonomous sub-system of society, is obliged to respect the autonomy of other sub-systems of society, including organisations and interactions. For jurists, this reads like a kind of legal-political programme along the lines of traditional liberal or neo-critical ideas of freedom. Everyone who wished to see in this program emancipatory intentions, that is who wished to see Habermas's proposals taken up, would read it in this way. However, according to the theoretical principles referred to here, what is put forward is no more than the simple statement of a fact, of a logical fact so to speak. This is the only possibility. The concept of autopoiesis, invented as a definition of life, is rigourously inflexible.

A system either continues its reproduction or it does not. Autonomy in this context can only mean that the reproduction of elements of the system is guaranteed, in recursively closed fashion, by the elements of the system. This either functions or it does not, and only the conditions for the process can be made complicated. Therefore, legal-theoretical, legal-dogmatic or legal-political conclusions could, at best, only be drawn by means of a detour (yet the reference to detours via high levels of abstraction underlines the potential fertility of this idea). And how do we arrive at this detour? By a detour!

II

Let us adopt the approach of Spencer Brown, whose logic has considerably influenced the formulation of this theory, and start by asking how it is possible for the world to observe itself (or more concretely: how is it possible that the world produces physicists in order to be able to observe itself).[1] The answer lies in a fundamental operation of distinction and indication, which violates the unity and the undifferentiatedness of the world by indicating something that leaves something out.[2] This fundamental process defines an observation.

1 Cf. Spencer Brown (1972). The problem was first formulated by Wittgenstein.

2 This idea has been formulated in innumerable ways. For cybernetics, see for example Maruyama (1985: 233–241), Wender (1968: 309–324), for a philosophical and linguistic-theoretical version: Derrida (1968). Gotthard Gunther says that

> these systems of self-reflection with centers of their own could not behave as they do unless they are capable of [drawing a line] between themselves and their environment. We repeat that this is something the Universe as a totality cannot do. It leads to the surprising conclusion that parts of the Universe have a higher reflective power than the whole of it, as has been recognized for a long time.
>
> (Gunther, 1976: 319)

According to Spencer Brown's logic, this observation cannot observe itself. This would be equivalent to its negation. An important addition by Varela abolishes this limitation and adds a third element (to the enactment or non-enactment of the fundamental operation), namely, the self-indication of the fundamental operation (see Varela, 1975; cf. also Dupuy, 1979: 97ff). This third element is the autonomy of the operation of indicative distinction. We do not at this point need to discuss the advantages of this addition as a contribution towards a contradiction-free theory of self-referential systems. The crucial point is that with reference to reality it implies the thesis that every observation, as the application of a distinction, makes possible not only an indication of that which is observed but also an indication of the observation itself. One therefore arrives at the possibility of saying 'I' by the application of any distinction. When this in turn is observed, the observer must decide whether he wishes to indicate the self-indication of the system observed or his own indication of this system.

This theoretical approach is concerned solely with the level of observation (the level which von Foerster calls 'second order cybernetics' (von Doerster, 1981). On the simple level of real processes, one can merely state that one does not see what one does not see, or that the blind man sees nothing (to take up von Foerster's examples). However, the question here concerns what the blind man sees when he sees that he sees nothing (or, as the reader can easily extrapolate, what the legal system regulates, when it regulates that it regulates nothing). If one combines this logic of observation with a theory of autopoietic systems (see Varela, 1979), then observation itself becomes an operation of autopoietic systems that consist of such operations and that use them in order to reproduce such operations.[3] The recursive closure of the production of the elements by the elements is, from a logical viewpoint, equivalent to the self-indication of the system. This is its unity, this is its autonomy. Accordingly, (and this is an insight that has long been familiar in the theory of self-consciousness – for a new version see Shoemaker, 1963) there can be no external criteria of self-determination, and likewise, everything that determines the system internally is in turn controlled by other elements of the system. There are no operations independent of the system, either from outside or from within. All operations are recursively conditioned and it is precisely this that constitutes the unity and the autonomy of the system. The system constitutes itself via criteria-less self-reference, by drawing limits, distinguishing itself from the environment, and thus, indicating itself.

When it then observes the objects in its environment or events, processes and structures in itself, this always implies that the system, in the process of observation, distinguishes and indicates itself as an observer – whatever the differentiation scheme and the object determining the observation in each case may be. Von Foerster's collection of essays quoted above underlines this in its ambiguous title: Observing Systems.

III

To avoid misunderstandings that can and do arise, particularly in connection with the concept of autonomy, it must be stressed that this theory of self-referential systems means not only self-regulation, for example, the right of a body to give itself its own statutes or of an individual or group to use its property as it sees fit. It is therefore not a matter of guarantees of freedom or of the decentralisation of power. The theory has something far more

3 Cf. Varela 'The physiological and cognitive organization of a selfconscious system may be understood as arising from a circular and recursive network, containing its own description as a source of further description' (1975: 3).

'substantial' in mind – if this formulation is allowed whereby the concept of substance is replaced by the concept of self-reference. From this alone, no legal-political programme can be derived just as the definition of life as autopoiesis does not say what forms of life exist or what life is worth living.

This refusal to make premature evaluations is compensated by advantages that should not be underestimated. On the one hand, it becomes clear that the plurality of self-referential systems leaves no alternative but self-referential law. The question can only be to what extent the theoretical apparatus of the legal system, and of legal dogmatics in particular, is capable of perceiving and taking into account autopoietic systems in its environment. The problem of cognitive competence is posed before that of legal-political intention. On the other hand, the entire theory is based on the primacy of difference-controlled observation. It is no longer simply a question of whether a cognition corresponds to its object (adaequatio) or whether a legal regulation of an imminent 'law-worthiness' (or whatever one chooses to call it) does justice to its object. The crucial question is rather: with the aid of what distinctions can a system observe internal or external objects in a sense which is system-internally autopoietically applicable? In other words, observations must be able system-internally to fit themselves into a network of processing self-indications and to continue its autopoiesis. If the legal system for this reason observes itself and everything else in terms of legal/illegal (see Luhmann, supra), i.e. if it must make indications with the aid of this distinction, then what limits are thereby imposed on insight into the autopoiesis of environmental systems? And, equally dramatically, what limits of the self-thematisation of law lie in the fact that law can observe itself only under the legal/illegal schema, although self-indication as the observer using this system refers the system to the unity of its own code?[4] External observation and self-observation ultimately come up against the same problems, the reason for this being that every observation, in order to indicate something, must be based on a distinction. Mysterious, usually anthropomorphic capacities – ratio, reason and the like, which can be morally bolstered – are no longer invoked. Instead, difference stands at the beginning, and with it, the possibility of self-indication, of the operation or of the system, which with the aid of this difference makes the operation possible.

The introduction of the major distinction is completely arbitrary. There is no 'reason' for it. The only condition it must fulfil is that of being applicable in an autopoietic system. But precisely this condition has a highly selective effect in the course of evolution. The system must be able to indicate itself as the unity of the operations that use precisely this schema to reproduce themselves. From the viewpoint of the legal system, the schema 'in accordance with/against the will of Allah' is less suitable than the schema legal/illegal, because only the latter permits a clear distinction between system and environment.[5] Everything that orientates itself by the schema legal/illegal can be grasped as legal system, regardless of whether an indication within this distinction refers to legal or illegal. But precisely here, in the process of reflection on the unity of the system, paradoxes arise (which are easier to cope with in the name of Allah). They hang on the question of whether the schema legal/illegal is introduced legally or illegally.

4 Günther would talk of 'rejection value' here. Perhaps more familiar is the centuries-old discussion of the question of whether the occasionally necessary derogation of law in emergencies or for the sake of higher purposes ('reason of *Stattrāsone*Mattei') 1953

5 We here presuppose that the differentiation of modern function systems takes place via communication codes and not via central ideas or concepts such as concentrated causality, domination or the like.

When a system uses a major difference as the code for the totality of its operations, the self-application of the code to the code must be ruled out. Self-reference is permitted only within the code, and here it is operationalised as negation. Legality is treated as the negation of illegality and illegality as the negation of legality. Thus, one defines the totality of all possibilities that could become relevant for the system. A contradiction (lawful = unlawful) is excluded *and this exclusion taker the place of the explication of the paradox.* The paradox is not a contradiction. It does not state that legal equals illegal, but legal *because* illegal or, conversely, illegal *because* legal.[6] This paradox, which one always encounters when one enquires into the correctness (or incorrectness) of the distinction between legal and illegal, is *deparadoxified* coding (see Luhmann, *supra*). It is transformed down into the form of a contradiction and then logically neutralised. According to this code, no operations are then allowed that indicate the distinction with the aid of the distinction itself. Self-indication, the third element, which Varela also calls autonomy, remains excluded. The resort to the paradox is not prohibited; for this would cause the paradox to become operatively effective, because the operation of prohibition would raise the question of whether the prohibition was legal or illegal. The paradox is concealed. No provision is made for operations that could point towards this paradox, and if such operations do occur, they are transformed into a contradiction and eliminated. The autonomy of the system is then nothing but the fact of operating *according to its own code*, because this code *deparadoxifies the paradox of self-reference.*

It is clear that this does not solve all problems and that an observer, a sociologist, for example, can form his own opinion about it. He may feel free to fall back on the paradox of 'legal because illegal'; he may, within the framework of the labelling approach, treat the distinctions and modes of labelling of the police almost as illegal or he may wish to recommend civil disobedience as a form of reason of state from below. Legal theory also sought forms of self-thematisation that would take paradox into account, but narrowly missed pinpointing them. In the 18th century, after theories of contract had collapsed because of the problem of self-implication, it was considered absolutely necessary to posit force as the origin of law. Today, the question of legitimation is posed in an equally pale and insecure fashion. In each case, the semantics of the legal system serve to restyle the paradox. It cannot yet be said with certainty whether insight into the necessity of the 'third element' of self-indication will open up other possibilities. It is an important step in itself to grasp that this is a possible option.

IV

Where does the perception of this possible option lead, especially in practical terms? Theory itself would have to answer this question by saying that it explains its own schema of observation. One could adopt van Parijs's terminology and describe this as 'parasitic clarification' (van Parijs, 1981: XI). At the moment, the theory of self-referential systems is primarily concerned with demonstrating that it is possible, indeed logically possible, that it can be operationalised in formal calculations, and that the traditional objections to the circular conclusions of self-reference have either been cleared away or else can be taken account of in the system as paradoxes. It should be stressed that what we are concerned with here is

6 In historical terms, legal thinking began in this form. Unlawful because lawful is the great subject of Greek tragedy – to which the institutionalresponse was the establishment of the Areopagus. The semantic response was the development of logic, which made possible the elimination of contradictions, but at the same time, led to the discovery of the logical problem of paradox (Epimenides).

a theory of empirical systems that includes the system of sciences and includes itself as a theory of the system of sciences, as one case among many others. To study whether and how this is possible is one of the great intellectual adventures of the present day and is a fascinating challenge in itself, even though we cannot even begin to foresee the practical consequences of this shift in thinking.

The logically baroque detour that we have just completed does not provide an immediate, clear view for legal sociology or for legal theory. However, the concept of 'reflexive law' cannot be adequately judged without the aid of such preliminary reflections.

'Reflexive law' is not a concept through which social knowledge could increasingly and, as it were, uninhibitedly flow into law.[7] On the contrary, the stress is on system subjectivity, if one may use this term, and thus, on the inevitable system relativity of all perspectives. It is also inconceivable that law could control and regulate the autopoiesis of all social systems – for example, in the sense of the regulation of self-regulation. It must be borne in mind that autopoiesis is concrete factual reproduction from moment to moment; it is that which will be said and done next. When one takes this concept as a basis, it immediately becomes clear that such a *supra*-regulation of society by law would be an illusion – however much the special significance of law, particularly in the development of European society, may predispose us to think along these lines. Reflexive law can only be self-reflexive law. Only in the manner in which it reproduces itself can it take account of the fact (and perhaps, take more account of the fact) that society (and hence, also law itself) reproduces itself autopoietically. This approach can only reinforce the self-sensitivity of law to its actual social conditions – but even this is a great deal.

Let me quote two examples, one from the area of legal dogmatics and one from a legal-political area, to illustrate what this could mean. In the following section, we will then discuss legal-theoretical questions raised by the advance of topical, rhetorical and argumentational perspectives.

V

The central dogmatic figure we wish to analyse here is that of action. Jurists have known for centuries that problems of the attribution of action to 'free will' arise here. The standard sociological theory of action, which is based on the work of Max Weber, seems to confirm this.[8] This school – polemically opposed to 'behaviorist' theories – advocates a 'subjective' conception of action. This means that only the subject can know whether he has acted or not and the conclusion is: the subject must be asked. The subject here must be conceived of as presocial – whether materially or transcendentally, but in all events pre-dating the social order. This corresponds to the 'liberal' tradition, in the widest sense, of modern Europe, and clearly correlates as semantics with the realities of a highly complex, functionally differentiated society.

The theory of autopoietic systems compels us to abandon this concept.[9] For it, action is the result of an observation of autopoietic processes (which must of course exist in order to

7 Teubner himself rejects this possibility by stressing the independence of legal-internal models of law as opposed to the proposals of the social sciences (Teubner, 1985). On the same subject of an untranscendable conceptual difference see also Aubert (1980: 117–136).

8 Within sociology, this currently dominant concept has been criticised. See Rubinstein (1977), which contains good arguments. Also Emerson (1985: 425–455).

9 One would have to argue the complete opposite if one wished to tie the concept of autopoiesis – given its biological origins – to life and then to conclude that action is an element in the reproduction of life. This version in Hejl (1982a, 1982b).

be observed – no fiction!). The observation may be either self-observation or external observation of mental or social systems, and there is no 'natural' guarantee that such observations will converge. The fixing of a behavioural unit emerges from the context of other actions in which it is embedded and to the reproduction of which it contributes.

Systems that in this way observe themselves as systems of actions themselves decide on what will function for them as a unit of action and operate according to possibilities of connections. For the directing of such connections attributions are necessary, for one must, if the case arises, know who to turn to if one wishes to praise or to blame, to reward or to punish, to continue or to break off incomplete projects, to interrupt what has been started or to ignore what has happened. To this extent, there is no action without attribution and the question can only be: which system controls attribution and under what conditions?

This interpretation – even before law begins to observe itself – explains a large amount of the usual disagreement in the definition of action as action – a subject that up to now has primarily been dealt with in psychiatric research (cf. Laing, Philippson and Lee, 1966). Furthermore, it here becomes clear that in many cases, no decision can be made on the spot about the meaning of an action. Often, this can only be done later, when consequences emerge and it is possible to react to the action, to regret, correct, deny, recount or boast about it. Definition processes of this kind operate and correct the continual production of action. Scientific observation that attempted to observe such behaviour as 'right' or 'wrong' would have to assume (erroneously) that there is such a reality as action independent of this; or it would have to work on the basis of an independent observation schema such as conscious/unconscious or internal/external control – a generally accepted scientific practice both in psychiatry and in social psychology.

The legal system can participate in the game of the definition of action only in fundamentally the same way. In doing so, it uses a schema, peculiar to law, which enables it, ultimately, to arrive at decisions about legality and illegality. Causality is treated as accusation causality – partly in order to find the guilty party, partly in order to shift the 'real causes' out of the facts of the case. The connection of specifically legal consequential actions is also controlled via theories of guilt. All this is in principle familiar and only very detailed analyses will be able to show whether and how improvements can be made. The reflexivity of 'reflexive law' could, however, bring home to jurists how little their observation system and that which they define as action coincides with the operations and self-observations of other autopoietic systems. Then, it would be more normal for a new definition of action to be worked out in the courtroom and taken down in records.[10] But, at the same time, this means that there is no guarantee whatsoever that this new action can then be transferred back into the autopoiesis of the mental and social environment of law.

VI

The next example is taken from the legal-political sphere. The tradition of European legal thought, derived as it was from natural law, fixated on legislation and confused by the problem of arbitrariness, related the contingency of law to the legislature and its legal legitimation, i.e. it interpreted it as a problem of the positivity of law and, finally, as a constitutional problem. When posed in this way the problem is: with what right (law) can law be made valid to the exclusion of other possibilities? It went, and it goes without saying, that

10 On the problem of the control of connections by documents, cf. Cicourel (1985).

law had to be obeyed once it became valid. If, on the other hand, one understands law as an autopoietic system in a world of autopoietic systems, this means that one has, perhaps without noticing it, broken with these presuppositions. The question then arises of what law means for the autopoiesis of life, of consciousness and of social communication generally. Attention is then directed towards a second contingency, a contingency 'from below'. For all autopoietic systems, the validity of law leads to a bifurcation: one may know it or not know it, obey it or not obey it or not obey it and obey it with the choice of this or that legal form without interrupting one's own autopoiesis, without ceasing to live, to think, to communicate.[11] How can law as reflexive law adjust to this and, thereby, adjust to itself?

The classical answer is: self-application, the use of law to solve problems to which it itself gave rise. Ignorance of law is prohibited or ignored for the purposes of law. The confusion of law by the interpretation of its regulations is forbidden. Non-compliance with the law is prohibited and punished. That which nonetheless can still escape the law is treated as a purely factual remnant and attributed to the relative impotence of law but not to its structure. The paradoxicality of law, the paradoxicality of 'commanded' bifurcation is thereby externalised.

From the legal-political perspective, the idea of reflexive law appears to wish to break with this externalisation. Even the traditional solution of the problem by self-application had a self-referential basis. This process can be described, to use the logic of Spencer Brown, as the 're-entry' of a distinction into that which was indicated with its aid (cf. Spencer Brown, 1972: 69ff). The question of whether law is complied with or not is in turn left to law to decide (analogously to: I see that I do not see what I see). The same structure can be found in the concessions made by law, above all in the double concession of bourgeois theory: legislative freedom for the 'state' and contractual freedom for 'society'. Here law reflects the bifurcation that it causes by externalising the definition of normative contents itself. The obligation entered into in freedom, that of the state to comply with its own laws and that of the citizen to honour his contracts, is the form by which the adjustment of law to motive situations and to interests is intended to be achieved and the difference between knowing/not knowing or complying/not complying with the law is intended to be defused. The legal technique of general results – which was originally intended in the concept of subjective law that could be activated at will – corresponds to this.

What, then, can explicitly 'reflexive' legal politics add?

A major possibility that has so far not been exploited, or at least not systematically considered, is that of building bifurcation into the law itself and then offering the environment a choice between variously conditioned legal forms: for example, limitations on liability in company law only in standardised conditions as an alternative to unlimited liability. This is merely the juridification of something which – in the context of contingency 'from below' – is already continually occurring in all areas of law. Everyone concerned considers whether it is worthwhile taking a case to court; whether it is worthwhile to insist on an agreement being put into writing; whether it is better to sell or to let the house that he has inherited.

11 Note that this applies to all autopoietic systems, including law itself. Law, too, may knowor not know itself, obey or not obey itself or obey in one form or another. The difference is only that this contingency in law leads to a paradox. Since the Middle Ages this subject has been discussed under the heading of the derogation of natural law by natural law, but with the positivity of law it was forgotten. Today one sees, precisely also in the fruitlessness of the medieval discussion and its continuation in the idea of reason of state, that the problem must be remodelled in the legal system itself. The text which encodes this problem perhaps most clearly is Borges (1972).

The different consequences a choice may have in terms of taxation have led to greater consciousness of the choice of forms. Questions of this kind have been discussed for some years from the viewpoint of an 'economic' analysis of law[12] or under the (curious) title of 'New Political Economy'.[13] However, it has not been clarified to what extent the contingency 'from below' is actually used in the strict form of a cost/benefit calculation and what consequences this has for law when it is switched on and switched off in this way. However, one can also loosen or completely cancel out the premises of economically calculating behaviour. One then arrives at the question of whether and how law could plan for evasive be/am/i or without getting caught up in its own paradoxicality or in the logical undecidability of the question of the right (or wrong) of deciding between legality and illegality.

There is now an extremely voluminous body of legal-sociological research that adopts quite different approaches to this problem. One approach, which can be summed up under the general heading of access to law, examines the conditions in which those affected by law either use the legal system or for a variety of reasons do not do so. These studies are conducted against a background norm of equality of opportunity. Negotiation, arbitration and settlement possibilities are examined with a view to finding out how conflicts could be solved without the circumstantiality, costs and risks of currently valid law. Both perspectives complement one another perfectly; in one case, the argument is that too little use is made of law and in the other that too much use is made of law. This is one method of making the critique of law complete, but the question remains: what can law learn by studying the results of this research?

As a counter-perspective to familiar problems of implementation, it is salutary and astonishing to examine the high degree to which law is not used. According to the findings of Blankenburg (1980: 47) a quarter to a half of those with legal problems do nothing and only 2%–7% finally go to court – and in less than a half of these cases does the court rule for or against either party (see also Felstiner, 1974, 1975; Greenberg, Ruback and Westcoll, 1982). Only 7%–15% said that they would consider going to court next time. If one then estimates that courts decide 2%–3% of legal disputes according to the law, this estimate will approximately correspond to the real situation. This of course is no criterion of respect for the law, but it dictates a reversal of classical thought patterns at least for the area of law accessible to private individuals: reflexive control lies not in the hands of the state but in the hands of those concerned. Whether or not a matter is dealt with in the framework of law is to this extent a matter of private calculation. The legal system simply does not get the opportunity to reflect upon legalisation and delegalisation. It is not asked.[14]

Society obviously has its own logic with which it deals with its law. The supposition that this could have something to do with the self-reproduction of social communication is reinforced by the experience that intact social systems are more reluctant to juridify their conflicts than fragmented systems (see Blankenburg, 1980: 37ff; see also Macaulay, 1963: 55–67). People obviously use law to 'get their own back' if social systems no longer

12 Most of the ideas in this field come from the United States. German publications on this subject are: Assmann, Kirchner and Schanze (1978), Adams (1981, n.d.a., n.d.b.)

13 See the *Jahrbuch für Neue Politische Ökonomie* (from 1982) which also contains essays on the economic analysis of law.

14 Far more striking deviations are to be found in other countries. They include mandatory law and certain forms of civil service legal practice. Cf. for example Falcão (1982). Falcão has told the author that of more than 200 cases concerning the protection of historical monuments that he examined, not a single one had been dealt with in accordance with the law.

function; or people attempt to rescue or save as much as possible from the system, which is heading for collapse anyway. This applies to private law relations and certainly also to relations to authorities such as the inland revenue that one continually has to cultivate.

Let us assume that the legal system finds this out, on whatever level. What would be the consequence? Could one push reflexion about 'reflexive law' so far that law reflects, and then decides in legal form, whether it wishes to intervene in the decision, so that law, together with the potential legal consumer would decide whether they wished to use law or not? Would this not inevitably be one of those paradoxical communications in which good intentions are professed and the opposite is achieved? Consumers are already practising 'reflexive law' when they consider whether it is worthwhile communicatively to relate to law, but law itself cannot react reflexively to this, unless in explicit paradoxicality. Or else one does what has always been done: puts law into the form of an offer of order that consumers may use *si eis placuit*.

VII

The last example leads us to the gates of legal dogmatics. Or to put this more precisely and less metaphorically: we will not attempt to draw up principles or even directives regarding content for useful dogmatics. Instead we will ask whether there are fundamental problems and relatively simple rules according to which legal systems can generate dogmatics. If one knew these problems and these rules, one would not be in a position to derive a system of dogmatics from them, no more than knowledge of a genetic code can enable us to describe the organism which the code structures. But one would arrive at a better understanding of the highly complex phenomenon of dogmatics if one could discover how dogmatics are developed and, if necessary, corrected. In other words, an observer of the system may be able to describe how that system operates when constructing dogmatics, but he cannot simulate or predict the construction. The system – for reasons that will be explained – must itself make the decisions.

Dogmatics (as opposed to decision-making programmes) is concerned with the fact that communication about law occurs in the form of *argumentation*. Before a decision, a sounding-out process typically occurs whose purpose is to find out what decisions with what consequences (this often means: with what minimum of change in law) can be fitted into law. This is meaningful under two pre-conditions: that there is a *majority* of *different* arguments (negentropy) and that the arguments are *not significant in relation to one another* (redundancy). Redundancy in the sense in which it is used here[15] means that the knowledge of an argument reduces the information value (surprise value) of other arguments.

In borderline cases of logically-closed systematisation (which for familiar reasons is not possible with self-referential systems), the order would be completely redundant. In fact, all real systems are to be found somewhere between crystal and smoke (to quote Atlan, 1979).

15 It should be noted that even the case of entropy, namely, the case of complete equality of all arguments (it is the will of Allah! It is the will of the party!) is a case of redundancy. For one knows all the other arguments having heard only one because one already knows what system one is dealing with. This case of entropic redundancy is based on the peculiarity of elements of the system. The case of negentropic redundancy dealt with in the text is based on the non-arbitrariness (limitationality) of relations between the elements of a system of non-arbitrariness. This in turn – in circular fashion – makes it possible for the elements of the system to distinguish themselves qualitatively from one another. This conception of redundancy is also used by Atlan (1979). Only this procedure enables him to regard redundancy as a measure of the connectivity of elements and of the complexity of the system.

Argumentation is the self-observation of the legal system and redundancy is nothing but the ordering of this system, from the aspect of the information necessary for this observation.[16] Arguments are therefore introduced in order to limit the information value of other arguments, with the effect that an observer can see an order in which the arguments mutually support one another. After a certain period in the practice of argumentation one finds that arguments with no connection value – for example: I do not want to – are excluded. They can then only be used provocatively – for example to state that redundancy is itself redundant and that the system must be traced back to its fundamental paradox – the inability to provide justification.

This theory of order is certainly not that which jurists have in mind if they are interested in 'argumentation theory'. This is clear from the fact that conflicts, and pathological systems in general, are highly redundant orders.[17] If one has read the deposition of one lawyer, the deposition of the opposing lawyer will scarcely be surprising, and the same applies the other way round. Redundancies are symmetrically structured. They concentrate order. They block out sidelong glances at other possibilities. What this does not do, what it indeed often makes more difficult, is the finding of justifications for a decision. In order to justify, one must asymmetrise an existent redundancy. This is the only way of getting out of the circle in which a justification is chosen because of its suitability as a means of justifying.

We know of course that this circle cannot be avoided in a self-referential system. The justification of justifications ends inevitably in the realisation that one is doing precisely this and nothing else. But if this is the case, one can still ask what strategies are available to the system in order to deparadoxify itself.

The tradition of rhetoric and dialectic had operated topially, i.e. presupposed reasons as 'topoi' (later as passages of text) in which arguments could be found. That which was to be found served the amplification of communication, i.e. its endowment with effects of temporal, factual and social generalisation. Looked at in terms of the history of evolution, this was intended as an antidote against the increasingly high information and improbability content of communication in developed societies.[18] It was not perhaps a happy idea to resuscitate this tradition against the verdict of history in order to resolve contemporary difficulties.[19] More recent developments of that which – in careful distance to the tradition – is called 'argumentation theory' dissociate themselves (without saying precisely why) from topics[20] but also presuppose an asymmetrical, non-circular structure of the context of justification. The theoretical advance lies in the emphasis on the operative, procedural nature of the discursive search for justifications. Asymmetry continues to be presupposed, on the assumption that there is, ultimately, a reason that would decide if one were prepared to listen to it.

System-theoretical analysis replaces this reason-hypostasis with the assumption of a problematic relation between redundancy and justification, autopoietic recursiveness and asymmetrised structure. The purpose here is not to replace a (bad) theory with a different,

16 These points are connected with the questions of distinction and indication dealt with in Section II. For information can be gained only with the aid of a schema that makes it possible to indicate something as selection in the context of a presupposed distinction.

17 This is why this idea plays an important pa.rt in modern psychiatry and in psychopathology of communication. Cf. Watzlawick, Beavin and Jackson (1967).

18 The significance of printing in this context has often been pointed out. Cf. Lechner (1962); Ong (1967, 1977).

19 The most influential study here is Viehweg (1955). For a critical study see Otto (1970: 1983–1997). Cf. also Haft (1978), Schreckenberger (1978), Esser (1979), Ballweg and Seibert (1982).

20 Cf. above all Alexy (1978). (On topics, see 39ff).

better one. Rather it is a matter of increasing understanding of the context in which legal argumentation takes place. (We do not here need to decide whether neo-rhetoric, semiotics or argumentation theory describe this process itself satisfactorily). The thesis is that the production of legal-dogmatic concepts and theories takes place 'between crystal and smoke', i.e. through a manipulation of redundancies that are sometimes dispersed, sometimes utilised, but always structured towards asymmetry.

On the one hand, redundancies in the operation of law, when 'one argument leads to another' must be reduced, new perspectives introduced and uncertainties increased by the fact that a not (yet) involved third party is brought in (see Luhmann, 1981: 92–112). On the other hand, the available redundancies must be used for the clarification, mediation and possible decision on the dispute. Precisely this procedure was described as topical in the tradition, but today it can no longer be understood as a kind of geographical orientation in the space of arguments. Rather it is a construction of irreversible asymmetries – of 'justifications' that are not valid merely because someone wishes to use them to justify something.[21] Tautology cannot be eliminated, but it can be straightened out and, as logicians say, 'unfolded' (cf. Loefgren, 1979: 205–229). Intellectual experimentation in this situation in the course of time produces what can be described as reusable semantics or 'legal dogmatics'. Reason is at best an aggregate term for convictions that function thus. It is certainly not a special competence that must be protected against and must prevail over the intervention of passions, interests, techniques or pure power. One can allow the concept of reason, which has always had the function of taking self-reference upon itself, and thereby, freeing the world of it, to stand, but one must concede that it is nothing but a general term for the maintaining of asymmetry.

On top of all this, the theory of autopoietic systems powerfully relativizes the practical significance of legal dogmatics, and even more so, the practical significance of legal theory. Legal theory cannot 'preformulate' the totality of events within the system, nor does legal dogmatics give norm instructions for the normal practice of law. Only a few collisions of a few arguments are actually controlled via these highly complex semantics[22] (and it seems above all to be the institutional connection of training and theory production that leads to an overestimation of the influence of theory and of theoretical disputes on so-called practice).

The autopoietic reproduction of law occurs via communications that transfer the quality of normative validity to other communications. Typically, the decisions in legal disputes depend more on questions of fact (questions of proof) than on legal questions. The opposite mistake, that of trivialising questions of theory, must of course also be avoided. But it would certainly be fatal for the legal system – above all politically fatal – if it could be revolutionised by the replacement of central theoretical elements or by a change of paradigm.

21 It is perhaps unnecessary but, in view of older social formations, important to note that asymmetrification is only allowed in one direction: only the justification can justify. Asymmetrification towards the person who needs the justification and who can, for example, bring his influence to bear is excluded: though not in topical rhetoric, where at least the moral quality, not the speaker, was an important argument for his arguments and moral quality obviously correlated with status.

22 Heller rightly sees the significance of legal theory as lying 'only in the liminal case where the content of settled practice comes into crisis' (although this obviously does not cover the entire sphere of legal dogmatics) He argues that the reproduction of law occurs directly from practice to practice and in the majority of cases without use of theory. 'What is necessary for the reproduction of theoretical practice is not control over the full run of legal outcomes, but rather continuing domination over paradigmatic or semiotically central events' (Heller, 1984,186, 189).

The race paradigm was imposed not by theory but by power, and even this certainly did not mean that all cases were decided differently from before.

All this has, in the first instance, little to do with reflexive law. But it leads to the question of whether this concept contains an excessive tendency to regard legal dogmatics as a legal-political instrument and, thus, to consider dogmatics as plannable. But if we have described it correctly, the genesis of dogmatics is an evolutionary process of the continual adjusting of arguments, and the result is a non-controllable complexity. In many cases, arguments today are more related to consequences and a layman's sociological perspective is perhaps gaining importance. But if 'reflexive law' is itself used as an argument, one makes a 'strange loop'[23] and lands precisely where one does not want to land: in the paradoxicality of law.

VIII

Would this be an accident, a blunder, an error? From the viewpoint of argumentative operation and dogmatics, it certainly would. However, for system-theoretical analysis, this is not at all surprising. The postulate of reflexive law is a programme of the combination of the self-reflection of law and reflection of the self-reflection of other autopoietic systems. The combination is either regarded as a matter of negotiating, i.e. as a matter of a 'third system' of negotiation, which, however, cannot be more powerful and complex than the systems involved in it. Or else it must be understood as a kind of co-evolutive adaptation. I do not wish to deny that these answers point in the right direction. Yet the question still remains of how the systems involved, and how, in particular, the legal system will cope with the burdens of reflection that this implies.

No system can transcend itself and carry out operations other than its own. The taking into account of the environment necessitates a re-entry of a distinction into that which it distinguished. When this happens, the legal system will realise that it is environment for the systems of its environment, for which law is relevant only in the context of their own autopoiesis. It will, for example, have to learn that the systems of its environment usually insert a different difference before that of legality/illegality, namely, that of being caught and not being caught. It must learn to see what it does not see and to regulate what it does not regulate. Other systems of intervention also face this problem.[24] Indeed all cognitions, in reflection on the conditions of their possibility, lead ultimately to the realisation that they do not realise what they do not realise.[25] This reflection confronts the system with the paradoxicality to which it owes its existence.

Paradoxicality, as explained in Section IV, does not simply mean: logical contradiction. We do not say: seeing = not seeing, regulating = not regulating, but seeing *because* not seeing, regulating *because* not regulating. Nor do we come to a 'dialectical' synthesis, which would have to presuppose a contradiction of thesis and antithesis. The problem lies in the fact that the paradox does not lie on a logical level; for a logical treatment, it would require

23 A term used by Hofstadter (1979).

24 Interesting parallels can be drawn to family therapy, which today increasingly uses system-analytical perspectives, and thus, comes up against the problem posed in the text. Cf. Thomm, Lannamann, and Mcnamee (n.d.).

25 «We do not see that we do not see', writes von Foerster (1979). This is precisely why 'second order cybernetics' must begin with observation, by means of which we can at least realize that one does not realize what one does not realize, although not what one does not realize when one does not realize. See also reversal of 'what' and 'how' in von Foerster (1981: 259).

a distinction of logical levels (or 'types'), which cannot itself be logically justified. What 'reflexive law' ultimately has in common with the self-references of the systems of its environment is the unsolvable paradox of self-reference. All system structures and all system operations serve the deparadoxification of this paradox. One can camouflage this process as 'combination' or 'negotiation', or as relationing of relations or as distinguishing of distinctions or as computation of computations (von Foerster, 1981: 226). In a logical treatment, one is faced with the question of whether this reference to itself – even if, as reference, it is a paradox – can be used as a 'third element,' and can thereby make possible a type-free logic.

Bibliography

Adams, Michael (1981), *Ökonomische Analyse des Zivilprozeßes*, Konigstein: Athenäum.

——— (n.d.a) "Ökonomische Analyse der Verschuldens- und Gefährdungshaftung". Paper for the Economic Institute of the University of Berne.

——— (n.d.b) "Der Wert des Lebens im Recht der unerlaubten Handlungen und der Einfluß der Kraftfahrzeughaftplichtversicherung auf das Unfallgeschehen". Paper for the Economic Institute of the University of Berne.

Alexy, Robert (1978), *Theorie der Juristischen Argumentation: Die Theorie des rationalen Diskurses als Theorie der juristischen Begrüdung*, Frankfurt a.M.: Suhrkamp.

Assmann, Heinz-Dieter, Kirchner, Christian and Schanze, Erich (eds.) (1978), *Ökonomische Analyse des Rechts*, Kronberg: Athenäum.

Atlan, Henri (1979), *Entre le cristal et la fumée*, Paris: Seuil.

Aubert, Vilhelm (1980), "On the Relationship between Legal and Sociological Concepts", *Jahrbuch für Rechtssoziologie and Rechtstheorie*, 6, 117.

——— (1983), *In Search of Law*, Oxford: Martin Robertson.

Ballweg, Ottmar and Seibert, Thomas Michael (eds.) (1982), *Rhetorische Rechtstheorie*, Freiburg: K. Alber.

Blankenburg, Erhard (1980), "Mobilisierung von Recht: Über die Wahrscheinlichkeit des Gangs zum Gericht, die Chance des Erfolgs und die daraus folgenden Funktionen der Justiz", *Zeitschrift für Rechtssoziologie*, 1, 35.

Borges, Jorge L. (1974), "El Jardin de senderos que se bifurcan", in *Obras Completas*, Buenos Aires: Emecè Editores, 427–480.

Cicourel, Aaron V. (1985), *The Social Organization of Juvenile Justice*, New York: Wiley.

Derrida, Jacques (1968), *L'écriture et la difference*, Paris: Seuil.

Dupuy, Jean-Pierre (1979), *Le signe et l'envie*, in: P. Dumouchel and J.P. Dupuy (eds.), *L'enfer des choses: Rene Girard et la logique de l'économie*, Paris: Seuil.

Emerson, Robert M. (1985), "Holistic Effects in Social Control Decision-Making", *Law & Society Review*, 17, 425.

Esser, Josef (1979), *Juristisches Argumentieren im Wandel des Rechsfindungskonzepts unseres Jahrunderts*, Heidelberg: Carl Winter.

Falcão, Joaquim A. (1982), *Justiça Social e Justiça Legal*, São Paulo: Florianopolis.

Felstiner, William (1974), "Influences of Social Organization on Dispute Processing", *Law & Society Review*, 9, 63.

——— (1975), "Avoidance as Dispute Processing: An Elaboration", *Law & Society Review*, 9, 695.

Foerster, Heinz von (1974), "Notes pour une épistémologie des objets vivants", in E. Morin and M. Piatelli-Palmarini (eds.), *L'unite de l'homme*, Paris.

——— (1979), "Cybernetics of Cybernetics", in K. Krippendorf (ed.), *Communication and Control in Society*, New York: Gordon and Breach.

——— (1981), *Observing Systems*, Seaside, CA: Intersystems Publications.

Greenberg, Martin S., Ruback, R. Barry and Westcoll, David R. (1982), "Decision-Making by Crime Victims: A Multimethod Approach", 17.

Günther, Gotthard (1976), "Cybernetic Ontology and Transjunctional Operations", in G. Günther (ed.), *Beiträge zur Grundlegung einer operationsfähigen Dialektik*, Vol. I, Hamburg: F. Meiner.
Haft, Fritjof (1978), *Juristische Rhetorik*, Freiburg: K. Alber.
Hejl, Peter M. (1982a), *Sozialwissenschaft als Theorie selbstreferentieller Systeme*, Frankfurt a.M.: Campus.
——— (1982b), "Die Theorie autopoietischer Systeme: Perspektiven für die soziologische Systemtheorie", *Rechtstheorie*, 13, 45.
Heller, Thomas C. (1984), "Structuralism and Critique", *Stanford Law Rewiev*, 36, 127.
Hofstadter, Douglas R. (1979), *Goedel, Escher, Bach: An Eternal Golden Braid*, New York: Basic Books.
Ietswaart, Heleen F.P. (1983), "The Conference on Reflexive Law and the Regulatory Crisis", July 18–21, University of Wisconsin, Madison, 5 Zeitschrift für Rechtssoziologie, 349.
Laing, Ronald D., Philippson, Herbert and Lee, A. Russell (1966), *Interpersonal Perception: A Theory and Method of Research*, London: Tavistock Publications.
Lechner, Joan M. (1962), *Renaissance Concepts of the Commonplaces*, New York: Pagaent Press.
Loefgren, Lars (1979), "Unfoldment of Self-Reference in Logic and in Computer Science", in F.V. Jensen, B.H. Mayoh and K.K. Moller (eds.), *Proceedings of the 5th Scandinavian Logic Symposium*, 17–19 January 1979, Aalborg: University Press.
Luhmann, Niklas (1981), "Konflikt und Recht", in N. Luhmann (ed.), *Ausdifferenzierung des Rechts*, Frankfurt a.M.: Suhrkamp.
Macaulay, Stewart (1963), "Non-Contractual Relations in Business: A Preliminary Study", *American Sociological Review*, 28, 55.
Maruyama, Magoroh (1933), "The Second Cybernetics: Deviation-Amplifying Mutual Processes", *General Systems*, 8, 233.
Maruyama, Magoroh (1985), "From Classificational Learning to Morphogenetic Learning", *Cybernetica*, 32.
Mattei, Rodolfo de (1953), *"Il problema della deroga e la Ragione di Stato"*, Roma: Bocca.
Ong, Walter J. (1967), *The Presence of the Word: Some Prolegomena for Cultural and Religious History*, New Haven, CT: Yale University Press.
——— (1977), *Interfaces of the Word: Studies in the Evolution of Consciousness and Culture*, Ithaca, NY: Cornell University Press.
Otto, Gerhard (1970), "Zwanzig Jahre Topik-Diskussion, Ertrag und Aufgaben", *Rechtstheorie*, 1, 183.
Parijs, Philippe van (1981), *Evolutionary Explanation in the Social Sciences: An Emerging Paradigm*, London: Tavistock Publications.
Rubinstein, D. (1977), "The Concept of Action in the Social Sciences", *Journal for the Theory of Social Behaviour*, 7.
Schreckenberger, Waldemar (1978), *Rhetorische Semiotik: Analysen von Texten des Grundgesetzes und von rhetorischen Grundstrukturen der Argumentationen des Bundesverfassungsgerichtes*, Freiburg.
Shoemaker, Sidney (1963), *Self-Knowledge and Self-Identity*, Ithaca, NY: Cornell University Press.
Spencer Brown, George (1972), *Laws of Form* (2nd ed.), New York: Julian Press.
Teubner, Gunther (1985), "Substantive and Reflexive Elements in Modern Law", *Law & Society Review*, 17, 259.
——— (1985), "After Legal Instrumentalism? Strategic Models of Post-Regulatory Law", in G. Teubner (ed.), *Dilemmas of Law in the Welfare State*, Berlin: de Gruyter.
Thomm, Karl, Lannamann, John and Mcnamee, Sheila (n.d.), "'No Interview Today': A Consultation Team Intervenes by Not Intervening", *Manuscript, Calgary.*
Varela, Francisco (1975), "A Calculus for Self-Reference", *International Journal of General Systems*, 2, 5.
——— (1979), *Principles of Biological Autonomy*, New York: Elsevier.
Viehweg, Theodor (1953), *Topik und Jurisprudenz*, Munchen: Beck.

Watzlawick, Paul, Beavin, Janet M., and Jackson, Don D. (1967), *Pragmatics of Human Communication: A Study of Interactional Patterns, Pathologies and Paradoxes*, New York: Norton.
Weizsaecker, C. Christian von (1985), "Effizienz und Gerechtigkeit". Paper of the Economic Institute of the University of Berne.
Wender, P. (1968), "Vicious and Virtuous Circles: The Role of Deviation-Amplifying Feedback in the Origin and Perpetuation of Behavior", *Psychiatry*, 31, 309.
Willke, Helmut (1985), *Entzauberung des Staates; Überlegungen zu einer sozietalen Steuerungstheorie*, Konigstein: Athenäum.

Index

For Product Safety Concerns and Information please contact our EU representative GPSR@taylorandfrancis.com
Taylor & Francis Verlag GmbH, Kaufingerstraße 24, 80331 München, Germany

www.ingramcontent.com/pod-product-compliance
Ingram Content Group UK Ltd.
Pitfield, Milton Keynes, MK11 3LW, UK
UKHW050754180926
475701UK00007B/1038
* 9 7 8 0 3 6 7 5 8 8 8 7 8 *